SMYTHE DIVISION CHAMPIONS
1974.75
1981.82
CANUCKS
RENA
2011
THE ODDS WITH PAUL ROGERS
WE LIVE FOR
SONY
make.believe
ROGERS
Mackenzie INVESTMENTS
Coca-Cola zero
HSBC
SPORTCHEK
RE/MAX
Tim Hortons
CRUZE
On the Run
Esso
STANLEY CUP FINAL

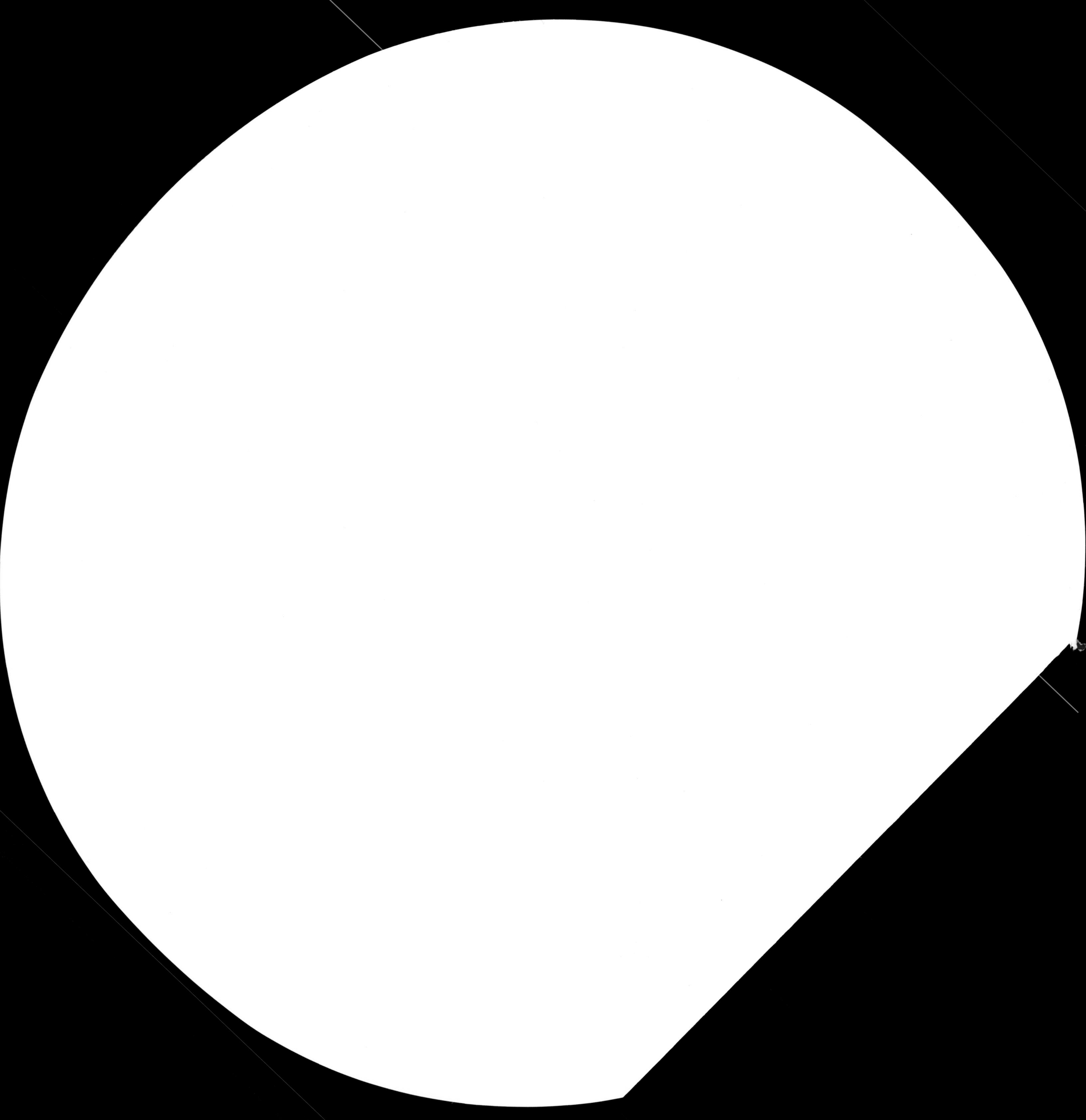

HOCKEY
RUCKUS
BOOKS

INTRODUCTION

The sport of hockey's roots may never be fully uncovered but it is estimated that some variation of the sport goes back nearly 4,000 years. The first versions of ice hockey are estimated to have taken place in the late 1700s in England using a bung, or a piece or cork or oak to serve as the stopper on a barrel, as the puck. It was English soldiers and immigrants that brought their version of hockey with them when they came to Canada and the United States and played them on the snow and ice in the winter months.

Today, the sport has ice hockey federations in 73 countries across the globe and is immensely popular in North America and throughout Europe. It's been a part of the Olympics since 1920; the International Ice Hockey Federation or IIHF has held the World Championships annually since 1930. Now there are professional and amateur leagues all over the map as Europeans, have increasingly become a factor in the sport after not being represented in the National Hockey League at all until the 1970s.

The game of hockey is more than just a game of sticks and pucks, penalties and goals. For some, it is a hobby. For some, a career. For others, it is passion, a vehicle for expression of national or cultural pride. Hockey is steeped in so much history, tradition, lore and love for the game that for many of us, our passion for hockey is part of our individual and collective identities.

From its ancient, rudimentary beginnings to the professional, big-money game it is today, hockey has undergone a metamorphosis in nearly every aspect. From the playing surface to the rules, from pick up games on the pond to sold-out games in every NHL arena, hockey today bears little resemblance to its earliest ancestors, but one thing remains: Those who love hockey love it passionately.

Hockey makes us form loyalties that wouldn't otherwise make sense. Why cheer on a team of players to whom we have no real allegiance? Because we love the game. Why have we gathered on ponds, hands frozen to the bone, just to spend a few hours knocking the puck around? Because we love the game. Why do little boys dream their whole lives of playing in the NHL, and spend their waking hours practising their slap shots and imagining the roar of the crowds? Because they love the game. Why do we, as families, gather around the television, dressed in the colors of our favorite teams, to urge our teams to victory over the "other guys"? Because, quite simply, we love the game.

This book is for all who know what it means to love hockey.

Hockey is at once a go-to resource for the history of the game and a portrait of the game as it exists today. It is a guide for those who have been in love with hockey for as long as they can remember as well as a resource for those people for whom the romance is just beginning.

STAPLES Center
i'm lovin' it.
BRIDGESTONE
Advil
DISCOVER
GATORADE
GEICO
Advil
Reebok

HOCKEY

The Birth of Ice Hockey, The Montreal Rules and Amateur Hockey

While we may not know the official origin of where the sport came from or how long the sport has been around, we do have some important facts in evidence.

The first organized indoor game of ice hockey as we know it took place on March 3, 1875 at Montreal's Victoria Skating Rink. James Creighton along with other McGill University students were part of the game, which featured nine players to a side. The rules of the game, being six feet in width and the game being 60 minutes in length are parts of the sport that still are in effect today.

In 1877, students at McGill, including Creighton, came up with seven rules for ice hockey that were adapted from the rules of field hockey.

The McGill University Hockey Club, which was founded in 1877, was the first hockey club in history. In 1881, the Montreal Victorias became the second club and the first so-called world championship took place in 1883 at Montreal's Winter Carnival. By now, the rules dictated that only seven players were on the ice at one time, down from the original nine. McGill was the first world champion as they won what was known as the Carnival Cup.

In 1885, the Montreal City Hockey League came into existence and a year later, the Amateur Hockey Association of Canada was born. This was the second league to be created in Canada after an initial league was devised in Kingston, Ontario in 1883. The league was created to provide a longer season and to help determine the champion of Canada instead of playing in the Winter Carnival in Montreal. Five teams were in the league when it was founded: McGill, the Montreal Victorias, Crystals, Ottawa and the Montreal Hockey Club. From 1886-1893, except for 1888, the champion was challenged by a new team every week; the first title change took place on January 14, 1887 when the Montreal Victorias beat the Crystals 4-0.

Beginning in 1893, the winner of the AHAC would be awarded the Stanley Cup as the best amateur team in the country. At this point, the league switched from the challenge format to a format more in line with what we see in the NHL today, where there is a schedule and teams face all the other teams in the league when they're slated for a contest. The Montreal Hockey Club won the Stanley Cup in both 1893 and 1894, thereby becoming the first team to win the Stanley Cup and repeat as champions; the Montreal Victorias won it the next four seasons between 1895 and 1898.

The league would reach its end in 1898. The Ottawa Capitals applied for membership in the league in 1897 but were turned down. The Capitals applied again in December of 1898 and were accepted; there was question about whether Ottawa was paying some of their players, thereby making them a professional or semi-pro team as opposed to an amateur one. When the Capitals were accepted, the Quebec Bulldogs, Montreal Victorias and the Ottawa Hockey Club all withdrew from the league. The Montreal Hockey Club followed suit after their attempt to convince the other three teams to reconsider failed. On December 14, that quartet met at the Windsor Hotel and created the Canadian Amateur Hockey League, adding the Montreal Shamrocks in the process.

The CAHL would last seven seasons, running from 1899 through the 1905 campaign. The biggest contribution that the CAHL would bring to the sport was the first use of netting on the goals in order to catch pucks that went into the goal. The nets became a permanent part of the CAHL after an exhibition series utilizing them in 1899. When the CAHL folded in 1905 and had its teams incorporated into the new Eastern Canada Amateur Hockey Association, the transition to

The Montreal Amateur Athletic Association posing with the first Stanley Cup circa 1893 in Montreal, Quebec. They would go on to win the Stanley Cup again in 1894, 1902 (March), and 1903 (February).

creating professional hockey leagues that could drive revenue was underway.

The Start of Professional Hockey

Pro hockey got its start in the early 1900s with the development of the Western Pennsylvania Hockey League in 1902, which was a pro-am league where some players were getting paid. In 1904, the WPHL merged with teams in Michigan and Ontario and formed the International Professional Hockey League; Jack Gibson, a dentist in Houghton, Michigan, was the league's founder. The league ceased operations in 1907 but professional hockey was born and on the map.

The first professional league in Canada came in 1905 with the Manitoba Professional Hockey League, which featured teams that were previously in the Manitoba Hockey Association, which was an amateur league. A year later was the birth of the Eastern Canada Amateur Hockey Association and a year after that, in 1907, came the birth of the Ontario Professional Hockey League.

With the number of professional leagues on the uptick, the salaries increased as leagues and teams were competing to reel in the top players available.

The IPHL closed up shop because of the rising salaries and with that was the end of professional hockey, at least for the moment, in the United States.

The OPHL didn't last long either, as it closed in 1908, while the MPHL closed its doors in 1909. The ECAHA went fully professional in 1908 as the amateur teams in the league separated themselves from the pro clubs and began competing for the Allan Cup, which was solely for amateur teams.

The ECHA, as it was now known, disbanded and formed a new league, known as the CHA, while leaving out the Montreal Wanderers. This was done because the Wanderers had moved from the Montreal Arena to the Jubilee Arena, which was a smaller venue but was owned by Wanderers' owner P.J. Doran. This meant less money in the pockets of the visiting teams on road trips, which didn't set well with the owners of the rest of the league.

The NHA and PCHA: Hockey From Coast to Coast

Several teams in Northern Ontario had found enough professional players that they wanted to be considered for admission in the CHA. Unfortunately, they found that the ECHA wasn't overly interested in expanding the league with their teams and were turned down. Rather than worry about it or become disgruntled and give up the dream of professional hockey all together, the group of teams came up with an idea to form a league of their own and the National Hockey Association, or NHA, was founded in 1909. Ambrose O' Brien, who was a silver miner and owner of the Renfrew Creamery Kings, along with Jimmy Gardner, who now owned the Wanderers, were the duo who decided to for the NHA. The other two teams, Cobalt and Halleysbury, were also owned by O'Brien.

On December 2, 1909, the NHA was officially founded. To add rivalry to the league, O'Brien and Gardner came up with an idea to put a team with a roster full of French speaking players and to be owned by a French speaking individual. That team was "Les Canadiens", the team known in the NHL today as the Montreal Canadiens; they came into existence on December 4, 1909. The Canadiens, as such, are the only team in NHL history to be in existence before the start of the NHL that existed continuously. The NHA began the 1909-10 season with five teams.

Money was thrown around to try and lure the best players to teams as they all wished to win the Stanley Cup. Frank and Lester Patrick were both signed by Renfrew for $3,000 each which at the time was the highest salary ever. That was passed shortly thereafter when Renfrew inked Cyclone Taylor, who played with the Ottawa Senators, to a deal reportedly worth $5,000 per season. The departure of star players from the CHA drove their attendance down as fans were intent on seeing the NHA's product.

On January 15, 1910, there was a meeting of the NHA about a potential merger with the CHA. Rather than work a merger, the NHA decided that they would bring the Senators and the Montreal Shamrocks into the league while the rest of the teams weren't even taken

The Ottawa hockey club poses with the Stanley Cup after winning the league championship, shown on this postcard, Ottawa, Ontario, c.1906.

into consideration for membership. At that point the CHA folded and the NHA threw out their previous games, choosing to restart their season at that point with seven teams. The Montreal Wanderers won the first NHA championship; they would go on to defend the Stanley Cup against Edmonton. After the season, Haileybury, Cobalt and the Montreal Shamrocks dropped out of the league while the Quebec Bulldogs joined; two teams in Toronto were planned to join in the future.

The league implemented a salary cap for the 1910-11 season, nearly causing the league to collapse as players threatened to form their own league. With ownership controlling the arenas, this was not a viable option; the players ended up taking pay cuts, some of them making half of what they had the season before as teams tried to stay under the $5,000 salary cap implemented. Ottawa would go on to win the Stanley Cup and defended it against Galt and Port Arthur. After the season, O'Brien decided to get out of the hockey business and the Renfrew team ceased to exist. Another key event that took place was the dropping of the "rover" position, reducing the number of players on the ice from seven to the six that are currently seen in the NHL today. Several attempts to try and bring seven man hockey back occurred through the 1920s but never materialized.

In 1911, the Patrick brothers built arenas in Vancouver and Victoria in British Columbia and formed the Pacific Coast Hockey Association, better known as the PCHA. The PCHA swiped a lot of the talent from the NHA because of the ability to offer higher salaries. Beginning in the 1912-13 season, the champions of the NHA and the PCHA met at the end of the season to do battle. Starting in the 1914-15 season, the champions of the two leagues met with the winner claiming the Stanley Cup. The Portland Rosebuds won the PCHA title in the 1915-16 season and after defeating the Montreal Canadiens; they became the first team from the United States to win the Stanley Cup.

With World War I ongoing, teams began losing players to the military and coupled with the raiding of NHA rosters by the PCHA, the NHA was facing a situation where they didn't have enough players to fill their teams. Before the 1915-16 season, Eddie Livingstone, who owned the Toronto Shamrocks, made a couple of moves that infuriated the rest of the NHA and the PCHA. Quebec was one of the teams that the PCHA would draft players from; Livingstone swung a deal with the Bulldogs in order to hide some of his players from the draft, which irritated the PCHA. He then bought the Toronto Blueshirts without permission from the league for its players; in retaliation for his moves, the PCHA raided the Blueshirts and left Livingstone with no players for the Shamrocks. The 1915-16 season was played with only five teams, meaning one team a week didn't play, cutting revenues and cash flow around the league.

In the 1916-17 season, the league put a second team in Toronto to replace the Shamrocks, called the 228th Battalion. The team was the league's highest scoring club before it was called to active duty for World War I and had to withdraw from the league. The NHA then chose to suspend the Blueshirts and disperse the players of the team to the other four teams in the league. Livingstone threatened to sue the league while the league mandated that Livingstone sell the Blueshirts between April and June of 1917. He refused to do so and instead followed through with his lawsuit of the league. At this point, the NHA was at a crossroads and a change was coming.

The Birth of the NHL

With Livingstone's lawsuit pending, the owners of the Ottawa Senators, Montreal Canadiens, Montreal Wanderers and the Quebec Bulldogs were fed up with the antics of the Toronto owner. They wanted to expel Livingstone from the league but found that wasn't an option under the constitution of the NHA. Faced with this situation, the other owners of the league chose to take the bold move of suspending operations of the NHA and form a new league, known as the National Hockey League, with their four respective teams, leaving Livingstone in the NHA by himself. On November 26, 1917, the National Hockey League was officially founded.

The Bulldogs lacked the financial stability to play in the first season of the NHL in 1917-18 so a team was

The Quebec Bulldogs team pose for a portrait circa 1912 after winning the Stanley Cup.

QUEBEC

Stanley Cup Champions—1912

Top Row—left to right: L. LAGUEUX (Committee) C. FREMONT (Committee) T. B. O'NIEL (Committee) A. DEROME (Committee) F. HILL (Committee)

Second Row: C. LOCKWELL (Committee) C. NOLAN (Coach) D. BELAND (Trainer) G. LEONARD G. CAREY J. SAVARD J. E. MATTE (Treasurer)

Third Row: B. J. KAINE (Secretary) Hon. P. A. CHOQUETTE (President) W. ROONEY G. PRODGER J. MALONE J. HALL P. MORAN M. J. QUINN (Vice-President) (Manager)

Bottom Row: J. MARKS J. McDONALD

Inset: E. OATMAN

placed in Toronto on a temporary basis. Known as the Arenas, the franchise inherited the contracted players of the Blueshirts to field their first team. The first games in NHL history kicked off on December 19, 1917; Joe Malone scored five goals in the Canadiens' 7-4 victory over the Senators and finished with 44 goals over the course of a 20 game season.

The league nearly fell apart in January 1918 when the Montreal Arena burned to the ground, forcing the Canadiens and the Wanderers into a situation where they had no home venue. The Canadiens moved into the Jubilee Arena while the Wanderers folded up shop after they were unable to get the other teams to give them players. The league finished the season with just three teams, with the Canadiens winning the first half of the season and the Arenas winning the second half. After Toronto won the league title by outscoring Montreal 10-7 on total goals, the Arenas went on to defeat the Vancouver Millionaires of the PCHA three games to two in order to win the Stanley Cup. The first major rule change in NHL history came in January of 1918 when the league allowed goaltenders to drop to the ice in order to make saves instead of having to be in the standing position all the time.

The 1918-19 season saw the Arenas suspend operations midway through the year, leaving Ottawa and Montreal to play for the league title. The Canadiens prevailed and went on to face the Seattle Metropolitans for the Stanley Cup. With the series tied 2-2 with one tie, the rest of the series was canceled due to the Spanish Flu epidemic. The epidemic whipped through the Montreal franchise and ended up killing Joe Hall. This marked the lone time in NHL history that the Stanley Cup failed to be awarded after the postseason had begun.

The Toronto franchise changed their name to the St. Patricks as they came back for the 1919-20 season while the Quebec Athletics became active for the first time, giving the league four teams once again. Malone set a NHL record that still stands when he scored seven goals in one game on January 20, 1920 against the St. Patricks; he led the league with 39 goals in 24 games but the Athletics went 4-20 on the season. It proved to be the final season for the team in Quebec City; they moved to Hamilton, Ontario and became the Hamilton Tigers.

The 1920s: Expansion into the United States and the WCHL

In the 1920s, the NHL looked to expand their horizons south of the Canadian border in an effort to boost the league's status. The league grew from four teams to six in the 1924-25 season as the Montreal Maroons and the Boston Bruins joined the NHL. The Bruins were the first team in the United States to be a part of the league; they were purchased by Charles Adams for a price of $15,000. The first NHL game played in the United States took place on December 1, 1924 with the Bruins prevailing over the Maroons by a 2-1 score at the Boston Arena.

At the same time, the NHL, already dealing with competition from the PCHA, would be forced to deal with another professional league when the Western Canada Hockey League began play in 1921. With three pro leagues looking to fight off each other for talent, the salaries of the players skyrocketed to the point that players were earning salaries along the lines of the top players in major league baseball. The WCHL had some quality teams but the competition and the money involved forced their hand; they ended up merging with the PCHA in 1924. The Victoria Cougars of the WCHL defeated the Montreal Canadiens in the 1925 Stanley Cup Finals, three games to one; they are the last non-NHL team to win the Stanley Cup in history.

After the 1925-26 season, the WCHL folded up shop, with the assets of the league purchased by the NHL for $300,000. The players of the Hamilton Tigers, who had their fair share of issues with their ownership after the owners made a tidy profit while declaring financial difficulties the season before, were purchased by Bill Dwyer, the owner of the expansion New York Americans with a price tag of $75,000. The Pittsburgh Pirates became the third team in the United States, starting play with the Americans in the 1925-26 campaign.

In 1926-27, the league added three more teams in markets in the United States. Tex Rickard, after seeing the success of the Americans, petitioned the league to add a second team in New York to play at Madison Square Garden. The league agreed to grant Rickard a team and the New York Rangers were born. Teams were

The New York Americans along with Mervin 'Red' Dutton, 7th from the right pose for a team photo circa 1930's in New York, New York.

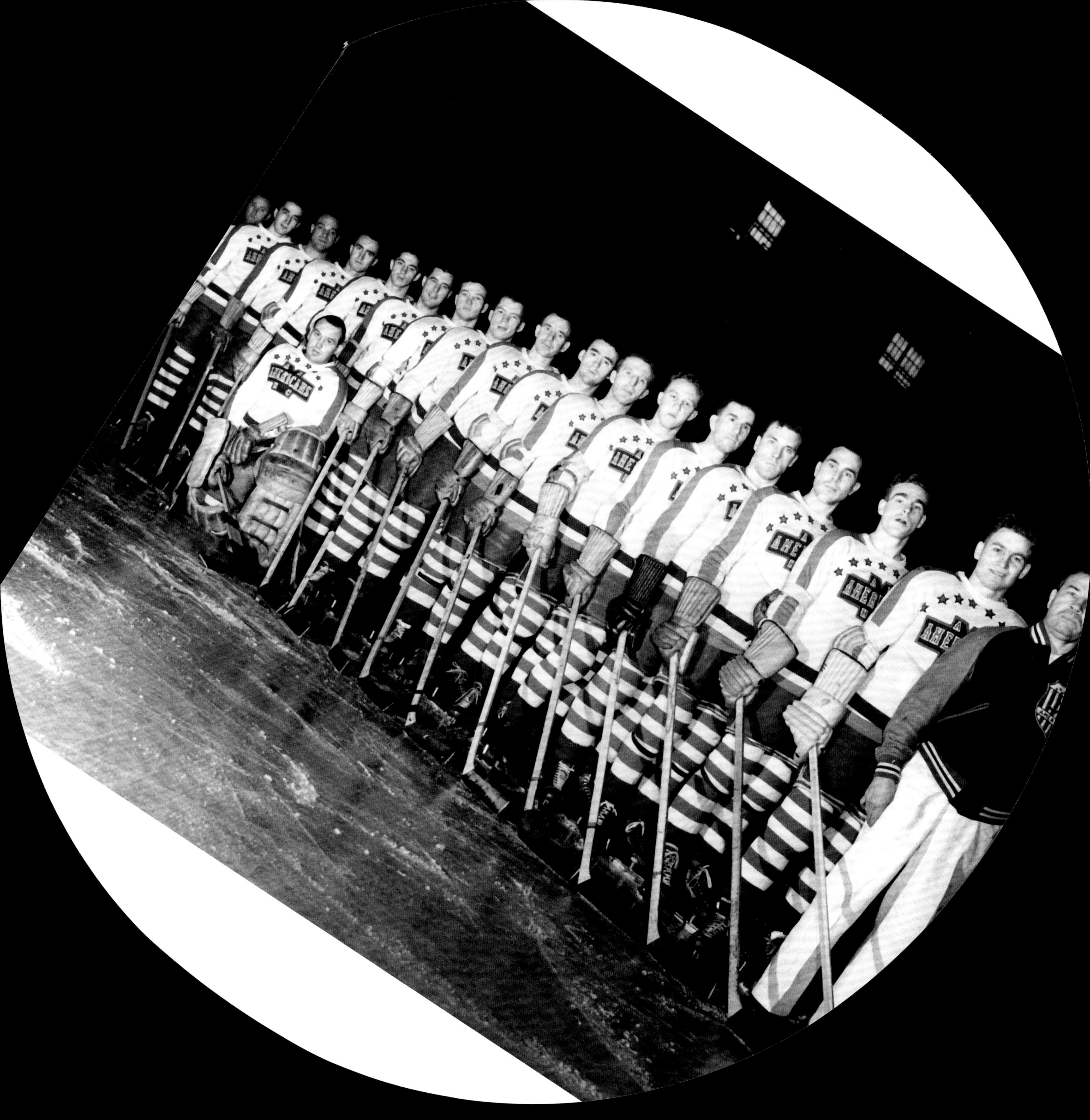
AMERICANS

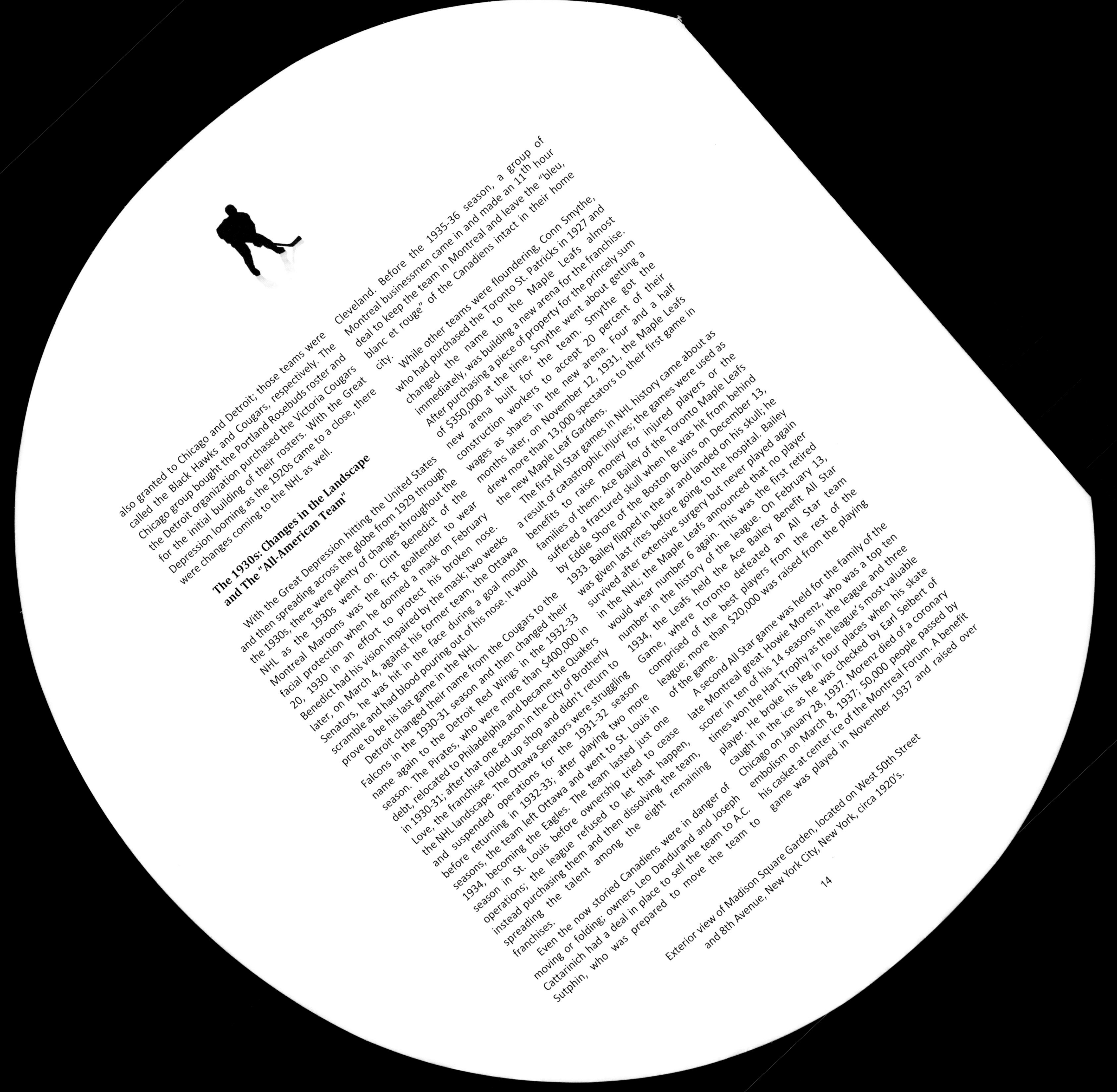

also granted to Chicago and Detroit; those teams were called the Black Hawks and Cougars, respectively. The Chicago group bought the Portland Rosebuds roster and the Detroit organization purchased the Victoria Cougars for the initial building of their rosters. With the Great Depression looming as the 1920s came to a close, there were changes coming to the NHL as well.

The 1930s: Changes in the Landscape and The "All-American Team"

With the Great Depression hitting the United States and then spreading across the globe from 1929 through the 1930s, there were plenty of changes throughout the NHL as the 1930s went on. Clint Benedict of the Montreal Maroons was the first goaltender to wear facial protection when he donned a mask on February 20, 1930 in an effort to protect his broken nose. Benedict had his vision impaired by the mask; two weeks later, on March 4, against his former team, the Ottawa Senators, he was hit in the face during a goal mouth scramble and had blood pouring out of his nose. It would prove to be his last game in the NHL.

Detroit changed their name from the Cougars to the Falcons in the 1930-31 season and then changed their name again to the Detroit Red Wings in the 1932-33 season. The Pirates, who were more than $400,000 in debt, relocated to Philadelphia and became the Quakers in 1930-31; after that one season in the City of Brotherly Love, the franchise folded up shop and didn't return to the NHL landscape. The Ottawa Senators were struggling and suspended operations for the 1931-32 season before returning in 1932-33; after playing two more seasons, the team left Ottawa and went to St. Louis in 1934, becoming the Eagles. The team lasted just one season in St. Louis before ownership tried to cease operations; the league refused to let that happen, instead purchasing them and then dissolving the team, spreading the talent among the eight remaining franchises.

Even the now storied Canadiens were in danger of moving or folding; owners Leo Dandurand and Joseph Cattarinich had a deal in place to sell the team to A.C. Sutphin, who was prepared to move the team to Cleveland. Before the 1935-36 season, a group of Montreal businessmen came in and made an 11th hour deal to keep the team in Montreal and leave the "bleu, blanc et rouge" of the Canadiens intact in their home city.

While other teams were floundering, Conn Smythe, who had purchased the Toronto St. Patricks in 1927 and changed the name to the Maple Leafs almost immediately, was building a new arena for the franchise. After purchasing a piece of property for the princely sum of $350,000 at the time, Smythe went about getting a new arena built for the team. Smythe got the construction workers to accept 20 percent of their wages as shares in the new arena. Four and a half months later, on November 12, 1931, the Maple Leafs drew more than 13,000 spectators to their first game in the new Maple Leaf Gardens.

The first All Star games in NHL history came about as a result of catastrophic injuries; the games were used as benefits to raise money for injured players or the families of them. Ace Bailey of the Toronto Maple Leafs suffered a fractured skull when he was hit from behind by Eddie Shore of the Boston Bruins on December 13, 1933. Bailey flipped in the air and landed on his skull; he was given last rites before going to the hospital. Bailey survived after extensive surgery but never played again in the NHL; the Maple Leafs announced that no player would wear number 6 again. This was the first retired number in the history of the league. On February 13, 1934, the Leafs held the Ace Bailey Benefit All Star Game, where Toronto defeated an All Star team comprised of the best players from the rest of the league; more than $20,000 was raised from the playing of the game.

A second All Star game was held for the family of the late Montreal great Howie Morenz, who was a top ten scorer in ten of his 14 seasons in the league and three times won the Hart Trophy as the league's most valuable player. He broke his leg in four places when his skate caught in the ice as he was checked by Earl Seibert of Chicago on January 28, 1937. Morenz died of a coronary embolism on March 8, 1937; 50,000 people passed by his casket at center ice of the Montreal Forum. A benefit game was played in November 1937 and raised over

Exterior view of Madison Square Garden, located on West 50th Street and 8th Avenue, New York City, New York, circa 1920's.

MADISON SQ. GARDEN
JAMES STEWART & CO.
BUILDERS

$20,000 for his family as the Canadiens beat the All-Stars by a 6-5 score.

Frederic McLaughlin, who owned the Chicago Black Hawks, wanted his general manager to field a team that was comprised solely of American-born players. The franchise made Bill Stewart, who was an umpire in major league baseball, the first American born coach in the history of the NHL. Eight of the 14 players on the Black Hawks roster were American-born in the 1937-38 season; while they struggled to a 14-25-9 record, the team still made the postseason and proceeded to upset the Canadiens, Americans and then stunned the Leafs in the Stanley Cup Finals. The Black Hawks are still the only team in NHL history to win the Stanley Cup after posting a losing record in the regular season.

Before the 1938-39 season, the Montreal Maroons, who were struggling on the ice and at the box office, suspended operations. The franchise couldn't keep up with the Canadiens and after being denied in their efforts to relocate to St. Louis; closed up shop. The New York Americans were in financial difficulty as well and were owned by the league at one point. With World War II underway and NHL players getting called up for active duty in the military, the Americans, who had moved to Brooklyn for the 1941-42 season, ceased operations after the season, bringing about the era that is known as the Original Six era. In that final season, the Maple Leafs became the first team in NHL history to rally from a 3-0 series deficit in the playoffs when they won four straight over the Detroit Red Wings to win the Stanley Cup. Through the 2013-14 season, three other teams have accomplished the feat in the NHL playoffs but none have done it in the Stanley Cup Finals.

1942-1967: The Original Six Era

With the departure of the Maroons and the Americans, the NHL was left with six teams in the 1942-43 season: the Toronto Maple Leafs, New York Rangers, Montreal Canadiens, Boston Bruins, Detroit Red Wings and the Chicago Black Hawks. These teams would comprise the league for the next quarter century and would be the backbone of the NHL going forward even to the present day. It is well known as the "golden age of hockey" by hockey fans and historians.

Frank Calder, who had been the president of the league, collapsed during a league meeting following a heart attack on January 25, 1943. He felt well enough to travel on February 3 back to Montreal but checked into Montreal General Hospital upon arriving in the city and suffered a fatal heart attack on February 4. He was replaced as league president by Red Dutton, who had owned the Brooklyn Americans; they had suspended operations after the 1941-42 season. Dutton took the job under the premise that the Americans would be reactivated after the close of World War II.

When World War II ended, Dutton found in 1946 that the other owners in the league weren't interested in bringing the Americans back and as such, had double-crossed him. Dutton resigned the presidency and Clarence Campbell took over the job. Dutton felt that the Rangers were to blame for the league's stance on the reinstatement of the Americans and he made the statement that the Rangers would never win another Stanley Cup while he was alive. As it turned out, he was correct; Dutton passed away in 1987 at the age of 89 and the Rangers hadn't won a Stanley Cup since 1940. They would finally break through and win a Cup in 1994, ending more than half a century of frustration.

The 1940s were exciting times for the NHL in the first years of the Original Six era. The ten minute overtime was removed from regulation contests in 1942 in order to allow teams to meet their trains on time instead of being delayed. This was partially due to the fact that there were travel restrictions during World War II. Regular season overtime didn't come back into the league until the 1983-84 season, well after even Campbell had finished his time as league president. Overtime was still present in playoff games, however.

Montreal's "Punch Line" of Maurice Richard, Elmer Lach and Toe Blake were 1-2-3 in the scoring race in the 1944-45 season, with Lach leading the way with 80 points, Blake following with 73 and Richard adding 67. Richard became the first player in NHL history to score 50 goals in a season that year, tallying his 50th goal at 17:45 of the third period of the 50th and final regular season game when he beat Harvey Bennett of the Boston Bruins. Richard never reached the mark again

Canadian professional hockey player Lorne 'Gump' Worsley of the New York Rangers poses in the goal, 1950s.

before retiring in 1960; it would be 16 years before the 50 goal plateau was reached again by any player.

The first official All Star Game in league history took place in Toronto's Maple Leaf Gardens on October 13, 1947. The game raised over $25,000 for the NHL Pension Society, which had been created shortly after Campbell assumed the presidency of the league. The All Stars defeated the Maple Leafs, 4-3, in the contest. Larry Kwong became the first non-white player and the first player of Asian ancestry to play in the National Hockey League when he played in one game for the New York Rangers against the Canadiens on March 13, 1948.

Every team had several stars to call upon in the 1940s: besides Blake, Lach and Richard, the Canadiens had Bill Durnan in net; the Bruins had Bill Cowley, Frank Brimsek, Detroit had Ted Lindsay, Gordie Howe, Sid Abel and Jack Stewart, Toronto had Syl Apps, Turk Broda, Babe Pratt and Lorne Carr, Chicago featured Max Bentley, Doug Bentley, Bill Mosienko and Earl Siebert while the Rangers featured Bryan Hextall, Lynn Patrick, Bud O'Connor and Neil Colville. A major rule change in time for the 1943-44 season led to the installation of the red line between the two blue lines for the offensive zones. The rule also allowed defensemen to pass the puck forward across the blue line instead of having to carry the puck up ice. Scoring increased 10 percent; four of the league's six teams scored at least 200 goals on the year.

Of course, the Original Six era was full of dynasties; in fact, during the quarter century that the era spanned, Montreal, Toronto and Detroit won 24 of the 25 Stanley Cups. Chicago's Stanley Cup victory in the 1960-61 season was the only time in the era that someone other than those three teams skated away with the Stanley Cup. Of course, there was a price to be paid for that victory; Chicago wouldn't win another Stanley Cup for another 49 years in the 2009-10 season. Montreal won ten Stanley Cups during that span, Toronto won nine and the Red Wings took five of their own.

Detroit reeled off seven straight division titles from 1948-49 through 1954-55; as of the 2013-14 season that feat has not been accomplished again. From 1944-45 through 1950-51, the Maple Leafs won five Stanley Cups in seven seasons. The 1951 Stanley Cup Finals was a thriller as all five games went to overtime between the Leafs and the Canadiens. Bill Barilko scored the Cup winning goal for Toronto in Game Five when he beat Montreal goaltender Gerry McNeil; he never played another game in the NHL as he died in a plane crash a few months later. The Leafs wouldn't win another Stanley Cup until 1962, which was the year that the plane Barilko was flying in when it crashed was found.

The Red Wings would take three of four Stanley Cups between 1951-52 and 1954-55 before yielding to the Canadiens, who made the Stanley Cup Finals in a record ten consecutive seasons from 1950-51 through 1959-60. Montreal lost four of the first five Stanley Cup Finals in the decade but then reeled off five straight Stanley Cup victories; they are the only team in NHL history to win as many as five consecutive Stanley Cups. A year after their impressive run, Bernie "Boom Boom" Geoffrion became the second player in NHL history to score 50 goals in a season; he posted 50 goals and 45 assists for 95 points in 64 games in the 1960-61 season. Geoffrion's numbers tapered off considerably after that as he failed to score more than 23 goals or 59 points in any of his final five seasons in the league.

In 1951, Conn Smythe came up with the idea of televising NHL games despite the fact that only one in ten Canadian homes owned a television. On October 11, 1952, CBC (the Canadian Broadcasting Company), aired their first NHL contest, which was a 2-1 Montreal victory over the Red Wings. Foster Hewitt called the first game in Maple Leaf Gardens on television on November 1, 1952 as the Leafs took on the Bruins. Hockey Night in Canada, as the program was called, quickly became CBC's top rated program. In 1956-57, CBS became the first station to broadcast hockey in the United States. When ratings proved to be a hit, the network ordered a 21 game slate for the following season and the era of hockey on television was born.

Of course, there were other big stories in the league during the 1950s: the first players union was created by Detroit's Ted Lindsay, who had been on the board of the NHL Pension Society since 1952 and was disgruntled with the fact that the owners wouldn't let the players see the books relating to the pension fund. The league was claiming financial difficulties, saying that the teams

Brothers Reg Bentley, Max Bentley and Doug Bentley of the Chicago Blackhawks pose on the ice on December 5, 1942 at Chicago Stadium in Chicago, Illinois.

BLACK HAWKS
CHICAGO
BLACK HAWKS
CHICAGO

were barely breaking even while the players had a different idea in mind. For his part in creating the union, Lindsay would be dealt by the Red Wings to the Chicago Black Hawks, who he played three years with before retiring after the 1959-60 season; he came out of retirement to play one final season with the Red Wings in 1964-65.

The league made a rule change in time for the 1956-57 season that allowed a player who had been sent to the penalty box to return to the ice if the opposing team scored a goal during the time he was in the box on a minor penalty. The offending player would stay in the box after a goal was scored only if he had been whistled for a major penalty; this was done because the Canadiens regularly scored multiple goals on the same penalty.

Maurice Richard became the first NHL player to score 500 career goals when he hit the mark on October 19, 1957; he would retire after the 1959-60 season with eight Stanley Cup championships and 544 goals to his credit. Willie O'Ree became the first black player in NHL history when he suited up for the Boston Bruins on January 18, 1958 against Montreal; he'd play 45 NHL games in his career. Montreal goaltender Jacques Plante became the first goaltender to wear a mask on a regular basis when he donned one on November 1, 1959 in a game at Madison Square Garden.

Plante was hit in the face by a shot off the stick of Andy Bathgate that cut him. In this era, there were no backup goaltenders, so the team's staff had to try to stitch Plante's face up to get him back on the ice. The gash took twenty stitches but Plante told coach Toe Blake that he wouldn't return to the ice without having the mask on. Blake caved, given the premise that Plante would take the mask off once his face healed. Montreal went on an 18 game unbeaten streak with the masked Plante in net; in the first game that he took the mask off, Montreal was defeated. Blake agreed to let Plante continue wearing the mask and the Canadiens went on to their fifth straight Stanley Cup. Other goaltenders around the league began to follow suit and the goalie mask became commonplace.

As the Original Six era wound down, the Maple Leafs were the dominant team in the league, winning three straight Stanley Cups in 1962, 1963 and 1964. Bob Baun became a folk hero in the 1964 Stanley Cup Finals; in Game 6 of the series with Toronto trailing three games to two, Baun took a slap shot from Gordie Howe off his ankle, breaking it in the process. Baun had the ankle taped and scored the game winning goal in overtime to force Game Seven. Toronto won that one and their third consecutive Cup thanks to some grit and determination.

With expansion franchises being approved and handed out in February 1966, the Original Six era would come to a close in the 1966-67 season. The Stanley Cup Finals pitted the Canadiens and the Maple Leafs, who were an aging roster with 37 year old Terry Sawchuk and 42 year old Johnny Bower in net, 39 year old Red Kelly and 36 year old George Armstrong up front along with 37 year old Tim Horton and 36 year old Marcel Pronovost on the blue line. Toronto's experience and leadership carried the team, known as the "Over the Hill Gang" to their fourth Stanley Cup in six years, defeating Montreal in six games. It's the last time, through the 2013-14 season, that the Maple Leafs have won the Stanley Cup or even played in the Stanley Cup Finals.

1967: First Expansion, Bill Masterton and Teams From Sea to Sea

As the 1966-67 season drew to a close, so did the Original Six era. Campbell had overseen a major expansion of the NHL, adding six new franchises that would double the size of the league overnight. The Philadelphia Flyers, Pittsburgh Penguins, Minnesota North Stars, Oakland Seals, Los Angeles Kings and St. Louis Blues all entered the league at the same time and took part in the expansion draft to put together their first rosters off the castoffs from the Original Six franchises. The fee for an expansion team at this time was $2 million.

St. Louis was awarded a team without making a bid or having an owner at the behest of James Norris and Arthur Wirtz, the owners of the Red Wings and Black Hawks; they owned the St. Louis Arena. The offer of a team in St. Louis was contingent on an owner coming forward to run the franchise; eventually a 16 man ownership group that included Baseball Hall of Famer

Bill Masterton #19 of the Minnesota North Stars poses for a portrait circa September, 1967 at the Met Center in Minneapolis, Minnesota. Masterton would die from a head injury on January 15, 1968.

Stan Musial stepped forward as the initial owners of the franchise. In picking the six cities that received teams, the league rejected bids that were submitted by Vancouver, Buffalo and Baltimore. The Original Six teams were clustered in the East Division while all six expansion teams were placed in the West Division. This kept the rivalries that had grown during the Original Six era intact while ensuring that an Original Six team would play for the Stanley Cup against a new club in the first couple years after the expansion took place.

A tragic incident took place in a January 13, 1968 game between the Oakland Seals and the Minnesota North Stars. Minnesota's Bill Masterton, who scored the first goal in franchise history earlier in the season, was hammered by Oakland's Ron Harris and Larry Cahan after dishing the puck off on a rush up the ice. Masterton fell backwards and landed on his head; he wasn't wearing a helmet, as was the case with the majority of players at that time. He lost consciousness from the hit and was bleeding heavily from the nose, ears and mouth. Despite ongoing treatment, Masterton never regained consciousness and died 30 hours after the hit on January 15, 1968. Through the end of the 2013-14 season, Masterton is the only NHL player to die of injuries sustained on the ice.

It would be another 11 years after the Masterton incident that the league mandated that players wear helmets, with that going into effect for the 1979-80 season. The Professional Hockey Writers Association came up with the Bill Masterton Memorial Trophy in 1968, which is awarded to the National Hockey League player who best exemplifies the qualities of perseverance, sportsmanship and dedication to hockey.

The 1970s: Further Expansion, Relocations and the WHA

Following the relative success of expansion for the league, Campbell wasn't done trying to make the NHL bigger and better going forward. Two of the cities that were rejected in the 1967 wave of expansion were granted teams in time for the 1970-71 season as the Buffalo Sabres and Vancouver Canucks joined the fold. The price of an expansion team tripled in that short span as Buffalo and Vancouver's ownership groups each had to pony up $6 million to have their respective teams become official.

The league wasn't done expanding in the decade; in 1972 the Atlanta Flames and the New York Islanders joined the league while in 1974, the Kansas City Scouts and the Washington Capitals joined the fray. What was a six team league as late as the 1967 Stanley Cup Finals had tripled in size to 18 teams by the time the 1974-75 campaign got underway. Like the Sabres and Canucks, the Flames, Islanders, Scouts and Capitals paid $6 million each to the league in order to get their franchises; the Islanders were forced to pay an additional $5 million to the Rangers for territorial infringement.

At the same time in 1972, there was a major threat to the NHL in the form of the World Hockey Association. The WHA was intent on making some noise as a force to be reckoned with alongside the NHL and promptly went out and threw around vast sums of money to raid NHL rosters of talent. Perhaps the biggest draw the WHA pulled in its early days was the signing of former Chicago great Bobby Hull, who signed a 10 year deal with the Winnipeg Jets; five years of the deal was as a player at a salary of $250,000 per season while the other five were for a front office position at $100,000 per season plus a $1 million signing bonus. By the time the WHA took to the ice for its first season, 67 NHL players, including future Hall of Famer and Stanley Cup winning goaltender Bernie Parent had jumped to the WHA.

It was the threat of the WHA that led to the expansion that brought the Islanders and Flames into the league in a preemptive strike to keep the fledgling league out of the recently built venues in those locations. The original plan was to not expand beyond 14 teams for a few seasons at least. The WHA received another shot in the arm when they signed Gordie Howe's sons, Mark and Marty, to play for the Houston Aeros. This prompted Gordie Howe to undergo wrist surgery so he could play again; he promptly signed with the Aeros as well and had the opportunity to play alongside his sons.

By the mid-1970s, both leagues were in some degree of financial difficulty due to the breakneck pace of spending the teams underwent in an effort to try and

Goalie Charlie Hodge #1 of the Vancouver Canucks makes the save on Brent Hughes #5 of the Philadelphia Flyers as Hodge's teammate Dave Tallon #19 checks Hughes' teammate Bobby Clarke #16 during their game in 1971 at the Pacific Coliseum in Vancouver, British Columbia.

ICTORIAVILLE

outdo the other. The NHL approved relocations of franchises for the first time since the 1930s in 1976, allowing the Scouts to move from Kansas City to Denver where they would become the Colorado Rockies. The Seals, who were floundering on the west coast, made the move to Cleveland and became the Barons. At the same time, the NHL rescinded potential expansion teams that were slated for Denver and Seattle in 1977; Denver wasn't overly affected thanks to getting the Rockies while Seattle still has yet to see a NHL team as of the end of the 2013-14 season.

Clarence Campbell retired as league president in 1977; John Ziegler took over the role as the first American president in NHL history. The rough times weren't over as far as relocations and the sort for the NHL. Cleveland struggled mightily in their first two seasons on the shores of Lake Erie. After potential attempts to merge the Barons with the Canucks and Capitals failed, the team merged with another financially struggling franchise in the Minnesota North Stars in 1978, which cut the league down to 17 teams for the 1978-79 season.

There had been talks about a potential merger with the WHA dating back to as far as 1976. A proposal was on the table where six WHA teams would join the NHL in the 1977-78 season and play in a division by themselves for one season until the scheduling could be figured out. The proposal was shot down by the NHL owners and four teams in the WHA promptly folded, leaving them with eight teams for the 1977-78 campaign. The loss of those teams led to increased questions about the stability and long term viability of the WHA given the loss of one-third of its brethren in one fell swoop.

The last big hurrah for the WHA was when they managed to get Wayne Gretzky to join them rather than go into the NHL Entry Draft. He was signed by the Indianapolis Racers and was later sold to the Edmonton Oilers after eight games with the team; along with goaltender Eddie Mio and Peter Driscoll, the Oilers paid $700,000 for the trio. The money still wasn't enough to bail out the Racers; they folded in December of 1978. Gretzky had 46 goals and 64 assists for 110 points in his lone season in the WHA, finishing third in the league in scoring. Peter Pocklington, the owner of the Oilers, signed Gretzky to a ten year personal services contract worth $3 million with options for an additional 10 years built into the contract.

Near the end of the 1978-79 season, the WHA thought that they had a deal on the table to merge with the NHL but the deal fell one vote short when it went to a vote by the NHL owners. Reports came out that the Canadiens and Canucks voted against the deal. Canadian fans were outraged by the vote and promptly organized a boycott of Molson products; Montreal was owned by the Molson Brewery and Vancouver served Molson products at Pacific Coliseum. A second vote was later held and both ownership groups reversed their previous votes, allowing the merger to proceed.

As part of the merger, the Hartford Whalers, Edmonton Oilers, Quebec Nordiques and the Winnipeg Jets joined the NHL in time for the 1979-80 season. Each franchise had to pay $6 million to the NHL to join the league along with an additional $1.5 million to the WHA to be dispersed among the remaining teams that would cease operations due to the merger. The merger wasn't really a merger when you look at it objectively as it was a form of expansion that didn't benefit the incoming WHA teams.

Instead of being put at the front of the NHL Draft order, the four WHA teams picked 18th, 19th, 20th and 21st in the draft. They also were allowed to protect just two skaters and two goaltenders from their rosters while the NHL teams that owned the rights to players that jumped leagues could reclaim their players without having to compensate the WHA teams. The NHL attempted to force Gretzky back into the entry draft but Pocklington forced the issue due to having him signed to a personal services contract and the league ultimately backed down, leaving Gretzky with the Oilers.

Perhaps one of the biggest reasons why the league eventually broke down and merged with the WHA was the overwhelming dominance of the Canadiens. In the seven seasons that the WHA existed, Montreal never posted fewer than 99 points in the standings and won five Stanley Cup championships, including four straight from 1975-76 through 1978-79. In that four year span, the Canadiens posted point totals of 127, 132, 129 and 115; they set a NHL record with the 132 points and their

Dave Keon #14 of the Hartford Whalers skates on the ice during an NHL game against the New York Rangers on October 28, 1979 at the Madison Square Garden in New York, New York.

Cooper
P.M.P. 14

eight losses that season (60-8-12) is also a NHL record for an 80 game season. The Canadiens were mainly able to keep the WHA from successfully raiding their roster, which kept their talented players on the roster while other teams in the league were getting wiped out by the upstart league.

The 1980s: The Great One, Super Mario, Islanders and Oilers Rule the Roost

The 1980s were a high flying, fast paced, up and down the ice decade that saw offensive numbers blow the roof off. Goals were scored at a ridiculous rate at times as offensive numbers that seemed unattainable just a decade or so before were blown by as if the skilled players in the league were going around pylons and shooting into an empty net.

There were still relocations and adjustments to the league; while there was no expansion in the 1980s, a couple of teams changed zip codes and hoped for greener pastures in a new location. The Flames, who were losing money by the truckload, finally gave up in Atlanta after the 1979-80 season and made the move to Alberta; they became the Calgary Flames. In the end, Calgary, who saw the Cowboys of the WHA fold after the initial merger proposal to join the NHL was rejected, ended up with a NHL franchise anyway. In 1982, the Colorado Rockies, formerly the Kansas City Scouts, picked up and moved for a second time, this time settling in New Jersey where they would become known as the New Jersey Devils.

The first players from behind the Iron Curtain played in the league in the decade as Peter and Anton Stastny defected from Czechoslovakia in 1980 and joined the Quebec Nordiques. Quebec owner Marcel Aubut played a key role in getting the Stastny brothers out of the country and they would be solid performers for the franchise; their defections opened the floodgates for Eastern European players to join the NHL. Michal Pivonka defected from Czechoslovakia in 1986, Alexander Mogilny did the same from the Soviet Union in 1989 and Petr Nedved walked into a police station in Calgary in 1989 after playing in a midget hockey tournament.

Gretzky quickly proved that he wasn't going to be a one hit wonder from his rookie season in the WHA as he scored 51 goals and added 86 assists for 137 points in his first season in the NHL. Gretzky tied Marcel Dionne of the Kings for the scoring lead but lost the Art Ross Trophy on goals scored as Dionne edged him in that category by a 53-51 margin. He still claimed the first of what would be eight consecutive Hart Trophies as the league's most valuable player; in 1980-81, he posted 55 goals and 109 assists for 164 points as he won the first of seven consecutive Art Ross Trophies as the league's leading scorer. By the time the decade was over, Gretzky would own eight of the ten highest single season point totals in NHL history.

The Great One is the only player to score at least 200 points in a season; he reached that mark a mind-blowing four times; including 212 points in 1981-82 when he set the NHL record for goals in a season with 92; he'd better the point record in 1985-86 when he posted 52 goals along with a league record 163 assists for 215 points. For good measure, Gretzky threw in seasons with 208 points in 1984-85 and 205 points in 1983-84; his LOWEST point total in the decade was his first season with 137 points, his next lowest was the 149 points he recorded in 1987-88 when he played in just 64 games. He would lead the league in assists every year in the decade, led in goals five different times and made the players around him better just by being on the ice.

While Gretzky was destroying opponents playing for the Oilers, another superstar center entered the league in the 1984 NHL Entry Draft. The Pittsburgh Penguins and New Jersey Devils were battling to see who would end up with the top pick in the draft, which was expected to be used on Mario Lemieux. As it turned out, the Penguins played just poorly enough to end up with the top selection and added Lemieux. There has been speculation since then that if the Penguins hadn't ended up with Lemieux, the team would have gone bankrupt. Lemieux didn't disappoint, winning the Calder Trophy in 1984-85 as the league's best rookie as he scored 43 goals and added 57 assists for 100 points.

Lemieux would go on to rack up impressive point totals of his own, leading the league in scoring in 1987-88 with 70 goals and 98 assists for 168 points and then

Wayne Gretzky in the jersey of the Campbell Conference (later renamed the Western Conference) on the ice during the 36th NHL All-Star game, New Jersey, January 31, 1984.

JOFA
TPM2020

narrowly missing joining Gretzky in the exclusive 200 point club as he tallied 85 goals with 114 assists for 199 points in 1988-89. He ripped off six straight 100 plus point seasons to start his career that carried him through the rest of the decade. The difference for Lemieux compared to Gretzky didn't have to do with their jersey number or where they played but with the talent pool surrounding them. Gretzky had bona fide stars and future Hall of Famers in Paul Coffey, Jari Kurri, Mark Messier, Glenn Anderson, Grant Fuhr and Andy Moog to help him out along with a terrific coach and general manager in Glen Sather. Lemieux was the focal point of the Penguins, who had a young of young, unproven talent as they tried to put together capable talent alongside him.

The decade opened with a dominant dynasty but it wasn't the Oilers. Instead, it was the New York Islanders who were setting the league ablaze. When Bill Torrey put together the Islanders in the expansion draft back in 1972, he chose to focus on building through the draft instead of going all in on veterans near the end of their careers with little left in the tank. He put together a nucleus featuring Denis Potvin, Billy Smith, Mike Bossy, Bryan Trottier, Clark Gillies, Bob Nystrom, John Tonelli and Ken Morrow. A late season trade in 1979-80 brought Butch Goring over from the Kings and things seemed to click for the Islanders.

New York would reel off four straight Stanley Cups from 1979-80 to 1982-83. In the process, they defeated the best that the league had to offer and even shut down Gretzky and the Oilers in the 1983 Stanley Cup Finals. The Islanders would win the Prince of Wales Conference again in the 1983-84 season but this time the Oilers were a year older, a year wiser and better prepared for what the four time defending champions would bring to the table. Edmonton picked up the first Stanley Cup in franchise history that year but the Islanders set a record for the four major professional sports leagues in North America by winning 19 consecutive postseason series in their run. The Oilers loss in the 1983 Stanley Cup Finals and subsequent victory by vanquishing the Islanders in 1984 proved to be the tip of the iceberg for Edmonton in the decade. The Oilers would win four Stanley Cups in five seasons and five in the span of seven seasons. Edmonton knocked off the Philadelphia Flyers in a relatively easy five games series in 1985 and bounced back after Steve Smith's own goal sunk them in the Smythe Division Finals against the Calgary Flames in 1986. The Oilers defeated the Flyers again in 1987, this time in a grueling seven game series after Edmonton blew a 3-1 series edge and crushed the Bruins in four straight games in 1988.

Gretzky was dealt by the Oilers to the Los Angeles Kings on August 9, 1988 along with Mike Krushelnyski and Marty McSorely in exchange for Jimmy Carson, Martin Gelinas, the Kings' first round picks in 1989, 1991 and 1993 along with $15 million in cash. The deal was less than well received by Oilers fans, who burned Pocklington in effigy in the parking lots of the Northlands Coliseum. Edmonton would blow a 3-1 series lead in the Smythe Division semifinals in 1989 against Gretzky and the Kings, losing the series four games to three. Even without Gretzky, the Oilers had enough firepower to return to the Stanley Cup Finals in the 1989-90 season and dispatch the Bruins in five games for their fifth Stanley Cup championship.

Gretzky would break Gordie Howe's league record for points in a career when he tallied his 1,851st career point with a goal in the third period on October 15, 1989 against his former team. Also happening in 1989 was the fact that Cliff Fletcher of the Calgary Flames reached a deal with the Soviet Union to allow Sergei Pryakhin to play in the NHL; this was the first time that a Soviet national player was allowed to play on a non-Soviet team. The famed "KLM" line of the Soviets, consisting of Vladimir Krutov, Igor Larionov and Sergei Makarov, would join the league that season as well. After just six European players were taken in the 1979 NHL Draft, 32 would be taken in 1989; that number would continue to climb in the following seasons, reaching 123 in the 2000 draft.

Gretzky #99 of the Los Angeles Kings looks on during a game in 1989 at the Great Western Forum in Inglewood, California. Wayne Gretzky played for the Kings from 1988 - 1996.

The 1990s: Gary Bettman, The Glowing Puck, Expansion and Labor Unrest

As the 1990s got underway, the league was seriously contemplating adding their first teams since the merger with the WHA back in 1979. The San Jose Sharks were the first team to be added to the team in the decade as they were admitted for the 1991-92 season. A year later, the Tampa Bay Lightning and the new version of the Ottawa Senators joined the league. All three franchises paid the league a $45 million expansion fee to join the league. The move to put teams in Tampa Bay and San Jose was part of adding teams in the south and the west coast in order to try and expand the fan base.

In 1993, the league added two more teams as they went from 21 in the 1990-91 season to 26 in time for the 1993-94 campaign by adding the Mighty Ducks of Anaheim and the Florida Panthers to the league. Those two teams had to shell out $50 million to join the league; half of Anaheim's expansion fee was paid to the Los Angeles Kings as a territorial fee to have the rights to share southern California with them. The league would add two more teams before the decade was out; the Nashville Predators joined in 1998 and the Atlanta Thrashers came in the league in 1999, both at a cost of $80 million.

There were relocations in the decade as well as teams moved in hopes of greener pastures and making more money. The Hartford Whalers closed up shop in Connecticut and moved to Raleigh, North Carolina and became the Carolina Hurricanes in 1997. The Minnesota North Stars were sold and eventually relocated to Dallas to become the Dallas Stars in 1993. Meanwhile, two Canadian teams ended up leaving the country as the Quebec Nordiques would relocate to Denver and became the Colorado Rockies in the 1995 season; a year later, the Winnipeg Jets pulled up stakes and moved to Phoenix to become the Phoenix Coyotes. The move of the Nordiques galled the population of Quebec, more so when Colorado swung a deal for former Montreal star Patrick Roy and won the Stanley Cup in their first season in the Rocky Mountains.

The league had its fair share of labor unrest during the decade. The first NHL strike took place on April 1, 1992 and lasted for ten days. It led to the ouster of Ziegler as league president; he was replaced on an interim basis by Gil Stein. The players were the winners in this standoff as they earned a hefty increase in playoff bonuses as well as increased control of their likenesses and the licensing with it while changes in free agency came about as well. The regular season schedule was expanded from 80 games to 84 as a result of the strike as well. In February of 1993, the league named Gary Bettman as the first commissioner of the NHL. Bettman had previously been the vice president of the NBA before taking the job as the NHL's top man.

As it turned out, that strike was merely the tip of the iceberg. After playing the entire 1993-94 season without a valid collective bargaining agreement, the owners locked the players out shortly before the regular season was due to start. The big issue at hand in the lockout was how to best fund the smaller market teams in the league; the owners were in favor of tying salaries to revenue in order to create more finances for smaller teams. The players were in favor of revenue sharing similar to the concepts that Major League Baseball and the NBA both have implemented where large market teams see a chunk of their revenues diverted to smaller markets in an effort to keep the playing field somewhat level.

When the two sides couldn't reach an agreement, the owners voted to lock out the players on October 1, 1994. It would drag on for over three months and didn't come to a close until January 11, 1995. The league lost 468 games from the schedule and as a result, had to cut the schedule from 84 games per team to 48 on the year. The season started on January 20 and ran through May 3 and to date remains the only time in NHL history that the regular season reached the month of May. There was no inter-conference play during the lockout shortened season due to the compressed schedule and future seasons were trimmed from 84 games down to 82. In addition, a salary cap on rookie contracts was put into place, with rookie contracts also having to be two way deals.

There were some major events that took place through the decade; Manon Rheaume became the first woman to play in an NHL game when she suited up in

National Hockey League Commissioner Gary Bettmann answers a question after announcing a counterproposal the NHL owners made to the players' union 07 January, as Quebec Nordiques' President Marcel Abut (L) listens.

net for the Tampa Bay Lightning in preseason action on September 23, 1992. Rheaume was also the first woman to sign a professional contract when she inked a deal with the Atlanta Knights, which was Tampa Bay's minor league affiliate. The Canadiens ripped off a league record ten straight overtime wins in the postseason en route to the Stanley Cup in 1993 over Gretzky and the Kings; it would prove to be the Great One's last run in the Stanley Cup Finals in his career. The New Jersey Devils won the Stanley Cup for the first time in franchise history in 1994-95, the Colorado Avalanche followed with their first win in 1995-96 as they bested a Florida Panthers team in just their third year of existence.

One of Bettman's first big deals was the signing of a television deal with Fox to get the NHL on the air in the United States. The deal was for five years with a price tag of $155 million for an average of $31 million per season. Fox's coverage was best known for the "FoxTrax", which was a technological advancement that was supposed to make it easier to follow the puck on television. The premise was that the puck would glow and have a comet trailing it on the ice. If the puck was traveling below 70 miles per hour, the comet was blue; if it went above 70 miles an hour, the comet would glow red. The problem was that blue didn't necessarily show up well on the white ice and it was widely panned to the point that comedians used it as part of their routines. The FoxTrax lasted from the 1996 All Star Game until the end of the 1998 Stanley Cup Finals before being scratched. After the end of the 1998-99 season, the NHL worked a deal with ESPN where ABC would be the network provider of NHL coverage, much to the chagrin and outrage of Fox.

The New York Rangers ended the Dutton Curse when they managed to pull off a seven game series win over the Vancouver Canucks in the 1994 Stanley Cup Finals. Seven former Edmonton Oilers were on that team, including captain Mark Messier. That Stanley Cup victory saw the first Russian names engraved on the chalice as Sergei Nemchinov, Sergei Zubov, Alexei Kovalev and Alexander Karpovtsev all were key members on that team. It was estimated that 285 million people tuned in to see the Rangers' victory and the program was CBC Sports' highest rated program in history to that point in time.

Just three years after the Rangers ended their long 54 year stretch without a Stanley Cup, the Detroit Red Wings did the same thing as they claimed the Cup in the 1996-97 season. The Cup victory was the first for Detroit since midway through the Original Six era back in the 1954-55 season. Detroit suffered tragedy shortly after winning the Cup as six days later; Vladimir Konstantinov was seriously injured in a limousine accident that left him with severe brain damage. The Red Wings would go on to repeat as Stanley Cup champions in 1997-98; through the end of the 2013-14 season they are the most recent repeat Stanley Cup champions.

In an effort to boost their image around the globe, the NHL began allowing their players to represent their home countries in the Winter Olympics beginning with the 1998 Winter Games in Nagano, Japan. Dominik Hasek, who was one of the top goalies in the league at the time while playing for the Buffalo Sabres, would lead the Czech Republic to the gold medal; he posted a 0.97 GAA with a sparkling .961 save percentage in six games during the Olympics. It's a trend that still goes on now; the NHL scheduled a break in the season schedule to allow players to take part in the 2014 Winter Olympics in Sochi, Russia.

The league saw two of its brightest stars retire during the decade as both Lemieux and Gretzky, cornerstones of the freewheeling, high scoring, end to end hockey that was prevalent throughout the 1980s, hung up their skates. Lemieux retired after the 1996-97 season after posting ten 100 plus point seasons and racking up six Art Ross Trophies. He was inducted into the Hockey Hall of Fame on November 18, 1997, with the decision made to waive the three year waiting period for induction. He led the Penguins to two Stanley Cup wins in 1991 and 1992; those were the first two Stanley Cups in franchise history.

One could write a book of its own about the accolades Gretzky accumulated during his storied career before hanging up the skates after playing his final game for the New York Rangers on April 18, 1999. When he retired, Gretzky owned a mind boggling 61 NHL records, including the marks for the most goals (894), assists (1,963 – he has more assists than any other player in NHL history has points) and points (2,857) to go along

Dominik Hasek of the Buffalo Sabres squirts water onto the ice during their 5-2 win over the New York Rangers at Marine Midland Arena in Buffalo, New York.

BAUER
BAUER
Cooper
SHK III

with nine Hart Trophies as the league's most valuable player, ten Art Ross Trophies as the league's leading scorer, five Stanley Cups, two Conn Smythe Trophies as the league's MVP in the playoffs, five Lady Byng Trophies for gentlemanly play and 15 seasons with at least 100 points. Like Lemieux, Gretzky had the three year waiting period waived and was inducted into the Hockey Hall of Fame on November 22, 1999.

The 2000s to Present: Crosby, Ovechkin and The Season That Never Was

Since the turn of the century and the new millennium, things have been up and down in the NHL, both in the performances on the ice and the popularity of the league. The one thing that hasn't changed is the fact that money is pouring in and the numbers seem to keep improving, regardless of how it's spun by the media, the owners or the players for that matter.

The most recent two expansion teams joined the NHL in time for the 2000-01 season as the Minnesota Wild, who were granted and would replace the Minnesota North Stars, who departed seven years earlier and the Columbus Blue Jackets both joined the league. The price tag involved was a hefty $80 million for the right to have a new team. Since their additions to the league, the NHL has had just one franchise relocate; the Atlanta Thrashers moved and proved for a second time that perhaps hockey and the state of Georgia don't mix well together as they were sold and relocated in 2011; the team is now known as the new version of the Winnipeg Jets. There was speculation that other teams like Nashville or Phoenix could move but those deals never materialized.

The league saw Lemieux, who by now owned the Penguins in a deal that turned the deferred money that the previous ownership owed him into equity in the franchise, come out of retirement during the 2000-01 season. In the process, he became the first player-owner in the history of the NHL. He picked up an assist 33 seconds into his first game back and added a goal later in the contest. Lemieux would go on to play parts of the next five seasons but missed huge chunks of most of them. He scored 76 points in 43 games in his comeback season and was a finalist for the Hart Trophy but played in just 24 games in 2001-02, including just one game after the 2002 Winter Olympics in Salt Lake City, where he led Canada to their first gold medal in more than 50 years in men's hockey. Lemieux finished eighth in the league in scoring in 2002-03 with 91 points in 67 games but that was his last big season; he played in just ten games in 2003-04 and retired 26 games in the 2005-06 season after being diagnosed with an irregular heartbeat. He announced his retirement on January 24, 2006.

Shortly after a thrilling postseason that saw the Tampa Bay Lightning win the first Stanley Cup in franchise history with a seven game victory over the equally small market Calgary Flames, rumblings of discord over a new collective bargaining agreement began. As is the norm when it comes to situations like this, the big sticking point was money: how much there was in the pot and how big a cut each side would get. Bettman and the owners wanted to install a salary cap in order to have a hard limit for owners' expenditures on player salaries. They called their concept cost certainty and based their thought process on a league commissioned report by Arthur Levitt, who formerly was the chairman of the United States Securities and Exchange Commission. The report stated that the NHL owners paid 76 percent of revenues in the form of player salaries and the teams lost a collective $273 million in 2002-03. There were several proposals made by Bettman and the owners, ranging from a hard cap to a soft cap with various exceptions similar to the one the NBA employs.

On the other side of the fence, the players were a proponent of the system that was in place where players tried to negotiate the best deals they could with teams and the owners paid what they deemed was market value. A report in the November 2004 issue of Forbes Magazine came up with an estimate that the league's report had nearly doubled the losses that the owners actually suffered in the 2002-03 season. Bob Goodenow, who was the president of the NHL Players' Association, emphatically vowed that the players would not accept a salary cap in any form.

Jamie McLennan #29 of the Minnesota Wild stops a shot by the Columbus Blue Jackets during the first period at the Xcel Energy Center in St. Paul, Minnesota.

SHER-WOOD
29
VAUGHN
VAUGHN

Negotiations continued back and forth with the players offering a proposal that included a luxury tax threshold similar to the NBA and a 24 percent rollback of salaries which was shot down by the league. As the league approached zero hour, the players offered a $52 million cap that wasn't tied to league revenues that Bettman refused; the owners countered with a $40 million figure with $2.2 million in benefits. That number was rejected by the players and on February 15, 2005 with the lockout already four and a half months old, Bettman sent a final proposal to the players; a cap figure of $42.5 million with an additional $2.2 million in benefits that was good until 11:00 am ET the following day. The players shot it down and offered a figure of $49 million, which was turned down again.

When 11:00 am ET came and went on February 16, 2005, Bettman made the announcement that the 2004-05 season was canceled due to the lockout. It marked the first time in history that an entire season was wiped out in any of the four North American professional sports leagues and just the second time that the postseason wouldn't be contested; the other was the 1994 Major League Baseball playoffs. It was the second time in league history that the Stanley Cup was not awarded and the first time since the 1918-19 season. As a result, many of the major leagues overseas as well as the minor league systems in the United States and Canada saw an influx of NHL players during the lockout.

The lockout finally came to an end on July 13, 2005 after 310 days. The owners got their salary cap while the players received 54 percent of revenues in the cap with a salary floor. Players also got their contracts guaranteed and revenue sharing would provide money from the top ten grossing teams in revenue to the bottom 15 in the league. Goodenow would resign as the head of the NHLPA five days after the deal was ratified; he was replaced by Ted Saskin. As a result of the new collective bargaining agreement, coupled with the launch of the NHL Network and a solid national TV deal in the United States, 26 of 30 franchises saw an increase in their franchise valuation in the following seasons.

Two of the biggest names to come on the scene were Sidney Crosby and Alexander Ovechkin. While they may not be Gretzky and Lemieux, the talented duo has filled scoresheets for the Pittsburgh Penguins and Washington Capitals since coming into the league. Crosby went first overall in the 2005 NHL Draft after the lockout was concluded, while Ovechkin was taken first overall in the 2004 NHL Draft before the lockout took place. Both players made their debuts in the 2005-06 season and finished first and second for the Calder Trophy as the league's best rookie, with Ovechkin getting the nod by scoring 52 goals and 54 assists for 106 points; Crosby posted 39 goals and 63 assists for 102 points.

The duo has put up impressive statistics in their careers; Crosby owns a pair of Art Ross Trophies as the league's leading scorer, one Rocket Richard Trophy for leading the league in goals, one Hart Trophy as league MVP and two Lester B. Pearson Trophies as the league's MVP as voted on by the players. Ovechkin has three Hart Trophies, three Pearson Trophies, four Rocket Richard Trophies and one Art Ross Trophy to go with his Calder. The biggest difference between the two is that Crosby owns two trips to the Stanley Cup Finals and led the Penguins to a championship in the 2008-09 season while Ovechkin and the Capitals haven't made it further than the Eastern Conference semifinals.

The two sides apparently didn't learn from the fallout that led to the cancellation of the 2004-05 season; on September 15, 2012, the owners locked the players out again. Again, money was the bone of contention; the owners wanted to reduce the players share of revenue from 57 percent to 46 percent and have the ability to cut it to 43 percent through the redefinition of what constituted hockey related revenue. The owners also wanted to limit contracts to four years in length while extending rookie deals from three years to five and necessitating ten years in the league to be a free agent as opposed to seven.

The players proposed a deal that would lower their cut of hockey related revenues from 57 percent to 52 and bounce back up to 54 in the final years of the deal. The owners countered with a deal that offered 49 percent at the beginning but tapered down to 47 by year six of the agreement. Both sides shot down the proposal of the other and when the old CBA expired, the lockout began. Four days later, on September 19, 2012,

National Hockey League Commissioner Gary Bettman announces that the 2004-05 season is being canceled during a news conference at the Westin New York, Times Square, February 16, 2005 in New York City. The NHL becomes the first North American professional league to cancel an entire season because of a labor dispute.

preseason games for the month of September were canceled. On October 16, Bettman canceled the rest of preseason action and regular season contests through November 1.

The owners came back with a proposal that had an even 50-50 split of hockey related revenue; two days after that, the players had three proposals of their own on the table. The owners refused to negotiate unless the players were going to use the 50-50 split as the starting point of negotiations and things went nowhere fast. On October 26, all regular season games for the month of November as well as the Hall of Fame Game were canceled. On November 2, the Winter Classic, scheduled for January 1, 2013 between the Maple Leafs and Red Wings, was canceled as well.

The two sides went back and forth with proposals, counterproposals and empty rhetoric while games were being canceled left and right. On January 6, 2013, the two sides finally came to terms on a tentative agreement that would bring the lockout to an end. The agreement included a salary cap floor of $44 million with a ceiling of $60 million beginning in the third year of the deal, which is the 2014-15 season. New contracts cannot be longer than seven years, unless a team is offering an extension to their own player; that can be eight years in length. The deal was officially ratified on January 12, 2013 with the regular season beginning a week later and ending on April 28. All games were played within their respective conferences, similar to the 1994-95 season.

The Chicago Blackhawks ended a 49 year drought without a Stanley Cup when they won it in the 2009-10 season; for good measure, they picked up a second title in four seasons with a Stanley Cup victory in 2012-13. They weren't the only team to break a long drought by hoisting the Stanley Cup: Boston picked up their first championship since 1971-72 in the 2010-11 season while the Los Angeles Kings won their first title in franchise history in 2011-12; they followed that up with a second championship in 2013-14. The Carolina Hurricanes won their first title in the 2005-06 season while Anaheim won their first one in 2006-07.

Major Firsts in NHL History

Every time that a commentator or journalist points out a major milestone or event that took place in a game recently, it's just the latest occurrence of that event. Somewhere, someone at some point in time accomplished that feat for the first time in league history. Here's a look at just some of the highlights of the first time something happened in the National Hockey League.

The first team to win a game in NHL history was the Montreal Wanderers, who beat the Toronto Arenas 10-9 on December 19, 1917. That same night, the Montreal Canadiens beat the Ottawa Senators by a 7-4 score. The win by the Wanderers would be the only NHL victory in franchise history; their arena burned down shortly thereafter and they disappeared from the NHL landscape. Charlie Gardiner of the Chicago Black Hawks was the first goaltender who was the team captain of a Stanley Cup winning team in the 1933-34 season. The Boston Bruins were the first team to pull their goalie late in a game, first attempting the feat on March 26, 1931 in a playoff game against Montreal when coach Art Ross pulled Tiny Thompson for an extra attacker in a game the Bruins lost 1-0.

Ralph Bowman of the St. Louis Eagles tallied the first penalty shot goal in league history in 1934. The Zamboni, the ice resurfacing machine which is as common in hockey now as the goal horn, made its debut in 1955 in a game between Montreal and Toronto. Jean Beliveau of the Montreal Canadiens was the first hockey player to appear on the cover of Sports Illustrated in 1956. Georges Vezina was the first goalie to record an assist in NHL history during the 1917-18 season for Montreal while Thompson of the Bruins was the first to record an assist after making an intentional pass during the 1935-36 season.Billy Smith of the New York Islanders was the first goaltender in league history to be credited with a goal on November 28, 1979 when Rob Ramage of the Colorado Rockies inadvertently put the puck in his own empty net; Smith was the last player on the Islanders to touch the puck. Ron Hextall of the Philadelphia Flyers was the first goalie to score a goal in the NHL by shooting the puck when he accomplished the feat into an empty net against the Bruins on December 8, 1987.

The Zamboni, the ice resurfacing machine which is as common in hockey now as the goal horn, made its debut in 1955.

CASINO NIAGARA
Hard Rock
CAFE
Hard Rock
CAFE

Garry Monahan was the first player ever selected in the NHL Entry Draft when he was taken first overall by the Montreal Canadiens in 1963. Ulf Sterner was the first Swedish born player to play in the NHL when he played four games for the Rangers in 1965. Jaromir Jagr was the first European born player to lead the league in scoring in the 1994-95 season. Niklas Lidstrom was the first European born player to win the Conn Smythe Trophy as the most valuable player in the playoffs in the 2001-02 season.

Phil Esposito was the first player in NHL history to score at least 100 points in a season when he posted 126 for the Boston Bruins in the 1968-69 campaign. Bobby Hull finished that season with 107 while Gordie Howe added 103 as the second and third players to reach the mark. Bobby Orr, Esposito's teammate, was the first defenseman to reach the 100 point plateau when he posted 120 points in the 1969-70 season. Orr was also the first defenseman to score 30 goals in a season, 40 goals in a season and was the first player in league history to post at least 100 assists in a season when he had 102 in 1970-71. The Bruins were the first team that had four 100 point scorers in the same season in that 1970-71 campaign. The Los Angeles Kings are the only team in NHL history to have two players post at least 150 points in the same season; they pulled that off in 1988-89.

Bobby Hull was the first player to score more than 50 goals in a season when he bagged 54 in the 1965-66 season; he, Bernie "Boom Boom" Geoffrion and Maurice Richard all had scored exactly 50 goals in a season. Esposito was the first to break the 60 goal barrier and the 70 goal barrier when he scored 76 goals in 1970-71. Howe was the first NHL player to score at least 1000 career points when he reached the mark in 1960-61 with the Red Wings; Denis Potvin of the New York Islanders was the first defenseman to reach the mark in the 1986-87 season.

The Stanley Cup: The Holy Grail of Hockey

The Stanley Cup is the championship trophy given to the National Hockey League champions. The Stanley Cup is named after Lord Stanley of Preston, who was the Governor-General of Canada from 1888 to 1893. The Cup was first awarded in 1893 to the Montreal Amateur Athletic Association on behalf of the Montreal Athletic Club. The Cup was originally known as the Dominion Hockey Challenge Cup, though it became almost immediately known as the Stanley Cup in honor of the man who brought it into existence.

Stanley purchased a punch bowl made in Sheffield, England for ten guineas, which translates to roughly $1,277 US dollars today. That original Stanley Cup is kept on permanent display at the Hockey Hall of Fame in Toronto, Ontario, Canada.

Lord Stanley never witnessed either a championship hockey contest or his namesake trophy presented to a championship team. Stanley's term as Governor-General was scheduled to end in September 1893, however, in April of that year (midway through the hockey season), Stanley's brother, the Fifteenth Earl of Derby, died. Lord Stanley resigned the Governor-Generalship and returned home to England on July 15, 1893 to become the Sixteenth Earl of Derby.

In 1910, the Cup was awarded solely to professional clubs. Following the demise of the PCHL in 1927, the Stanley Cup has only been awarded to NHL franchises. For his contributions to the game, Stanley was inducted to the Hockey Hall of Fame in 1945, one of fourteen inductions that year.

Jonathan Toews #19 of the Chicago Blackhawks hoists the Stanley Cup Trophy after defeating the Boston Bruins in Game Six of the 2013 NHL Stanley Cup Final at TD Garden on June 24, 2013 in Boston, Massachusetts. The Chicago Blackhawks defeated the Boston Bruins 3-2.

Road to the Stanley Cup

In the current playoff format, where eight teams from both the Eastern and Western Conference make the postseason, a team must win four best of seven series in order to claim the Stanley Cup.

Only twice has the Cup failed to be awarded. In 1919, with the series between the Montreal Canadiens and Seattle Metropolitans tied at 2-2-1, the series was put on hold when Montreal's Newsy Lalonde, Joe Hall, Billy Coutu, Newsy Lalonde, Jack MacDonald and coach George Kennedy were hospitalized with the flu. Hall died four days later, and the series never completed. This marked the only time in NHL history that the Stanley Cup was not awarded once the postseason began. The other campaign where no Cup was awarded was of course, the

HOCKEY HALL of FAME

2004-2005 season, which was completely wiped out by the lockout.

When it comes to Stanley Cup victories, the Montreal Canadiens have won the most, hoisting the Cup 24 times. Next are the Toronto Maple Leafs with 13, while the Detroit Red Wings have the most Stanley Cup victories among teams based in the United States with eleven.

Stanley Cup Lore

The Stanley Cup is the only trophy in the four major pro sports in North America to use the same trophy every year. In baseball, football and basketball, a new trophy is given to that particular year's winner. In hockey, the trophy is given to the team that wins and remains in their possession until the next champion is crowned.

The Stanley Cup has seen its fair share of bizarre incidents. In 1905, the Ottawa Silver Seven had a contest to see if one of them could kick the Cup into the Rideau Canal. After succeeding, the team left, with the Cup floating in the canal until the next day.

In 1907, the Montreal Wanderers were the champions. After having a photo taken to commemorate the event, they left the trophy at the home of the photographer. The photographer's mother thought that the trophy would be a terrific flower pot, and so it was for several months before it was relocated. The 1924 Montreal Canadiens left the Cup in a snowbank when the vehicle they were driving to the celebration got a flat. The Cup had been in the trunk, so when they took the spare out, they put the Cup on the side of the road. They managed to remember it and find it still in its location.

The original bowl and collar for the Cup were retired to the Hockey Hall of Fame in 1962 after the Maple Leafs won the Cup, only to be stolen in 1970. They were missing for seven years before an anonymous phone call pointed police in the direction of a back room of a Toronto cleaning store. There, the collar and bowl were located.

The Cup was nearly stolen in 1977 by a group of men who, when their vehicle was inspected, were found to have detailed plans of the Hall and a list of the equipment needed to pull off the job. Then in 1996, Colorado Avalanche defenseman Sylvain Lefebvre christened his child in the bowl of the Cup following his team's win.

These are just some of the zanier tales in the storied history of Lord Stanley's chalice.

Pantheon of Greatness: The Hockey Hall of Fame

The premise of a Hall of Fame for hockey first became mulled about on April 17, 1941 when the Canadian Amateur Hockey Association appointed a three man committee to look into the origins of hockey. Later in 1941, Leo Dandurand, who owned the Montreal Canadiens between 1921 and 1935, brought up the idea of a Hall of Fame with the National Hockey League. On September 10, 1943, after a meeting between the CAHA and the NHL, a decision was made to create a Hockey Hall of Fame in Kingston, Ontario, which is where Sutherland said organized hockey was born in 1886. Kingston mayor Stuart Crawford was installed as the Hall's first president.

The first induction class in the Hockey Hall of Fame came in 1945 and featured 14 individuals: 12 players and two builders, were enshrined in the inaugural class. They were: Howie Morenz, Georges Vezina, Hobey Baker, Dan Bain, Dubbie Bowie, Chuck Gardiner, Eddie Gerard, Frank McGee, Tommy Phillips, Harvey Pulford, Art Ross and Hod Stuart as players along with Sir Montagu Allan and Lord Frederick Stanley in the builders' category. Sutherland himself along with Cyclone Taylor, two of the biggest proponents for the Hall, was enshrined in 1947.

When Sutherland died in 1955, the construction for the Hockey Hall of Fame had yet to even begin in Kingston. NHL President Clarence Campbell was fed up with the delays and the lack of funds for the construction and in 1958, he removed the league's support for the Hall in Kingston. Instead, Campbell and the NHL chose to relocate the Hall of Fame to Toronto. The legendary Conn Smythe, who once owned the

Fans inside the Hockey Hall of Fame tent outside of Comerica Park during the Hockeytown Winter Festival Great Lakes Invitational - Day 2 of college hockey games played outdoors at Comerica Park on December 28, 2013 in Detroit, Michigan.

Detroit Red

Toronto Maple Leafs and was the chairman of the owners' committee, was the man in charge to find a suitable location.

After working with the rest of the league's owners and the league itself, Smythe managed to find enough resources to finance a building on property that was acquired from the city of Toronto on the grounds of the Canadian National Exhibition. Smythe supervised the construction of the building and construction was completed on May 1, 1961. The Hall of Fame officially opened for visitors on August 26, 1961.The Hall stayed in that location until it relocated to the former BCE Place, now Brookfield Place, just a short distance from Union Station in Toronto. After a $27 million renovation by Bell Canada, the new venue for the Hockey Hall of Fame opened on June 18, 1993.

For a person to be inducted to the Hockey Hall of Fame, they must be nominated by an elected 18-person selection committee which consists of Hockey Hall of Fame members and media personalities. Each committee member is allowed to nominate one person in each category per year, and candidates must receive the support of 75% of the members of the committee that are present, or a minimum of ten votes. In any given year, there can be a maximum of four male players, two female players, and a combined two in the builders and on-ice officials categories. For a player, referee, or linesman to be nominated, the person must have been retired for a minimum three years.

As of the Class of 2013, 259 players (256 men, 3 women), 101 builders and 15 on-ice officials have been inducted into the Hockey Hall of Fame. Fifteen of those who are enshrined were done posthumously. Ten players had their three year waiting period waived due to being exceptionally notable; they included Dit Clapper, Maurice Richard, Ted Lindsay, Red Kelly, Terry Sawchuk, Jean Beliveau, Gordie Howe, Bobby Orr, Mario Lemieux and Wayne Gretzky. After Gretzky's induction, the Hall announced that there would be no more bypassing the waiting period unless there were certain humanitarian circumstances. Lemieux is one of three players to play in the NHL after being inducted in the Hockey Hall of Fame, Howe and Guy Lafleur are the others. As of the 2013 class, the Toronto Maple Leafs have the most players inducted into the Hall of Fame with 56.

The inductees for the 2014 class of the Hockey Hall of Fame are slated to be announced on June 24, 2014 with the induction of those members scheduled for November 10, 2014.

The Stanley Cup is on display prior to the HHoF induction press conference and photo opportunity at the Hockey Hall of Fame on November 12, 2012 in Toronto, Ontario.

HOCKEY HALL of
LE TEMPLE de

ANAHEIM DUCKS

First Year of Existence: 1993-94
Owner: Henry Samueli
Coach: Bruce Boudreau (November 30, 2011-present)

The Anaheim Ducks entered the NHL in the 1993-94 season as one of two expansion teams with the Florida Panthers as the other.

The team was originally owned by the Walt Disney Company and was known as the Mighty Ducks of Anaheim. The franchise named Ron Wilson its first head coach on June 30, 1993.

The team took part in the 1993 NHL expansion draft along with the Panthers to piece together their initial rosters. The Mighty Ducks assembled a group that featured goaltenders Guy Hebert and Ron Tugnutt, veteran defensemen Alexei Kasatonov, Bobby Dollas and Randy Ladouceur along with forwards Terry Yake, Stu Grimson, Troy Loney and Joe Sacco. With their first selection in an entry draft, the Mighty Ducks made Paul Kariya their choice with the 4th overall pick in 1993.

The Mighty Ducks played their first game at home on October 8, 1993 against the Detroit Red Wings. Anaheim was crushed 7-2, with Sean Hill scoring the team's first goal. Five days later, the team picked up their first win by recording a 4-3 victory over the Edmonton Oilers with Tugnutt in net.

Anaheim finished the season with 71 points, which was ninth in the West, 11 points behind San Jose for the final playoff spot. The Mighty Ducks set an expansion record along with the Panthers for the most victories by a team in its first year. Bob Corkum led the team with 23 goals while Yake was the team leader in points with 52. Hebert was 20-27-3 with a 2.83 GAA, a .907 save percentage and two shutouts.

The Mighty Ducks made the playoffs for the first time in 1996-97. In a major deal that took place on February 7, 1996, the Ducks sent Chad Kilger, Oleg Tverdovsky and a 3rd round pick to the Winnipeg Jets for Marc Chouinard, a 4th round selection and Teemu Selanne.

The Mighty Ducks finished the 1996-97 season 36-33-13, which was second in the Pacific Division. Selanne led the team with 51 goals and 109 points while Kariya put up 44 goals and 99 points. Hebert went 29-25-12 in 67 games with a .919 save percentage, a 2.67 GAA and four shutouts on the season. The Mighty Ducks faced the Phoenix Coyotes in the opening round of the playoffs and won the first two games in the series, with Selanne scoring the first playoff goal in team history. Anaheim lost the next three games before rallying for wins in the final two games to take the series 4-3. The Ducks were swept in the conference semifinals by the Red Wings; one game went to overtime, a second to double overtime and a third ended in triple overtime.

Anaheim returned to the playoffs in 1998-99 but was beaten in the quarterfinals by Detroit in a sweep. With Mike Babcock at the helm in 2002-03, the Mighty Ducks went 40-27-9-6 and returned to the postseason. Anaheim swept Detroit in the first round and followed that up with a 4-2 win over the Dallas Stars to advance to the Western Conference Finals for the first time.

Anaheim swept the Minnesota Wild to advance to the Stanley Cup Finals for the first time. The Mighty Ducks took the New Jersey Devils to seven games but ran out of steam as they were shut out 3-0 to lose the series 4-3. Giguere won the Conn Smythe Trophy for the MVP in the playoffs. Sykora led the team with 34 goals in the regular season while Kariya added 25 goals and a team leading 81 points.

The Mighty Ducks drafted Corey Perry and Ryan Getzlaf in the first round of the 2003 NHL Draft but were dealt a blow when Kariya signed a free agent deal with the Colorado Avalanche. They added Sergei Fedorov and Vaclav Prospal but missed the playoffs in 2003-04. They finished 29-35-10-8 for 76 points.

Anaheim went 43-27-12 in 2005-06 to return to the playoffs in Randy Carlyle's first season as head coach. After beating the Calgary Flames 4-3 in the opening round, the Ducks followed that up with a sweep of the Avalanche. In the conference finals, the Ducks ran out of gas as they were beaten 4-1 by the Edmonton Oilers. Selanne returned to the team as a free agent after an injury-plagued season with Colorado and led the team with 40 goals and 90 points. Andy MacDonald had 34 goals along with 85 points while Giguere played in 60 games, going 30-15-11 with a 2.66 GAA, .911 save percentage and two shutouts.

The 2006-07 saw a transfer of ownership as Disney sold the team to Henry Samueli. Along with general manager Brian Burke, Samueli decided to make the change in team name from the Mighty Ducks of Anaheim to the Anaheim Ducks. The team finished 48-20-14 for 110 points and their first division championship. Anaheim handled the Wild 4-1 in the opening round and followed that up with a 4-1 series win over the Vancouver Canucks in the conference semifinals. The Ducks then bested Detroit 4-2 in the conference finals to advanc to the Stanley Cup Finals for the second time.

This time Anaheim would not be denied as they knocked off the Ottawa Senators 4-1 fo their lone Stanley Cup. Defenseman Scott Niedermayer won the Conn Smythe Trophy as the Ducks became the first California team to win the Stanley Cup. Selanne led the team with 48 goals and 94 points while Giguere was stellar in net, posting a 36-10-8 record with a 2.26 GAA, a .918 save percentage and four shutouts.

The Ducks would make the playoffs in three of the next four seasons under Carlyle, but couldn't find the same success. Carlyle was fired 24 games into the 2011-12 season and was replaced by Bruce Boudreau. The Ducks won their second division title in the lockout shortened 2012-13 season but were beaten in the opening round by the Red Wings 4-3.

The 2013-14 season was a solid one for the Ducks as they set franchise records in wins and points (116) as the team was 54-20-8. Perry led the team with 43 goals while Getzlaf had 31 goals to go along with team highs in assists (56) and points (87) on the season. Jonas Hiller was solid in net, playing in 50 games and posting a 29-13-7 record with a 2.48 GAA, .911 save percentage and five shutouts. The Ducks eliminated the Dallas Stars, 4-2, in the opening round of the Western Conference playoffs. Anaheim held a 3-2 series lead in the conference semifinals but lost 4-3 to the Los Angeles Kings.

Andrew Cogliano #7 of the Anaheim Ducks skates the puck out of the Ducks zone in the second period during Game Six of the Second Round of the 2014 NHL Stanley Cup Playoffs against the Los Angeles Kings at Staples Center on May 14, 2014 in Los Angeles, California. The Kings defeated the Ducks 2-1.

COGLIANO
7
EASTON
EASTON

ARIZONA COYOTES

First Year of Existence: 1972-73 (WHA), 1979-80 (NHL)
Owner: IceArizona Acquisition Company, LLC
Coach: Dave Tippett (September 24, 2009-present)

The Phoenix Coyotes franchise began in the World Hockey Association in the 1972-73 season as the Winnipeg Jets. When the WHA ran into financial difficulties and folded in 1979, the Jets were brought into the NHL along with the Edmonton Oilers, the Quebec Nordiques and the New England (Hartford) Whalers.

When Winnipeg joined the NHL, they had to deal with a steep price for becoming part of the league. Three of their top six scorers from the 1979 Avco Cup winning team were given up in a reclamation draft. The Jets selected 18th of the 21 teams in the NHL Entry Draft. Tom McVie was the first coach of the franchise. The Jets lost the first game in franchise history as a NHL team 4-2 on the road to the Pittsburgh Penguins on October 10, 1979. They picked up the first win in franchise history on October 14, 1979 with a 4-2 win over the Colorado Rockies.

The Jets finished their first NHL season 20-49-11 for 51 points and tied for last in the league. Morris Lukowich led the team with 35 goals and 74 points on the season. The Jets picked Dave Babych with the second overall pick in the 1980 NHL Draft.

The Jets put up a dismal 9-57-14 mark in 1980-81, finishing with the worst record in franchise history. McVie was the interim coach but was fired again after the team started the year 1-20-7. The team picked Dale Hawerchuk with the top pick in the 1981 NHL Draft, who became a #1 center and won the Calder Trophy as Rookie of the Year in 1981-82.

Hawerchuk exploded in his rookie season, scoring 45 goals and adding 58 assists for 103 points. Under Tom Watt, the Jets were 33-33-14 and they made the playoffs for the first time as a NHL franchise. The Jets were brushed aside 3-1 by the St. Louis Blues in the Norris Division semifinals. The following season, 1982-83, the Jets were moved to the Smythe Division, which buried them with powerhouse teams like the Edmonton Oilers and the Calgary Flames.

Winnipeg made the playoffs in six straight seasons in the 1980s but won just two playoff series. Winnipeg beat Calgary 3-1 in the 1984-85 Smythe semifinals before being swept by the Oilers. Hawerchuk posted career highs with 53 goals and 130 points. In 1986-87, the Jets won in the Smythe Division semifinals, 4-2 over the Flames as the Jets were no match for the Oilers.

Between 1988-89 and 1995-96, the Jets would make the playoffs just three times and were eliminated in the division semifinals, once by Edmonton and twice by Vancouver. Hawerchuk was dealt in a blockbuster deal during the 1990 NHL Draft. He went to Buffalo with Winnipeg's 1st round pick, which turned into Brad May. Winnipeg received Phil Housley, Scott Arniel, Jeff Parker and Buffalo's top pick, which the Jets parlayed into Keith Tkachuk. The team also saw the emergence of the Finnish Flash, Teemu Selanne, who set NHL records with 76 goals and 132 points during his rookie season of 1992-93.

The franchise faced major financial problems due to skyrocketing salaries and the fact that Winnipeg was a small market with a small arena. In December 1995, Jerry Colangelo, along with a group of others, bought the Jets with the intent to move them to Phoenix in time for the 1996-97 season. After mulling over several potential names, a contest to name the team came up with the Coyotes.

The team played its first game as the Coyotes on October 5, 1997 on the road against the Hartford Whalers and lost 1-0. They picked up the first win as the Coyotes two days later with a 5-2 road win over the Boston Bruins. Phoenix finished the season 38-37-7 and made the playoffs, but was eliminated in the first round 4-3 by the Mighty Ducks of Anaheim.

That trend continued for the next few seasons and despite a solid array of talent, the Coyotes struggled in the postseason. Phoenix made the playoffs in five of their first six seasons in the desert but was eliminated in the opening round each time. With financial problems beginning to loom, the franchise was sold to Steve Ellman with Wayne Gretzky part owner of the franchise.

Phoenix opened a new arena, the Glendale Arena (now the Jobing.com Arena) in 2003 but that didn't help matters. Ellman sold the franchise to Jerry Moyes in 2005. The Coyotes finished above .500 just once in that span. Gretzky coached the team for four seasons before stepping aside after 2008-09 when Dave Tippett took over.

Moyes put the team in bankruptcy in 2009 hours before a deal was to be presented for him to sell the team to Reinsdorf. He planned on selling the team to Jim Balsillie, who was going to buy the team and move it to Hamilton. Several potential ownership groups have come forward only to fall through: Reinsdorf, Michael Hulsizer, Greg Jamison, Ice Edge Holdings an Darin Pastor all failed to come up with a proposal that met the league's approval.

Phoenix went 50-25-7 in Tippett's first season as the coach in 2009-10, setting a franchis record with 107 points. The team failed to advance past the first round of the playoffs, losin 4-3 to the Detroit Red Wings. The Coyotes returned to the playoffs in 2010-11 only to b swept in the opening round by the Red Wings. In 2011-12, Phoenix was 42-27-13 and won the Pacific Division, the first division title in franchise history at the NHL level. Phoenix knocked off the Blackhawks 4-2 in the opening round of the playoffs for their first playoff series win in 25 years. They followed that up with a 4-1 triumph over Nashville. Phoenix advanced to the Western Conference Finals for the first time, but was knocked off 4-1 by the Los Angeles Kings.

The team missed the playoffs the last two seasons, but things are looking better off the ice. On July 2, 2013 the Glendale City Council approved a 15 year lease with Renaissance Sports and Entertainment with the premise that the team would be sold for $225 million. There is an agreement in place where if RSE accumulates $50 million in losses, they can move the team in five years. On January 29, 2014, the team announced that they would be changing the name to the Arizona Coyotes beginning with the 2014-2015 season.

Mikkel Boedker #89 of the Phoenix Coyotes skates with the puck during the NHL game against the Minnesota Wild at Jobing.com Arena on March 29, 2014 in Glendale, Arizona. The Wild defeated the Coyotes 3-1.

89
BAUER
PHX
89
89

BOSTON BRUINS

First Year of Existence: 1924-25
Owner: Delaware North Companies
Coach: Claude Julien (June 22, 2007-present)

The Boston Bruins are one of the Original Six franchises in the National Hockey League, starting play in the 1924-25 season. At the convincing of Charles Adams, the NHL made the decision to expand to the United States and Boston was awarded a franchise on November 1, 1924. Along with the Montreal Maroons, the team was one of the first expansion teams in NHL history. The franchise's first coach was Art Ross, who was a solid player earlier in his career.

Boston played their first game on December 1, 1924 against the Maroons. Fred Harris scored the first goal in franchise history while Carson Cooper banged home the winner in a 2-1 victory. Boston finished the season 6-24-0 and in the cellar of the NHL. Jimmy Herbert led the team with 17 goals and 22 points while Doc Stewart was the team's top goaltender with a 5-16-0 mark, a 3.08 GAA and a pair of shutouts.

The Bruins took advantage of the collapse of the Western Hockey League to add talent, including Eddie Shore, to the mix. Boston went 21-20-3 in 1926-27 to make their first playoff appearance. The Bruins beat the Chicago Blackhawks on goal differential in the quarterfinals and followed that up on goal differential over the New York Rangers in the semifinals to advance to the Stanley Cup Finals for the first time. Boston was defeated by the Ottawa Senators, 2-0-2, in the first Stanley Cup Finals exclusively between NHL clubs.

Boston won four straight division titles between 1927-28 and 1930-31, including setting a NHL record for winning percentage in 1929-30. The Bruins won their first Stanley Cup in 1928-29 season under coach Cy Denneny. The team lost the Stanley Cup Finals the next season with Ross behind the bench. The Bruins added Stanley Cup titles in 1938-39 and 1940-41.

Boston became the first team in NHL history to own a Zamboni machine after having a test run on New Years' Day 1954; their initial Zamboni would be sent to the Hockey Hall of Fame in 1988. The Bruins also were trendsetters in breaking the color barrier as Willie O'Ree was the first black player to play in a NHL game on January 18, 1958.

The Bruins missed the playoffs eight straight times to close out the Original Six era though they did make a couple of major moves. Boston signed defenseman Bobby Orr in 1964, who won the Calder Trophy as Rookie of the Year in 1966-67. Orr would go on to win eight straight Norris Trophies as the league's best defenseman and three straight Hart Trophies as the league's MVP. He also is the only defenseman in league history to win the Art Ross Trophy as the league leader in points; he did it twice.

The Bruins picked up key players Phil Esposito, Ken Hodge and Fred Stanfield in a deal with the Chicago Blackhawks that sent Gilles Marotte, Pit Martin and Jack Norris to Chicago right before rosters were frozen for the expansion draft. Esposito went on to become the first player to score at least 100 points in a season and won the Art Ross Trophy four years in a row. He is one of four players to do that.

The Bruins would make the playoffs 29 straight times from the 1967-68 season through the 1995-96 season. Boston ended a 29 year Stanley Cup drought in 1969-70 as the Bruins swept the St. Louis Blues with Orr scoring the Cup winning goal in overtime. Esposito led the team with 43 goals while Orr had 33 goals along with team highs in assists (87) and points (120) on the season. Gerry Cheevers (24-8-8, 2.72 GAA, four shutouts) and Eddie Johnston (16-9-11, 2.98 GAA, three shutouts) had a near-even split in net.

Boston would set franchise records with 57 victories and 121 points in 1970-71 but was upset 4-3 by the Canadiens with Ken Dryden leading Montreal in net. The Bruins bounced back to win the Cup in 1971-72 with a 4-2 win over the New York Rangers behind Esposito's 66 goal, 133 point season along with Orr's 37 goals and 117 points. It was a near even split in net as Cheevers was 27-5-8 with a 2.50 GAA and two shutouts while Johnston went 27-8-3 with a 2.71 GAA and two shutouts. Boston returned to the Stanley Cup Finals but lost to the Philadelphia Flyers 4-2 in 1974-75.

The team won four straight division titles under Don Cherry from 1975-76 through 1978-79 as part of a five season run of at least 100 points; they were eliminated in the semifinals twice and lost the Stanley Cup Finals in 1976-77 and 1977-78, both times tc Montreal. Boston would have to wait nearly a decade to return to the Stanley Cup Finals i 1987-88 with Terry O'Reilly as the head coach. Boston couldn't close things out as they we swept by the Edmonton Oilers. In 1989-90, Boston returned to the Stanley Cup Finals but w handled by the Oilers again, 4-1.

The Bruins have made the playoffs in each of the seven seasons under coach Claude Juli with two Stanley Cup Finals appearances in that span. Boston won the Stanley Cup in 20 11 by beating the Vancouver Canucks 4-3. The Bruins trailed the series 2-0 before outsco Vancouver 21-4 over the last five games.

When it came to defending their title, Boston fell short as they lost in the opening rou 4-3 by the Washington Capitals in 2011-12. The Bruins returned to the Stanley Cup Finals 2012-13 after rallying from a 4-1 deficit in the third period of Game 7 to beat the Maple Le in overtime to take a 4-3 series win. They followed that up with a 4-1 series win over th New York Rangers in the conference semifinals and then swept the Pittsburgh Penguins In the Stanley Cup Finals, Boston fell short as they lost to the Chicago Blackhawks 4-2 ir a battle of Original Six franchises.

In the 2013-14 season, the Bruins finished 54-19-9 for 117 points as they won the Atlantic Division. The Bruins were led by Patrice Bergeron's 30 goals while David Krejci had 19 goals along with team highs in assists (50) and points (69) on the season. Tuukka Rask was the main man in goal, playing in 58 games and posting a 36-15-6 record with a 2.04 GAA, .930 save percentage and seven shutouts. Boston whipped the Detroit Red Wings, 4-1, in the Eastern Conference quarterfinals but was eliminated by the Canadiens 4-3.

Tuukka Rask #40 of the Boston Bruins makes a save against the Montreal Canadiens during Game Seven of the Second Round of the 2014 NHL Stanley Cup Playoffs at the TD Garden on May 14, 2014 in Boston, Massachusetts.

BRUINS
40
EPIC

BUFFALO SABRES

First Year of Existence: 1970-71
Owner: Hockey Western New York Hockey, LLC
Coach: Ted Nolan (November 13, 2013-present)

The Buffalo Sabres were part of the second wave of expansion in the National Hockey League, joining with the Vancouver Canucks in 1970-71. The franchise was originally owned by Seymour Knox III, Northrup Knox and Robert O. Swados. The Knox brothers had tried to bring in a team before, starting with a bid during the league's original expansion in 1967 and then attempting to purchase the Oakland Seals and move the team, but were rebuffed both times. Punch Imlach was named the first coach in team history.

Buffalo took part in the 1970 NHL Expansion Draft and pieced together their initial roster. Among the players selected by the Sabres in the expansion draft were defensemen Reg Fleming, Paul Terbenche, Jim Watson and Al Hamilton with forwards Phil Goyette, Don Marshall and Gerry Meehan. Buffalo won a spin on the roulette wheel giving them the top pick in the 1970 NHL Entry Draft. They selected winger Gilbert Perreault, who set a series of franchise records over the course of his career.

The Sabres played their first game on the road against the Pittsburgh Penguins on October 10, 1970. Watson scored the first goal in franchise history on an assist from Meehan and Perreault bagged the winning goal in a 2-1 Sabres win. It proved to be one of the high points of the season for the Sabres, who finished the year with a 24-39-15 mark. Perreault led the team with 38 goals and 72 points. Roger Crozier played 44 games in net, going 9-20-7 with a 3.69 GAA and one shutout while Joe Daley posted a 12-16-8 mark with a 3.70 GAA and one shutout.

Buffalo drafted Rick Martin with the 5th overall pick in the 1971 NHL Draft and acquired Rene Robert in a late-season trade with the Pittsburgh Penguins. Those two, paired with Perreault, formed the famed "French Connection" line that was a major key to the Sabres' success. Buffalo made the playoffs for the first time in 1972-73 as they posted a 37-27-14 mark, but were knocked off in the first round 4-2 by the Montreal Canadiens. Robert led the team with 40 goals while Perreault had team highs in assists with 60 and points with 88. Crozier was 23-13-7 with a 2.76 GAA and three shutouts while Dave Dryden was 14-13-7 with a 2.65 GAA and three shutouts.

In Floyd Smith's first season as head coach in 1974-75, the Sabres won their first division title and set a franchise record with 113 points. Buffalo knocked off the Chicago Blackhawks 4-1 in the opening round of the playoffs and followed with a 4-2 elimination of the Canadiens in the semifinals to advance to the Stanley Cup Finals for the first time. Buffalo lost the finals, 4-2, to the Philadelphia Flyers in a series that is well remembered for Game 3 at the Memorial Auditorium. The game was full of fog due to unseasonably warm weather and a lack of air conditioning in the Memorial Auditorium. Players, officials, and the puck were invisible to many spectators. During a face-off and through the fog, Sabres center Jim Lorentz spotted a bat flying across the rink and swung at it with his stick, killing it. It was the only time that any player killed an animal during an NHL game. The Sabres won that game thanks to Robert's goal in overtime but couldn't hang on in the series.

Buffalo was knocked off by the New York Islanders in the 1979-80 semifinals 4-2, missing their best chance at a Stanley Cup Final for more than a decade. The Sabres would go no further than the Adams Division Finals in their next five playoff appearances through 1984-85. Buffalo would see Perreault reach the 500 goal plateau in his career during 1985-86, retiring 17 games into 1986-87.

Buffalo picked up goaltender Dominik Hasek in a deal with the Chicago Blackhawks in exchange for Stephen Beauregard and future considerations, which eventually materialized into a draft pick used to select Eric Daze. Hasek won two Hart Trophies as the league's most valuable player and six Vezina Trophies as the league's best goaltender during his tenure in Buffalo.

Buffalo went to the Eastern Conference Finals in Lindy Ruff's first season as head coach in 1997-98 but was knocked off by the Washington Capitals 4-2. The Sabres put together a 37-28-17 mark in 1998-99; Buffalo swept Ottawa in the opening round and followed that up with a 4-2 win over the Bruins in the conference semifinals. The Sabres knocked off the Toronto Maple Leafs, 4-1 in the Eastern Conference Finals to advance to the Stanley Cup Finals. Buffalo lost to the Dallas Stars 4-2 with Brett Hull scoring the controversial series winning goal in triple overtime of Game 6.

Hasek was dealt to the Red Wings after the 2000-01 season. Buffalo made back to back conference finals appearances, losing to the Carolina Hurricanes in 2005-06 and then by the Ottawa Senators in 2006-07. The Sabres have struggled since, making the playoffs just twice in the last seven seasons. Ruff was fired partway through the 2012-13 season and was replaced by Ron Rolston.

In the 2013-14 season, things couldn't have gone worse for the Sabres. Rolston was fired 20 games into the season and was replaced by Ted Nolan, who was back for his second stint as coach. General Manager Darcy Regier was also dismissed. Pat LaFontaine was named the President of Hockey Operations. He left the team on March 1, 2014 to return to his post with the NHL.

On January 9, 2014, the Sabres named Tim Murray the new General Manager. Buffalo finished the season with a 21-51-10 record for 52 points and the worst record in the league. Buffalo traded goaltender Ryan Miller along with Steve Ott to the St. Louis Blues for Jaroslav Halak, Chris Stewart, William Carrier and a pair of draft picks. Halak ended up never playing for the Sabres and was traded with a third round pick to the Capitals for Michael Neuvirth and Rostislav Klesla at the trade deadline on March 5, 2014.

Buffalo was led by Tyler Ennis, who scored 21 goals, Christian Ehrhoff had a team best 27 assists while Cody Hodgson had a team best 44 points. Miller played in 50 games before the deal, posting a 15-22-3 mark with a 2.72 GAA and a .923 save percentage.

Alexander Sulzer #52 of the Buffalo Sabres passes the puck away as Tanner Glass #15 of the Pittsburgh Penguins reaches in from behind at First Niagara Center on February 5, 2014 in Buffalo, New York. Pittsburgh defeated Buffalo 5-1.

15
BAUER
FIRST
NIAGARA
52
CCM

CALGARY FLAMES

First Year of Existence: 1972-73
Owner: Calgary Flames LP
Coach: Bob Hartley (May 31, 2012-present)

The Calgary Flames began their tenure in the National Hockey League as the Atlanta Flames in the 1972-73 season. The Flames were awarded an expansion franchise on November 9, 1971 with owner Tom Cousins purchasing the team at a cost of $6 million. The team named former Montreal Canadiens great Bernie "Boom-Boom" Geoffrion as their first head coach.

The Flames took part in the 1972 NHL Expansion Draft to put together their initial roster along with the New York Islanders. Atlanta put together a roster featuring Phil Myre in net, defensemen Pat Quinn, Bill Plager and Ron Harris along with forwards Bob Leiter, Larry Romanchych, John Stewart and Bill MacMillan. With the second overall pick in the 1972 NHL Draft, the Flames selected Jacques Richard.

The Flames played their first game in franchise history on the road on October 7, 1972 against the Islanders. Atlanta took a 3-2 victory in the game with Morris Stefaniw tallying the first goal in franchise history and it proved to be the lone goal of his NHL career. Atlanta finished the season with a 25-38-15 mark; Leiter led the team with 26 goals, 34 assists and 60 points. Myre was 16-23-5 with a 3.03 GAA and two shutouts while Dan Bouchard was 9-15-10 with a 3.09 GAA and two shutouts.

Atlanta made the postseason for the first time in franchise history in the 1973-74 season as they posted a 30-34-14 mark. The Flames were swept by the Philadelphia Flyers; in eight seasons in Atlanta, the Flames made the postseason six times but won a total of two playoff games.

Cousins sold the team to Daryl and Byron Seaman along with Nelson Skalbania on May 21, 1980 for $16 million, which at the time was the highest price paid for a NHL team. With the announcement of the sale came the statement that the team was moving to Calgary to become the Calgary Flames.

The team made the playoffs in the first season in Calgary as the team went 39-27-14, which put them third in the Patrick Division. The Flames won their first postseason series in franchise history with a sweep of the Chicago Blackhawks in the preliminary round. They followed that up with a 4-3 win over the Philadelphia Flyers in the quarterfinal round before losing 4-2 by the Minnesota North Stars in the semifinals. Kent Nilsson led the team with 131 points while Guy Chouinard bagged 52 goals. Pat Riggin was 21-16-4 with a 3.83 GAA as the number one goalie while Reggie Lemelin was 14-6-7 with a 3.24 GAA and two shutouts.

Calgary moved to the Smythe Division in 1981-82 as the league shuffled teams. The team struggled to a 29-34-17 mark and was swept by the Vancouver Canucks in the Smythe semifinals. Chouinard led the team with 57 assists and 80 points while Lanny MacDonald had a team-high 34 goals. The goaltending struggled; Riggin was 19-19-11 with a 4.23 ERA with two shutouts while Lemelin went 10-15-6 with a 4.34 GAA.

The 1985-86 season was a solid one for the Flames as they posted a 40-31-9 record for 89 points. Calgary beat the Winnipeg Jets 3-0 in the Smythe semifinals and followed that with a 4-3 series win over the Edmonton Oilers in the Smythe Finals to advance to the conference finals for the first time. Calgary advanced when Edmonton defenseman Steve Smith's attempt to clear the puck bounced off goaltender Grant Fuhr's leg and into the net, providing the winning goal in Game 7. The Flames survived the St. Louis Blues 4-3 in the conference finals to advance to the Stanley Cup Finals for the first time. The two long series took their toll on the Flames as they were beaten 4-1 by the Montreal Canadiens in the Finals.

The 1987-88 saw the Flames win their first division title with a 48-23-9 mark for 105 points. In the process, Calgary won the President's Trophy for having the league's best record for the first time. Joe Nieuwendyk won the Calder Trophy as the league's best rookie. He was the second rookie in NHL history to score at least 50 goals as he potted 51 while Hakan Loob had 50 goals and a team high 106 points on the season. They were defeated in the Smythe Division Finals in a sweep by the Oilers.

In 1988-89, the Flames set franchise records with 54 wins and 117 points, winning their second division title in the process and second straight President's Trophy. After getting past the Vancouver Canucks 4-3 in the Smythe semifinals, the Flames swept the Los Angeles Kings and knocked off Chicago 4-1 to advance to their second Stanley Cup Finals appearance. In a rematch of 1985-86, this time it was the Flames emerging victorious 4-2 for their only Stanle Cup championship. Joe Mullen led the team with 51 goals and 110 points on the season whil Mike Vernon was the top goaltender, posting a 37-6-5 record, a 2.65 GAA and a .897 sav percentage. Al MacInnis was named the Conn Smythe Trophy winner as he posted seven goa and 31 points in 22 postseason games. The Flames wouldn't win another playoff series for 1 seasons.

The Flames turned things around in 2003-04, going 42-30-7-3. Calgary knocked of Vancouver 4-3 in the opening round of the playoffs for their first series win since hoisting the Stanley Cup. The Flames followed that up with 4-2 series win over the Detroit Red Wings and then eliminated the San Jose Sharks 4-2 to advance to the Stanley Cup Finals for the third time. Calgary battled tooth and nail but lost the Finals, 4-3, to the Tampa Bay Lightning.

Miikka Kiprusoff became the first goaltender to record a shutout in an outdoor game when he posted a 4-0 blanking of the Canadiens in the Heritage Classic on February 22, 2011. Jarome Iginla scored his 1,000th career point on April 1, 2011 against the St. Louis Blues and his 500th career goal on January 7, 2012 against the Minnesota Wild.

The 2013-14 season was another down one for the Flames as they finished the season 35-40-7. Mike Cammalleri led the Flames with 26 goals while Jiri Hudler posted team highs with 37 assists and 54 points. Karri Ramo saw the most action in net for the Flames, posting a 16-15-4 record with a 2.65 GAA, .911 save percentage and two shutouts. Reto Berra was 9-17-2 with a 2.95 GAA with a .897 save percentage.

Karri Ramo #31 of the Calgary Flames makes a save against the Ottawa Senators at Canadian Tire Centre on March 30, 2014 in Ottawa, Ontario.

31

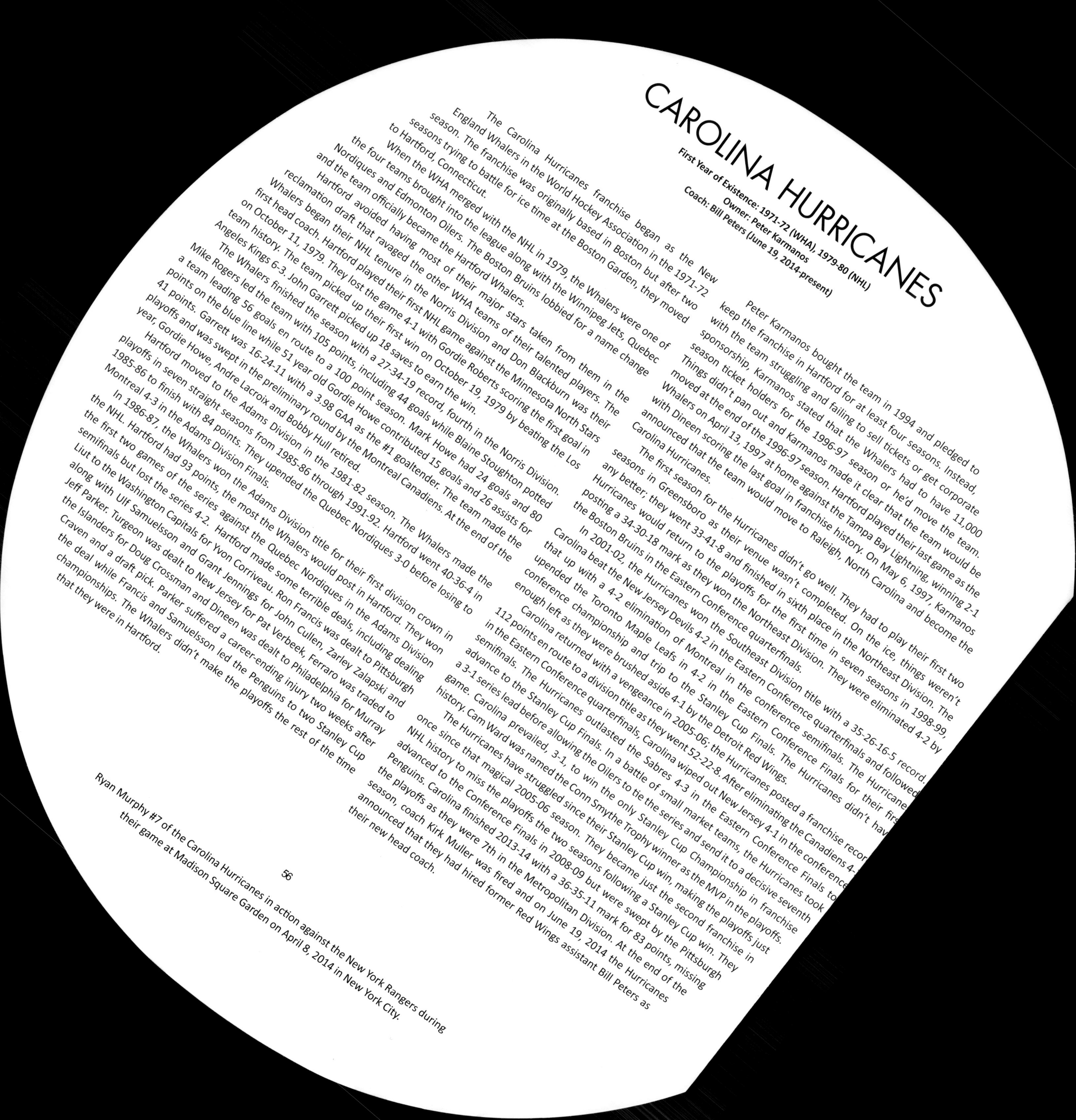

CAROLINA HURRICANES

First Year of Existence: 1971-72 (WHA), 1979-80 (NHL)
Owner: Peter Karmanos
Coach: Bill Peters (June 19, 2014-present)

The Carolina Hurricanes franchise began as the New England Whalers in the World Hockey Association in the 1971-72 season. The franchise was originally based in Boston but after two seasons trying to battle for ice time at the Boston Garden, they moved to Hartford, Connecticut.

When the WHA merged with the NHL in 1979, the Whalers were one of the four teams brought into the league along with the Winnipeg Jets, Quebec Nordiques and Edmonton Oilers. The Boston Bruins lobbied for a name change and the team officially became the Hartford Whalers.

Hartford avoided having most of their major stars taken from them in the reclamation draft that ravaged the other WHA teams of their talented players. The Whalers began their NHL tenure in the Norris Division and Don Blackburn was their first head coach. Hartford played their first NHL game against the Minnesota North Stars on October 11, 1979. They lost the game 4-1 with Gordie Roberts scoring the first goal in team history. The team picked up their first win on October 19, 1979 by beating the Los Angeles Kings 6-3. John Garrett picked up 18 saves to earn the win.

The Whalers finished the season with a 27-34-19 record, fourth in the Norris Division. Mike Rogers led the team with 105 points, including 44 goals while Blaine Stoughton potted a team leading 56 goals en route to a 100 point season. Mark Howe had 24 goals and 80 points on the blue line while 51 year old Gordie Howe contributed 15 goals and 26 assists for 41 points. Garrett was 16-24-11 with a 3.98 GAA as the #1 goaltender. The team made the playoffs and was swept in the preliminary round by the Montreal Canadiens. At the end of the year, Gordie Howe, Andre Lacroix and Bobby Hull retired.

Hartford moved to the Adams Division in the 1981-82 season. The Whalers made the playoffs in seven straight seasons from 1985-86 through 1991-92. Hartford went 40-36-4 in 1985-86 to finish with 84 points. They upended the Quebec Nordiques 3-0 before losing to Montreal 4-3 in the Adams Division Finals.

In 1986-87, the Whalers won the Adams Division title for their first division crown in the NHL. Hartford had 93 points, the most the Whalers would post in Hartford. They won the first two games of the series against the Quebec Nordiques in the Adams Division semifinals but lost the series 4-2. Hartford made some terrible deals, including dealing Liut to the Washington Capitals for Yvon Corriveau. Ron Francis was dealt to Pittsburgh along with Ulf Samuelsson and Grant Jennings for John Cullen, Zarley Zalapski and Jeff Parker. Turgeon was dealt to New Jersey for Pat Verbeek, Ferraro was traded to the Islanders for Doug Crossman and Dineen was dealt to Philadelphia for Murray Craven and a draft pick. Parker suffered a career-ending injury two weeks after the deal while Francis and Samuelsson led the Penguins to two Stanley Cup championships. The Whalers didn't make the playoffs the rest of the time that they were in Hartford.

Peter Karmanos bought the team in 1994 and pledged to keep the franchise in Hartford for at least four seasons. Instead, with the team struggling and failing to sell tickets or get corporate sponsorship, Karmanos stated that the Whalers had to have 11,000 season ticket holders for the 1996-97 season or he'd move the team. Things didn't pan out and Karmanos made it clear that the team would be moved at the end of the 1996-97 season. Hartford played their last game as the Whalers on April 13, 1997 at home against the Tampa Bay Lightning, winning 2-1 with Dineen scoring the last goal in franchise history. On May 6, 1997, Karmanos announced that the team would move to Raleigh, North Carolina and become the Carolina Hurricanes.

The first season for the Hurricanes didn't go well. They had to play their first two seasons in Greensboro as their venue wasn't completed. On the ice, things weren't any better; they went 33-41-8 and finished in sixth place in the Northeast Division. The Hurricanes would return to the playoffs for the first time in seven seasons in 1998-99, posting a 34-30-18 mark as they won the Northeast Division. They were eliminated 4-2 by the Boston Bruins in the Eastern Conference quarterfinals.

In 2001-02, the Hurricanes won the Southeast Division title with a 35-26-16-5 record. Carolina beat the New Jersey Devils 4-2 in the Eastern Conference quarterfinals and followed that up with a 4-2 elimination of Montreal in the conference semifinals. The Hurricanes upended the Toronto Maple Leafs in 4-2 in the Eastern Conference Finals for their first conference championship and trip to the Stanley Cup Finals. The Hurricanes didn't have enough left as they were brushed aside 4-1 by the Detroit Red Wings.

Carolina returned with a vengeance in 2005-06; the Hurricanes posted a franchise record 112 points en route to a division title as they went 52-22-8. After eliminating the Canadiens 4-2 in the Eastern Conference quarterfinals, Carolina wiped out New Jersey 4-1 in the conference semifinals. The Hurricanes outlasted the Sabres 4-3 in the Eastern Conference Finals to advance to the Stanley Cup Finals. In a battle of small market teams, the Hurricanes took a 3-1 series lead before allowing the Oilers to tie the series and send it to a decisive seventh game. Carolina prevailed, 3-1, to win the only Stanley Cup Championship in franchise history. Cam Ward was named the Conn Smythe Trophy winner as the MVP in the playoffs.

The Hurricanes have struggled since their Stanley Cup win, making the playoffs just once since that magical 2005-06 season. They became just the second franchise in NHL history to miss the playoffs the two seasons following a Stanley Cup win. They advanced to the Conference Finals in 2008-09 but were swept by the Pittsburgh Penguins. Carolina finished 2013-14 with a 36-35-11 mark for 83 points, missing the playoffs as they were 7th in the Metropolitan Division. At the end of the season, coach Kirk Muller was fired and on June 19, 2014 the Hurricanes announced that they had hired former Red Wings assistant Bill Peters as their new head coach.

Ryan Murphy #7 of the Carolina Hurricanes in action against the New York Rangers during their game at Madison Square Garden on April 8, 2014 in New York City.

BAUER
7
bauer
bauer
bauer
bauer
ups

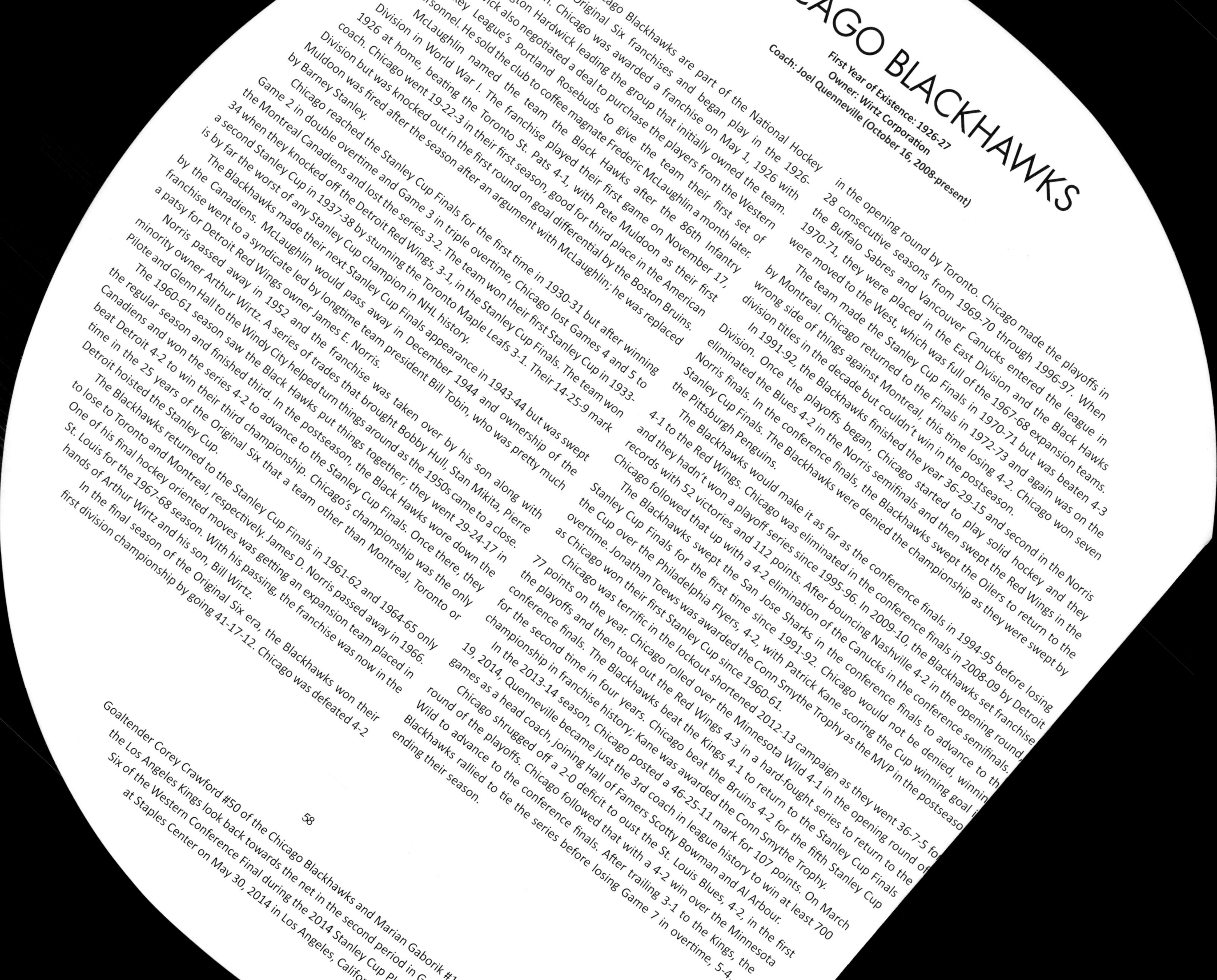

CAGO BLACKHAWKS

First Year of Existence: 1926-27
Owner: Wirtz Corporation
Coach: Joel Quenneville (October 16, 2008-present)

ago Blackhawks are part of the National Hockey Original Six franchises and began play in the 1926- n. Chicago was awarded a franchise on May 1, 1926 with ton Hardwick leading the group that initially owned the team. ick also negotiated a deal to purchase the players from the Western key League's Portland Rosebuds to give the team their first set of rsonnel. He sold the club to coffee magnate Frederic McLaughlin a month later. McLaughlin named the team the Black Hawks after the 86th Infantry Division in World War I. The franchise played their first game on November 17, 1926 at home, beating the Toronto St. Pats 4-1, with Pete Muldoon as their first coach. Chicago went 19-22-3 in their first season, good for third place in the American Division but was knocked out in the first round on goal differential by the Boston Bruins. Muldoon was fired after the season after an argument with McLaughlin; he was replaced by Barney Stanley.

Chicago reached the Stanley Cup Finals for the first time in 1930-31 but after winning Game 2 in double overtime and Game 3 in triple overtime, Chicago lost Games 4 and 5 to the Montreal Canadiens and lost the series 3-2. The team won their first Stanley Cup in 1933-34 when they knocked off the Detroit Red Wings, 3-1, in the Stanley Cup Finals. The team won a second Stanley Cup in 1937-38 by stunning the Toronto Maple Leafs 3-1. Their 14-25-9 mark is by far the worst of any Stanley Cup champion in NHL history.

The Blackhawks made their next Stanley Cup Finals appearance in 1943-44 but was swept by the Canadiens. McLaughlin would pass away in December 1944 and ownership of the franchise went to a syndicate led by longtime team president Bill Tobin, who was pretty much a patsy for Detroit Red Wings owner James E. Norris.

Norris passed away in 1952 and the franchise was taken over by his son along with minority owner Arthur Wirtz. A series of trades that brought Bobby Hull, Stan Mikita, Pierre Pilote and Glenn Hall to the Windy City helped turn things around as the 1950s came to a close.

The 1960-61 season saw the Black Hawks put things together; they went 29-24-17 in the regular season and finished third. In the postseason, the Black Hawks wore down the Canadiens and won the series 4-2 to advance to the Stanley Cup Finals. Once there, they beat Detroit 4-2 to win their third championship. Chicago's championship was the only time in the 25 years of the Original Six that a team other than Montreal, Toronto or Detroit hoisted the Stanley Cup.

The Blackhawks returned to the Stanley Cup Finals in 1961-62 and 1964-65 only to lose to Toronto and Montreal, respectively. James D. Norris passed away in 1966. One of his final hockey oriented moves was getting an expansion team placed in St. Louis for the 1967-68 season. With his passing, the franchise was now in the hands of Arthur Wirtz and his son, Bill Wirtz.

In the final season of the Original Six era, the Blackhawks won their first division championship by going 41-17-12. Chicago was defeated 4-2 in the opening round by Toronto. Chicago made the playoffs in 28 consecutive seasons from 1969-70 through 1996-97. When the Buffalo Sabres and Vancouver Canucks entered the league in 1970-71, they were placed in the East Division and the Black Hawks were moved to the West, which was full of the 1967-68 expansion teams.

The team made the Stanley Cup Finals in 1970-71 but was beaten 4-3 by Montreal. Chicago returned to the Finals in 1972-73 and again was on the wrong side of things against Montreal, this time losing 4-2. Chicago won seven division titles in the decade but couldn't win in the postseason.

In 1991-92, the Blackhawks finished the year 36-29-15 and second in the Norris Division. Once the playoffs began, Chicago started to play solid hockey and they eliminated the Blues 4-2 in the Norris semifinals and then swept the Red Wings in the Norris finals. In the conference finals, the Blackhawks swept the Oilers to return to the Stanley Cup Finals. The Blackhawks were denied the championship as they were swept by the Pittsburgh Penguins.

The Blackhawks would make it as far as the conference finals in 1994-95 before losing 4-1 to the Red Wings. Chicago was eliminated in the conference finals in 2008-09 by Detroit and they hadn't won a playoff series since 1995-96. In 2009-10, the Blackhawks set franchise records with 52 victories and 112 points. After bouncing Nashville 4-2 in the opening round, Chicago followed that up with a 4-2 elimination of the Canucks in the conference semifinals. The Blackhawks swept the San Jose Sharks in the conference finals to advance to th Stanley Cup Finals for the first time since 1991-92. Chicago would not be denied, winnin the Cup over the Philadelphia Flyers, 4-2, with Patrick Kane scoring the Cup winning goal i overtime. Jonathan Toews was awarded the Conn Smythe Trophy as the MVP in the postseaso as Chicago won their first Stanley Cup since 1960-61.

Chicago was terrific in the lockout shortened 2012-13 campaign as they went 36-7-5 fo 77 points on the year. Chicago rolled over the Minnesota Wild 4-1 in the opening round of the playoffs and then took out the Red Wings 4-3 in a hard-fought series to return to the conference finals. The Blackhawks beat the Kings 4-1 to return to the Stanley Cup Finals for the second time in four years. The Blackhawks beat the Bruins 4-2 for the fifth Stanley Cup championship in franchise history; Kane was awarded the Conn Smythe Trophy.

In the 2013-14 season, Chicago posted a 46-25-11 mark for 107 points. On March 19, 2014, Quenneville became just the 3rd coach in league history to win at least 700 games as a head coach, joining Hall of Famers Scotty Bowman and Al Arbour.

Chicago shrugged off a 2-0 deficit to oust the St. Louis Blues, 4-2, in the first round of the playoffs. Chicago followed that with a 4-2 win over the Minnesota Wild to advance to the conference finals. After trailing 3-1 to the Kings, the Blackhawks rallied to tie the series before losing Game 7 in overtime, 5-4, ending their season.

Goaltender Corey Crawford #50 of the Chicago Blackhawks and Marian Gaborik #1 the Los Angeles Kings look back towards the net in the second period in G Six of the Western Conference Final during the 2014 Stanley Cup Pl at Staples Center on May 30, 2014 in Los Angeles, Califo

STAPLES Center
verizon
Advil
MERCURY
INSURANCE COMPANY
Alberta
EASTON
50
4
Reebok
KING
BAUER
DISCOVER
TOYOTA

COLORADO AVALANCHE

First Year of Existence: 1979-80
Owner: Colorado Avalanche LLC, A Division of Kroenke Sports Entertainment
Coach: Patrick Roy (May 23, 2013-present)

The Colorado Avalanche joined the National Hockey League in the 1979-80 season as part of a four team addition to the league with the folding of the World Hockey Association. As part of the price the Nordiques had to pay, they were allowed to protect just three players from their roster in the WHA. In the 1979 NHL Expansion Draft, the Nordiques selected goaltender Ron Low, defensemen Gerry Hart and Dave Farrish along with forwards Hartland Monahan, Alain Cote and Pierre Plante.

In the first round, the Nordiques selected Michel Goulet; Dale Hunter was chosen in the 2nd round and Anton Stastny in the 4th. Jacques Demers was named as the first head coach in the team's history in the NHL.

Quebec would play their first game at home on October 10, 1979, in a 5-3 defeat to the Atlanta Flames. Real Cloutier scored the first goal and scored all three Quebec goals on the night. In doing so, Cloutier became the second NHL player in NHL history to score a hat trick in his first NHL game.

The Nordiques earned their first win against the Colorado Rockies 5-2, on October 18, 1979. Quebec struggled during their first season as they finished with a 25-44-11 record and 61 points. Demers was out as coach after the season and was replaced by Maurice Filion at the start of the 1980-81 season.

Filion would last just six games before being replaced by Michel Bergeron. Quebec was bolstered by the signings of Peter and Anton Stastny, who joined the team after defecting from Czechoslovakia. After starting the season 1-9-5, the Nordiques came together as a unit and went 29-23-13 the rest of the way and earned the team's first playoff berth. Peter Stastny won the Calder Trophy as the league's rookie of the year after scoring 39 goals and a team high 109 points. Quebec was ousted in the preliminary round of the playoffs, 3-2, by the Philadelphia Flyers.

In 1981-82, Quebec posted their first winning season as they went 33-31-16. The Nordiques won their first playoff series by ousting Montreal 3-2 in the Adams semifinals. They followed that with a 4-3 defeat of the Boston Bruins to advance to the conference finals for the first time; the Nordiques were swept by the New York Islanders.

Quebec returned to the conference finals in 1984-85 after finishing the regular season 41-30-9. Quebec knocked off the Buffalo Sabres, 3-2, in the Adams Division semifinals and followed that up with a 4-3 series win over the Canadiens before being defeated 4-2 by the Flyers.

The Nordiques went 43-31-6 for 92 points in 1985-86, winning their first division title. Quebec's euphoria didn't last long and they were swept in the Adams Division semifinals by Hartford. The Nordiques slumped to 31-39-10 in 1986-87 and knocked off the Whalers 4-2 in the Adams semifinals, but lost to the Canadiens 4-3.

Quebec dealt Hunter and Malarchuk to Washington during the 1987 NHL Draft, receiving Alan Haworth, Gaetan Duchesne and Washington's first round pick, which turned into Joe Sakic. Bergeron left the team and took the head coaching job with the New York Rangers. The Nordiques received New York's first round selection in the 1988 NHL Draft as compensation.

Poor finishes gave Quebec the top pick in the 1989, 1990 and 1991 NHL Drafts, which they used to select Mats Sundin, Owen Nolan and Eric Lindros, respectively. Lindros never played for the team; he held out for over a year before being dealt to the Flyers for the rights to Peter Forsberg, Ron Hextall, Chris Simon, Mike Ricci, Kerry Huffman, Steve Duchesne, first round picks in 1993 and 1994 plus $15 million in cash.

Quebec wasn't making money. The franchise was in the smallest market in the NHL and when owner Marcel Aubut asked for a bailout from the province plus a new arena funded by the public, his pleas fell on deaf ears. He sold the team to COMSAT Entertainment Group, the deal was made official on July 1, 1995 and on August 10, 1995, the team was branded the Colorado Avalanche.

The Avalanche played their first game on October 6, 1995, beating the Detroit Red Wings by a 3-2 score. In a major deal on December 6, 1995, Colorado sent Jocelyn Thibault, Martin Rucinsky and Andrei Kovalenko to the Canadiens for goalie Patrick Roy and Mike Keane. Roy was humiliated after he allowed nine goals on 26 shots against Detroit and vowed that he wouldn't play for Montreal again.

Colorado finished 1995-96 with a 47-27-10 record and the Pacific Division crown. Colorad beat the Vancouver Canucks 4-2, the Chicago Blackhawks 4-2 and then upended Detroit 4- to advance to the Stanley Cup Finals for the first time. Colorado swept the Florida Panthers t win their first championship with Sakic taking the Conn Smythe.

From 1995-96 to 2001-02, the Avalanche went to the conference finals six times and wo two Stanley Cup titles. In 2000-01, the Avalanche set franchise records with 52 wins and 11 points. Colorado swept Vancouver in the opening round, ground out a 4-3 series victory ove the Los Angeles Kings and then dusted the St. Louis Blues 4-1 to return to the Stanley Cup Finals. Roy and the Avalanche rallied from a 3-2 series deficit, winning Game 7 over Martin Brodeur and the New Jersey Devils; Roy won the Conn Smythe Trophy.

On May 23, 2013, the Avalanche announced that Roy would come back to the organization as head coach. Roy is the only coach in the NHL currently who has the powers of a general manager. The Avalanche posted a 52-22-8 record for 112 points and won the Central Division. Ryan O'Reilly led the team with 28 goals while Matt Duchene had team highs in assists (47) and points (70) on the year. Semyon Varlamov was the anchor in net for Colorado, going 41-14-6 with a 2.41 GAA, .927 save percentage and two shutouts.

Colorado faced the Minnesota Wild in the opening round of the playoffs and led the series three games to two; they dropped Game 6 on the road to force a Game 7 at home. Colorado lost 5-4 on Nino Neiderreiter's second goal of the game at 5:02 of the extra session. The loss gave the Wild a 4-3 series victory and ended the Avalanche's season.

Gabriel Landeskog #92 and Paul Stastny #26 of the Colorado Avalanche skate against Nate Prosser #39 of the Minnesota Wild in Game Seven of the First Round of the 2014 NHL Stanley Cup Playoffs at Pepsi Center on April 30, 2014 in Denver, Colorado.

SHER-WOOD
CCM
STYLE

COLUMBUS BLUE JACKETS

First Year of Existence: 2000-01
Owner: John P. McConnell
Coach: Todd Richards (January 9, 2012-present)

The Columbus Blue Jackets entered the NHL in the 2000-01 season as one of the two NHL teams in the most recent expansion, with the Minnesota Wild being the other. The franchise was awarded to the city on June 25, 1997. The choice was made for the Blue Jackets in reference to the state of Ohio's contributions to the Civil War.

Columbus took part in the expansion draft for the original population of their roster on June 23, 2000. With the first selection in the expansion draft, the Blue Jackets selected goaltender Rick Tabaracci, who had previously played for the Colorado Avalanche. The Blue Jackets picked up goaltender Dwayne Roloson, defenseman Mathieu Schneider along with forwards Dallas Drake and Turner Stevenson; none of them played for the franchise. Dave King was named as the franchise's first coach.

With the first pick in franchise history in the NHL Draft, the Blue Jackets took defenseman Rostislav Klesla with the fourth overall selection in the 2000 NHL Draft. Columbus played the first game in franchise history on October 7, 2000 at home against the Chicago Blackhawks. The Blue Jackets were defeated 5-3 in the game. Bruce Gardiner scored the first goal in franchise history and Ron Tugnutt was the goaltender in the contest. The team won the first game in franchise history as they were victorious on the road, 3-2, over the Calgary Flames on October 12, 2000.

Geoff Sanderson led the team with 30 goals and 56 points on the season while Espen Knutsen had a team best 42 assists for the year. Tugnutt was solid in net, going 22-25-5 with 2.44 goals against average and a .917 save percentage. He tied a NHL record for wins by a goaltender on an expansion team that was previously set by Lorne Chabot of the Rangers back in the 1926-27 season.

Things were worse in the 2001-02 season for the Blue Jackets despite using the eighth overall pick on goaltender Pascal Leclaire. Knutsen was the first player in franchise history to be selected to the All Star Game. He tallied a goal and an assist as the World Team was victorious over the North American squad, 8-5. The Blue Jackets finished the season with a 22-47-8-5 mark for 57 points, leaving them second worst in the league.

Tugnutt was dealt to Dallas with a second round pick in exchange for the Stars' 20th overall selection in the 2002 NHL Draft. Columbus was slotted to pick 3rd in the draft but swung a deal with the Florida Panthers and they dealt it plus the option to swap picks in 2003 to get the top overall selection. The Blue Jackets used that pick to select Rick Nash. King was fired partway through the season and was replaced by Doug MacLean. Marc Denis set a league record by playing 4,511 minutes and logged the second-most games in league history for a goalie with 77. Whitney scored 24 goals with 52 assists, giving him a franchise record 76 points while Sanderson potted 34 goals. Nash had 17 goals and 22 assists in his rookie campaign.

Nash potted a franchise record 41 goals in the 2003-04 season but that didn't generate much success in the grand scheme of things. The 2008-09 season saw improvement for the Blue Jackets as they had success under Hitchcock. Rookie Steve Mason became the first Columbus goaltender to post three straight shutouts on the season while Nikita Filatov became the first rookie to score a hat trick.

Ken Hitchcock won his 500th NHL game on February 19, 2009 while on March 7, 2009, Nash became the first NHL player since Maurice Richard back in the 1947-48 season to score an unassisted hat trick. The Blue Jackets clinched the first playoff berth in franchise history. Columbus finished the season 41-31-10 for 92 points for their first playoff berth and were swept by the Detroit Red Wings. Mason won the Calder Trophy for the league's best rookie and he was the first Blue Jacket to win a major award.

Late in the 2009-10 season, Hitchcock, who had coached his 1,000th career NHL game earlier in the year, was let go as head coach with the team sporting a 22-27-9 mark and was replaced by Claude Noel. Columbus went 10-8-6 down the stretch. Their 32-35-15 mark left them on the outside looking in when the postseason took place. Scott Arniel took over the coaching job after the season came to an end, signing a three year deal in June of 2010.

Arniel's tenure proved to be unsuccessful, posting a 45-60-18 mark as the head coach. After going 34-35-13 in 2010-11, he was 11-25-5 in 2011-12 before getting relieved anc replaced by Todd Richards. Jeff Carter, who was a major acquisition before the season begar was dealt away to the Kings after just 39 games. The Blue Jackets went 18-21-2 under Richarc in the second half of the season to finish the year 29-46-7 for 65 points.

At the 2012 NHL Draft, the Blue Jackets dealt 2nd and 4th round picks to the Philadelph Flyers for goaltender Sergei Bobrovsky. A month later, on July 23, 2012, Columbus dealt Nas who owned several franchise records, to the New York Rangers. In exchange, the Blue Jacke received Tim Erixon, Brandon Dubinsky, Artem Anisimov and a first round pick in 201 Columbus dealt for Marian Gaborik and set a franchise mark for consecutive games earnin a point with an 8-0-4 stretch. The Blue Jackets finished the season 24-17-7 and missed the postseason as the Wild had more non-shootout victories. Bobrovsky went 21-11-6 with a 2.00 GAA and a .932 save percentage and won the Vezina Trophy for his work.

In the 2013-14 season, the Blue Jackets moved from the Central Division in the Western Conference to the Metropolitan Division in the Eastern Conference. The Blue Jackets went 43-32-5-2 on the season, finishing with a franchise record 93 points. Ryan Johansen led the team with 33 goals and 63 points while Bobrovsky went 32-20-5 with a 2.38 GAA, a .923 save percentage with five shutouts. They made the playoffs for the second time and picked up the first playoff win in franchise history with a 4-3 double overtime win in Pittsburgh on April 19, 2014. The Blue Jackets were eliminated in the Eastern Conference quarterfinals, 4-2, by Pittsburgh.

David Savard #58 of the Columbus Blue Jackets skates against the Pittsburgh Penguins in Game Five of the First Round of the 2014 NHL Stanley Cup Playoffs at Consol Energy Center on April 26, 2014 in Pittsburgh, Pennsylvania.

58
CCM
COLUMBUS
BLUE JACKETS
58

DALLAS STARS

First Year of Existence: 1967-68
Owner: Dallas Stars, LP
Coach: Lindy Ruff (June 21, 2013-present)

The Dallas Stars got their start in the NHL as part of the first wave of expansion in 1967-68 as the Minnesota North Stars. The franchise was awarded on February 9, 1966 and the team name the North Stars was announced following a public contest on May 25, 1966.

Minnesota took part in the 1967 NHL Expansion Draft to populate their initial roster. In the expansion draft, the North Stars added goaltender Cesare Maniago, defensemen Bob Woytowich, Jean-Guy Talbot and Elmer Vasko along with forwards Bill Goldsworthy, Murray Hall, Andre Pronovost and Dave Balon.

Wren Blair was the first head coach in franchise history while Woytowich was the team's first captain.

The North Stars played their first game on October 11, 1967 when they faced fellow expansion team St. Louis. The teams battled to a 2-2 tie with Bill Masterson scoring the first goal. On October 21, 1967, the North Stars recorded their first win with a 3-1 win over the Oakland Seals.

One of the lowest points in league history and perhaps the worst moment for the North Stars came on January 13, 1968. In a game at home against the Seals, Bill Masterton was checked by Ron Harris and Larry Calan and fell backwards onto the ice. The back of Masterton's head hit the ice and the force generated from the fall damaged the pons of his brain. He was taken to the hospital and died two days later. Masterton's is the only death in NHL history that stemmed from an on-ice incident. In his honor, the Professional Hockey Writers' Association created the Bill Masterton Trophy in 1968, which is awarded to the player who best exemplifies the qualities of perseverance, sportsmanship and dedication to hockey.

Minnesota finished their inaugural season 27-32-15. The North Stars won their first playoff series with a 4-3 series win over the Los Angeles Kings in the quarterfinals before succumbing to the Blues 4-3 in the semifinals.

The team picked up their first winning season in 1971-72 as they went 37-29-12. Things didn't go the North Stars' way in the playoffs as they were ousted 4-3 in the quarterfinals by the Blues. Over the next six seasons, Minnesota struggled, both on the ice and financially. Gordon and George Gund III, who owned the Cleveland Barons, which was the transplanted Seals franchise, came up with a radical concept to merge the Barons with the North Stars.

With an infusion of talent from the merger, the North Stars put together their first winning season since 1972-73 in 1979-80 by posting a 36-28-16 mark. Minnesota knocked off the Toronto Maple Leafs, 3-0, in the preliminary round and followed that up with a 4-3 elimination of the Montreal Canadiens to advance to the conference finals for the first time. Minnesota lost to the Philadelphia Flyers 4-1 to end their season.

The North Stars built on that momentum with a 35-28-17 mark in 1980-81. Minnesota brushed aside the Boston Bruins 3-0 in the preliminary round and followed it up with a 4-1 win over the Buffalo Sabres. Minnesota knocked off the Calgary Flames 4-2 before being knocked off by the New York Islanders 4-1 in their first Stanley Cup Finals appearance.

Minnesota won their first division title in 1981-82 in their first season in the Norris after they relocated from the Adams Division. They would win a second division title in 1983-84 as they went 39-31-10. Minnesota knocked off the Chicago Black Hawks 4-1 in the Norris semifinals and followed that up with 4-3 series win over the Blues in the Norris finals. They fell short in the conference finals as they were swept by the Edmonton Oilers.

The North Stars' next big season came in 1990-91. Despite finishing the season 27-39-14, Minnesota got on a roll in the postseason. They beat Chicago 4-2 in the Norris semifinals and then beat the Blues 4-2 in the Norris finals. The North Stars followed that with a 4-1 whipping of the Oilers in the conference finals to advance to the Stanley Cup Finals for the second time. They were knocked off by the Pittsburgh Penguins 4-2 in the Stanley Cup Finals.

Attendance was again bad for the North Stars and the Gunds were threatening to move the team to San Francisco. They sold the team to Norm Green, Howard Baldwin and Morris Belzberg while assuming control of the new expansion team in San Jose. Green was looking to move the franchise in 1992 with an eye on the Los Angeles area, but the NHL was putting a team in Anaheim. The compromise struck there was that if Green left Anaheim open for expansion, he would be approved for to relocate anywhere. In January 1993, Gree announced that the team would be moving to Dallas in time for the 1993-94 season.

In 1998-99, Dallas went 51-19-12 for a franchise record 114 points as they won th President's Trophy. Dallas swept the Oilers in the Western Conference quarterfinals, bea the Blues 4-2 in the semifinals and the Colorado Avalanche 4-3 in the conference Finals. I the Stanley Cup Finals, the Stars beat the Sabres, 4-2, on Hull's controversial goal in tripl overtime to give the team their only Stanley Cup.

The Stars returned to the Stanley Cup Finals in the 1999-00 season as they were 43-23-10-6. Dallas knocked off the Oilers 4-1 in the quarterfinals and then eliminated the Sharks 4-1 in the semifinals. The Stars survived 4-3 in the conference finals against the Avalanche, but lost in the Stanley Cup Finals 4-2 to the New Jersey Devils.

At the end of 2012-13, the team fired GM Joe Nieuwendyk and coach Glen Gulutzan. Jim Nill was brought in as general manager and Lindy Ruff took over as coach. In 2013-14, the Stars finished the season 40-31-11, which was fifth in the Central Division and snuck them into the playoffs. Tyler Seguin, who was acquired before the season began in a deal that brought Rich Peverley and Ryan Button from Boston for Loui Eriksson, Reilly Smith, Matt Fraser and Joe Morrow, led the team with 37 goals, 47 assists and 84 points. Kari Lehtonen was the team's top goalie, he posted a 33-20-10 record with a 2.41 GAA, a .919 save percentage and five shutouts. Dallas was eliminated in the Western Conference quarterfinals 4-2 by the Anaheim Ducks.

The Dallas Stars' Vernon Fiddler, middle, celebrates after the tying goal in the second period against the Anaheim Ducks in Game 4 of a Western Conference quarterfinal at American Airlines Center in Dallas on Wednesday, April 23, 2014.

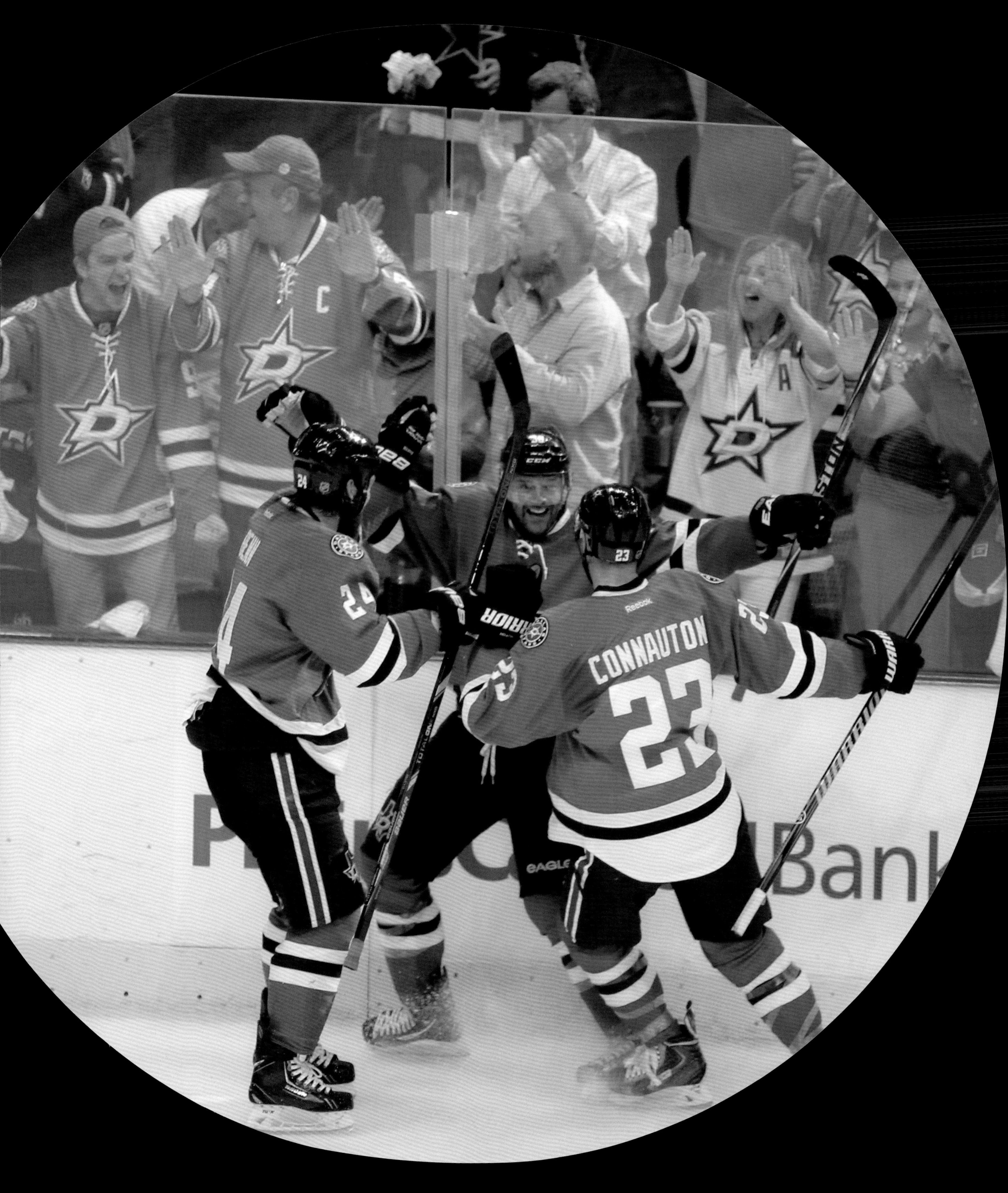
CONNAUTON
23
24
Reebok
Bank

DETROIT RED WINGS

First Year of Existence: 1926-27
Owner: Ilitch Holdings
Coach: Mike Babcock (July 5, 2005-present)

The Detroit Red Wings franchise came into existence in time for the 1926-27 season. On May 15, 1926, the NHL awarded an expansion franchise to Detroit. The Detroit ownership bought the Victoria Cougars from Frank and Lester Patrick for $100,000 in order to put together their first roster. The franchise was named the Detroit Cougars to pay homage to the Victoria franchise.

Art Duncan was the team's first head coach. The Red Wings played their first game on November 18, 1926 against the Boston Bruins and lost 2-0. The team's first goal was on November 20, 1926 against the Pittsburgh Pirates with Harold "Slim" Halderson potting the goal in a 4-1 loss. The Cougars finished 12-28-4 and missed the playoffs.

With Jack Adams behind the bench for the Red Wings, they made the playoffs for the first time in 1928-29. Detroit lost in the quarterfinals as they were outscored 7-2 by the Toronto Maple Leafs. The team changed their name to the Falcons in 1930 as the ownership group hoped that a name change would alter their fortunes.

The team was sold to James E. Norris in 1932 and the first thing he did was change the franchise's name to the Red Wings. The name became official on October 5, 1932. Detroit won the first Stanley Cup in franchise history in 1935-36. Detroit swept the Maroons 3-0 in the semifinals in a series that will be remembered for Detroit's 1-0 win in Game 1. Mud Bruneteau scored the winning goal in the sixth overtime and the 176 minutes and 30 seconds that elapsed made it the longest game in NHL history. The Red Wings took a 3-1 series win over Toronto for the Stanley Cup. Detroit defended their title in 1936-37. They defeated the Rangers 3-2 after knocking off the Montreal Canadiens 3-2 in the semifinals.

Detroit made the Stanley Cup Finals in three straight seasons in 1940-41, 1941-42 and 1942-43. In 1940-41, they beat the Rangers and Chicago to advance to the Stanley Cup Finals where they were swept by the Bruins. The following season, Detroit beat Montreal and Boston. The Red Wings took a 3-0 series lead over Toronto in the Stanley Cup Finals, but lost four straight to drop the series and become the first team in NHL history to lose a best of seven series after leading 3-0. In 1942-43, the Red Wings exacted revenge by beating Toronto 4-2 in the semifinals and swept the Bruins to win the Stanley Cup.

Detroit made three more Stanley Cup Finals appearances in the 1940s but lost each one. Toronto defeated Detroit 4-3 in 1944-45 and swept in the 1947-48 and 1948-49 seasons. Detroit won four Stanley Cups in the 1950s while falling in the Stanley Cup Finals once. The Red Wings edged the Rangers 4-3 in the 1949-50 season, swept the Canadiens in 1951-52 and edged Montreal 4-3 in both 1953-54 and 1954-55. Montreal beat Detroit 4-1 in the 1955-56 Stanley Cup Finals.

It was during this time that the tradition of throwing an octopus on the ice in Detroit came to life. On April 15, 1952, Pete and Jerry Cusimano, who owned Detroit's Eastern Market, hurled an octopus on the ice at the Olympia. The eight arms of an octopus symbolized the number of playoff games that a team had to win to claim the Stanley Cup in the Original Six era.

Detroit made the Stanley Cup Finals four times in the 1960s but failed each time. Chicago beat them in 1960-61, the Maple Leafs beat them in 1962-63 and 1963-64 while Montreal sunk them in 1965-66.

Detroit made the conference finals in 1986-87, sweeping Chicago in the Norris semifinals and beat Toronto 4-3 in the Norris finals. The Red Wings lost to the powerhouse Edmonton Oilers 4-1. Detroit won their first division title in 23 years in 1987-88, beating the Maple Leafs 4-2 and the St. Louis Blues 4-3 to advance to the conference finals. They were knocked off 4-1 by the Oilers.

Detroit has made the playoffs for 23 consecutive seasons. The Red Wings returned to the Stanley Cup Finals in 1994-95. Detroit beat the Dallas Stars in the quarterfinals 4-1 and followed that up with a sweep of the San Jose Sharks. In the conference finals, the Red Wings handled Chicago 4-1 to advance to the Stanley Cup Finals; they were swept by the New Jersey Devils.

The Red Wings won consecutive Stanley Cups in the 1996-97 and 1997-98 seasons. In 1996-97, Detroit beat the Blues 4-2 in the quarterfinals, swept the Mighty Ducks of Anaheim and beat the Avalanche 4-2 in the conference finals. In the Stanley Cup Finals, the Red Wings swept the Philadelphia Flyers to win their first Stanley Cup since 1954-55. Mike Vernon won the Conn Smythe Trophy as the playoff MVP.

In 1997-98, the Red Wings beat the Phoenix Coyotes 4-2 in the quarterfinals, beat th Blues 4-2 in the semifinals and dropped the Stars 4-2 in the conference finals. In the Stanle Cup Finals, the Red Wings swept the Washington Capitals to win their second straight Stanle Cup. Yzerman won the Conn Smythe Award as playoff MVP.

In 2001-02, Detroit won the second of eight straight division titles with a 51-17-10- record. Detroit knocked off the Vancouver Canucks 4-2 in the quarterfinals, eliminated th Blues 4-1 in the semifinals and defeated the Avalanche 4-3 in the conference finals. In the Stanley Cup Finals, the Red Wings beat the Carolina Hurricanes 4-1 and Nicklas Lidstrom won the Conn Smythe Trophy.

Detroit won the Stanley Cup in 2007-08. In the quarterfinals, Detroit knocked off the Nashville Predators 4-2, swept the Avalanche and eliminated the Stars in the conference finals 4-2. In the Stanley Cup Finals, the Red Wings beat the Pittsburgh Penguins 4-2 to hoist the Cup for the 11th time. The Red Wings returned to the Stanley Cup Finals in 2008-09, but lost 4-3 to the Penguins.

The Red Wings finished 2013-14 39-28-15 for 93 points, clinching the playoff berth in the final week of the season. Gustav Nyquist scored a team leading 28 goals while Niklas Kronwall had 41 assists and a team best 49 points. Jimmy Howard was the main man between the pipes, playing in 51 games and going 21-19-11 with a 2.66 GAA, .910 save percentage and two shutouts. The Red Wings were knocked off 4-1 by the Bruins in the Eastern Conference quarterfinals.

Niklas Kronwall #55 of the Detroit Red Wings celebrates his first-period goal with Henrik Zetterberg #40 while playing the Boston Bruins in Game Four of the First Round of the 2014 NHL Stanley Cup Playoffs at Joe Louis Arena on April 24, 2014 in Detroit, Michigan.

WARRIOR
WARRIOR
40
CCM
CCM
CCM

EDMONTON OILERS

First Year of Existence: 1979-80
Owner: Rexall Sports Corporation
Coach: Dallas Eakins (June 10, 2013-present)

The Edmonton Oilers came into existence as the Alberta Oilers in the 1972-73 season in the World Hockey Association and joined the National Hockey League as one of four teams absorbed when the WHA folded in time for the 1979-80 season.

The franchise was originally awarded as one of the original 12 franchises in the WHA on November 1, 1971. The Oilers also made a major personnel move in 1978 when they picked up, among others, Wayne Gretzky, from the Indianapolis Racers.

Edmonton ended up losing the majority of their players through the reclamation draft as part of the terms of joining the NHL. Along with the other WHA teams, they were forced to pick at the end of the first round but managed to retain Gretzky's rights thanks to Pocklington signing him to a 21 year personal services contract. The Oilers' first pick in the NHL Entry Draft was Kevin Lowe, who they selected with the 21st pick in the first round. The Oilers added Mark Messier and Glenn Anderson later in the draft.

The Oilers played their first game as a NHL franchise on October 10, 1979 against the Chicago Black Hawks. Lowe scored the team's first goal in a 4-2 loss. Edmonton would record their first win on October 19, 6-3, over Quebec Nordiques. The Oilers finished in fourth place in the Smythe Division with a 28-39-13 record for 69 points. The Oilers made the playoffs but were swept by the Philadelphia Flyers in the preliminary round.

In the 1980 NHL Draft, the Oilers selected Paul Coffey, Jari Kurri and goaltender Andy Moog. Edmonton finished 29-35-16, again finishing 4th in the Smythe. The Oilers swept the Montreal Canadiens in the preliminary round before getting knocked off in the quarterfinals 4-2 by the New York Islanders. In the 1981 NHL Draft, the Oilers added Grant Fuhr and defenseman Steve Smith.

In 1981-82, the Oilers won their first division title but lost to the Kings 3-2 in the Smythe Division semifinals. It was merely the tip of the iceberg as Edmonton would advance to the Stanley Cup Finals six times in the next eight years.

Edmonton's first trip to the Stanley Cup Finals came in 1982-83. The Oilers swept the Jets in the Smythe semifinals and took out the Calgary Flames 4-1 in the Smythe finals. In the conference finals, the Oilers swept Chicago to advance to the Stanley Cup Finals. The Oilers were swept by the Islanders, who won their fourth straight Stanley Cup.

The Oilers returned to the Stanley Cup Finals in 1983-84 as they set franchise records in wins with 57 and points with 119. In the postseason, Edmonton handled the Jets in the Smythe semifinals in a sweep before eliminating the Flames 4-3 before they swept the Minnesota North Stars in the conference finals to set up a rematch in the Stanley Cup Finals. This time, it was the Oilers that came up with a 4-1 series win to win their first Stanley Cup.

Edmonton won their second straight Stanley Cup in 1984-85. They swept the Kings in the Smythe semifinals then followed that up with a sweep of the Jets before bouncing Chicago 4-2 to make their third straight Stanley Cup Finals. Edmonton handled the Flyers 4-1 as they continued their dominance. The 1985-86 season proved to be a disappointment when the Oilers were knocked off 4-3 by the Flames in the division finals.

The Oilers roared back in 1986-87 as they won the President's Trophy for the league's best record for the second straight season. Edmonton bounced the Kings 4-1 in the Smythe semifinals before sweeping the Jets. In the conference finals, the Oilers handled the Detroit Red Wings 4-1 to advance to their fourth Stanley Cup Finals in five years. The Oilers blew a 3-1 series lead to end up in a Game Seven before beating the Flyers 3-1 to take the series, 4-3.

Edmonton won their fourth Stanley Cup in five years in 1987-88 even with personnel changes. Coffey held out the first 21 games and was dealt to Pittsburgh while Moog chose not to report and was dealt to the Bruins for Bill Ranford. The Oilers eliminated the Jets 4-1 and swept the Flames. In the conference finals, the Oilers demolished Detroit 4-1 to return to the Stanley Cup Finals; the Oilers swept the Bruins.

On August 9, 1988, Gretzky, who had long been the face of the franchise, was dealt along with Marty McSorely and Mike Krushelnyski. The Oilers received Jimmy Carson, Martin Gelinas, the Kings' first round picks in 1989, 1991 and 1993 plus $15 million. The Oilers fell to third in the Smythe in 1988-89. Despite leading the Kings 3-1 in the division semifinals, Gretzky led Los Angeles to three straight wins to eliminate his former team.

The Oilers went 38-28-14 in 1989-90. Edmonton rallied from a 3-1 series deficit and 3-1 deficit in Game 7 to eliminate the Jets and then swept Gretzky and the Kings. The Oilers eliminated Chicago 4-2 in the conference finals to return to the Stanley Cup Finals where they defeated the Bruins 4-1 to win their fifth Stanley Cup.

The Oilers made the conference finals in 1990-91 before getting knocked off by the Minnesota North Stars. The Oilers returned to the conference finals in 1991-92 but were swept by Chicago and it was more than a decade before they advanced that far again.

The Oilers have made the playoffs just seven times in the 21 years since the end of the Oilers' powerhouse era. Edmonton's best season since came in 2005-06 as the Oilers went 41-28-13 for 95 points. The Oilers defeated Detroit 4-2 in the quarterfinals, the San Jose Sharks 4-1 in the semifinals and the Mighty Ducks of Anaheim 4-1 in the conference finals to return to the Stanley Cup Finals. The Oilers battled from a 3-1 series deficit to force a Game 7 against the Carolina Hurricanes. The Oilers fell short in Game 7, losing 3-1.

The Oilers haven't been back to the playoffs. In 2013-14, under head coach Dallas Eakins, the Oilers finished the year 29-44-9 for 67 points. Jordan Eberle and David Perron led the team with 28 goals while Taylor Hall recorded a team high 53 assists and 80 points. Devan Dubnyk played a team high 32 games in net, he recorded an 11-17-2 record with a 3.36 GAA, .894 save percentage and two shutouts.

Tristan Jarry #30 of the Edmonton Oil Kings stops a shot in the warm-up prior to play against the Val'Dor Foreurs in Game Five of the 2014 MasterCard Memorial Cup at Budweiser Gardens on May 20, 2014 in London, Ontario. The Foreurs defeated the Oil Kings 4-3 in double overtime.

Reebok
JARRY
30

FLORIDA PANTHERS

First Year of Existence: 1993-94
Owner: Sunrise Sports and Entertainment
Coach: Gerard Gallant (June 21, 2014-present)

The Florida Panthers joined the National Hockey League in the 1993-94 season as part of a two team expansion that season with the Mighty Ducks of Anaheim. Wayne Huizenga, who owned the Miami Dolphins of the National Football League at the time and was the owner of Blockbuster Video, was awarded the franchise on December 10, 1992 with the price tag being $50 million. The team's name was revealed on April 20, 1993. Bill Torrey, who was the architect of the New York Islanders when they came into the league as an expansion team, was named team president while Bobby Clarke was the team's first general manager.

In the 1993 NHL expansion draft, the Panthers and Ducks went about populating their rosters for the first time. Florida added players like goalies John Vanbiesbrouck and Daren Puppa, defensemen Joe Cirella, Gord Murphy and Stephane Richer along with forwards Tom Fitzgerald, Scott Mellanby and Dave Lowry. Roger Neilson was the team's first head coach and with the 5th overall pick in the 1993 NHL Entry Draft, the Panthers added Rob Niedermayer to the mix. Brian Skrudland was the first captain in Panthers' history.

The Panthers played their first game on October 6, 1993 on the road against the Chicago Blackhawks. Mellanby scored the first goal in franchise history as the teams skated to a 4-4 tie. When it was all said and done, the inaugural season in Panthers' history was pretty successful; they posted a 33-34-17 record for 83 points, the most by a first year expansion team in the history of the NHL. Florida fell just one point shy of the last playoff spot in the Atlantic Division. Mellanby led the team with 30 goals and 60 points on the year. Vanbiesbrouck was solid in the net; he was 21-25-11 with a 2.93 GAA, a .924 save percentage and one shutout.

The Panthers made the playoffs for the first time in 1995-96, which was their first winning season in franchise history. Florida, in their first season under coach Doug MacLean, went 41-31-10 for 92 points. Mellanby again paced the Panthers with 32 goals and 70 points and he inspired a craze in south Florida with his antics early in the season. On October 8, 1995, Mellanby saw a rat in the locker room of the Miami Arena. He slapped the rat like he would shoot the puck off a pass for a one-timer and the rat hit the wall and died. Mellanby went out and scored a pair of goals in a 4-3 Florida win over the Calgary Flames and within weeks, fans were tossing rubber rats on the ice after Panther goals.

Vanbiesbrouck was rock solid in net again, posting a 26-20-7 with a 2.68 GAA, a .904 save percentage and two shutouts. Florida knocked off the Boston Bruins 4-1 in the Eastern Conference quarterfinals for their first playoff series win. The Panthers followed that up with a 4-2 elimination of the top-seeded Philadelphia Flyers in the semifinals and then eliminated the second seeded Pittsburgh Penguins 4-3 in the Eastern Conference Finals with Fitzgerald scoring the winning goal. That sent Florida to their only Stanley Cup Finals. The magic ran out for the Panthers as they were swept by the Colorado Avalanche.

The Panthers would go 35-28-19 in 1996-97 to make the playoffs for the second consecutive year. It is the only time that Florida made the playoffs in back to back seasons. Florida did nothing in the playoffs as they were knocked out in the quarterfinals by the New York Rangers 4-1. The Panthers won the first game 3-0 but dropped the next four with two of those losses coming in overtime.

Florida posted a franchise record 98 points in 1999-00 as they went 43-27-6-6 in the regular season. Pavel Bure, who came over in a big deal with the Vancouver Canucks, was a force to be reckoned with as he led the team with 58 goals and 94 points on the season. Talented winger Ray Whitney scored 29 goals and racked up 71 points while young center Viktor Kozlov had 17 goals and a team high 53 assists for 70 points. Mike Vernon was 18-13-2 with a 2.47 GAA, .919 save percentage and one shutout between the pipes while Trevor Kidd posted a mark of 14-11-2 with a 2.63 GAA, a .915 save percentage and one shutout. Florida went nowhere in the playoffs as they were swept by the New Jersey Devils in the quarterfinals. The Panthers were held to six goals in the series.

The Panthers would miss the playoffs in each of the next 10 seasons and went through seven head coaches in that span. Terry Murray, Duane Sutter, Mike Keenan, Rick Dudley, John Torchetti, Jacques Martin and Peter DeBoer all had the reins for at least 25 games during that span but couldn't get the Panthers to the postseason. The era of futility was punctuated b poor personnel decisions, none more one-sided than the deal that sent Roberto Luongo, Luka Krajicek and a 6th round draft pick to Vancouver for a banged-up Todd Bertuzzi, Alex Auld an Bryan Allen.

Florida finally made their way back to the postseason in 2011-12 under coach Kevi Dineen and won their only division championship in franchise history. The Panthers finishe the season 38-26-18 for 94 points and the Southeast Division crown. In the playoffs, Florid fell short and after leading their Eastern Conference quarterfinals series against the New Jersey Devils 3-2, they dropped Game 6 in overtime and Game 7 in double overtime to lose the series 4-3.

The Panthers haven't returned to the playoffs since; they finished 2013-14 29-45-8 for 66 points, which left them 7th in the Atlantic Division. Brad Boyes led the team with just 21 goals while Nick Bjugstad led the team with 38 points. Tim Thomas was the anchor in net for the Panthers as he played in a team high 40 games, going 16-20-3 with a 2.87 GAA and a .909 save percentage. Dineen was fired on November 8, 2013 after 16 games and Peter Horachek was named as the interim coach. Horachek went 26-36-4 the rest of the way but on April 29, 2014, the team informed Horachek that he would not be back as coach. On June 21, 2014, the Panthers announced that they had hired former Columbus head coach and Montreal assistant Gerard Gallant as the new head coach of the franchise.

Jimmy Hayes #12 of the Florida Panthers is unable to take the puck from Nicklas Grossmann #8 of the Philadelphia Flyers as he circles the net with the puck at the BB&T Center on April 8, 2014 in Sunrise, Florida.

Blue
12
8
EASTON
EASTON
8

LOS ANGELES KINGS

First Year of Existence: 1967-68
Owner: Los Angeles Kings Hockey Club, L.P.
Coach: Darryl Sutter (December 17, 2011-present)

The Los Angeles Kings joined the National Hockey League as part of its first wave of expansion along with five other teams in time for the 1967-68 NHL season. The expansion brought an end to the Original Six era as the league doubled in size. Jack Kent Cooke was the franchise's first owner, having plunked down $2 million to put a franchise in Los Angeles.

Red Kelly was named the team's first coach. The Kings took part in the 1967 NHL expansion draft where talent was rather thin as the Original Six teams tried to protect as much of their talent as possible. The Kings selected goaltenders Terry Sawchuk and Wayne Rutledge, defensemen Poul Popiel and Brent Hughes along with forwards Real Lemieux, Bill Flett, Lowell MacDonald, Ted Irvine and Eddie Joyal. With the first pick in the 1967 NHL Draft, the Kings selected defenseman Rick Pagnutti; he never played in the NHL.

The team played their first game on October 14, 1967 at home against fellow expansion team Philadelphia and won, 4-2. Brian Kilrea netted the team's first goal. Los Angeles finished their first season with 72 points and finished one point behind the Flyers for the top spot in the West Division. The Kings were knocked off 4-3 in the quarterfinals by the Minnesota North Stars.

Los Angeles made the playoffs again in 1968-69 and won their first playoff series with a 4-3 triumph over the Seals, but were swept by the Blues in the semifinals. They posted a franchise record 105 points in 1974-75; things didn't pan out for the Kings in the playoffs as they lost, 2-1, to the Toronto Maple Leafs in the preliminary round.

The Kings shuffled from the West Division to the Norris Division in the 1974-75 season and the Smythe Division when the league realigned again in 1981-82. Los Angeles managed to climb to 4th in the Smythe in 1986-87 and 1987-88 only to be eliminated 4-1 by the Edmonton Oilers and Calgary Flames in the Smythe semifinals.

Bruce McNall bought the team in 1987 and in an effort to make the Kings a Stanley Cup contender, he made a move to bolster the team. McNall made a deal with the Oilers, sending Jimmy Carson, Martin Gelinas, first round picks in 1989, 1991 and 1993 plus $15 million in exchange for Marty McSorely, Mike Krushelnyski and Wayne Gretzky. The addition of the league's best player had a positive effect on the attendance but not as much on the ice as the Kings were swept in the Smythe Finals by the Flames. The Kings won their first division title in 1990-91.

The 1992-93 season was their first season under coach Barry Melrose. Los Angeles finished the season 39-35-10 despite Gretzky playing just 45 games because of a herniated thoracic disc. Los Angeles whipped the Flames 4-2 in the Smythe semifinals and beat the Vancouver Canucks 4-2 in the Smythe Finals. The Kings escaped the Toronto Maple Leafs 4-3 in the Campbell Conference Finals but there was controversy involved. In overtime of Game 6, Gretzky clipped Toronto center Doug Gilmour with a high stick to the face. Referee Kerry Fraser missed the call and Gretzky scored the game winning goal moments later. Los Angeles won Game 7 to advance to the Stanley Cup Finals for the first time.

The Kings took the first game of the series but lost momentum late in Game 2 when the Montreal Canadiens had officials measure the curve of McSorely's stick blade. It was found to be illegal and he went to the penalty box. Montreal scored on the ensuing power play to tie the game, won in overtime to square the series and took the next three to win the Stanley Cup.

McNall would have to sell the team and eventually pled guilty to five counts of conspiracy and fraud. The next owners, Jeffrey Sudikoff and Joseph Cohen, had to go into bankruptcy in 1995 and the financial difficulties led to the departure of key players to cut payroll. Gretzky was unhappy with the way the team was going and wanted to be dealt. On February 27, 1996, he was traded to the Blues.

In the last three years, the Kings have taken position as one of the elite teams in the NHL. In 2011-12, the Kings went 40-27-15 and caught fire when Darryl Sutter took over on December 17, 2011. The team went 25-13-11 down the stretch. The Kings dusted the Canucks 4-1 in the quarterfinals and followed that up with a sweep of the Blues to advance to the conference finals for the first time since 1992-93.

The Kings beat the Phoenix Coyotes 4-1 in the Western Conference Finals. In the Stanley Cup Finals, the Kings defeated the New Jersey Devils 4-2 to win their first Stanley Cup. Quic was awarded the Conn Smythe Trophy as the MVP in the postseason, went 16-4 with a 1.4 GAA, .946 save percentage and three shutouts.

The 2013-14 season was another solid one for the Kings. Before the season, they trade backup goaltender Johnathan Bernier to the Toronto Maple Leafs for Ben Scrivens, Ma Frattin and a second round pick in either 2014 or 2015. Los Angeles posted a 46-28-8 record Kopitar scored a team high 29 goals along with 70 points. Quick played in 49 games, goin 27-17-5 with a 2.07 GAA, .915 save percentage and six shutouts.

The Kings looked to be doomed to an early exit as they trailed 3-0 to the San Jose Sharks in the quarterfinals. The Kings won four straight games in the series to become the fourth team in NHL history to rally from a 3-0 deficit in the postseason to win a series. Los Angeles followed that up with a 4-3 series win over the Anaheim Ducks and after nearly blowing a 3-1 series lead, the Kings prevailed in Game 7 with a 5-4 overtime win over Chicago to return to the Stanley Cup Finals.

In the Stanley Cup Finals, the Kings rallied from a two goal deficit to win Game 1 3-2 and rallied for a 5-4 double overtime win in Game 2. The Kings took a 3-0 series lead before the Rangers staved off elimination with a Game 4 win. Alec Martinez's goal at 14:43 of the second overtime gave the Kings a 3-2 win in Game 5 and their second Stanley Cup championship. The Kings set an NHL record by playing in 26 playoff games to win the Stanley Cup. Justin Williams was awarded the Conn Smythe Trophy.

Mike Richards #10 of the Los Angeles Kings celebrates with the Stanley Cup after the Kings 3-2 double overtime victory against the New York Rangers in Game Five of the 2014 Stanley Cup Final at Staples Center on June 13, 2014 in Los Angeles, California.

FINAL
LA

MINNESOTA WILD

First Year of Existence: 2000-01
Owner: Minnesota Sports and Entertainment
Coach: Mike Yeo (June 17, 2011-present)

The Minnesota Wild was one of the last two expansion teams in the NHL, beginning play in the 2000-01 season. The Wild replaced the Minnesota North Stars, who had relocated to Dallas. The franchise was awarded on June 25, 1997 and a list of six potential franchise names was handed out on November 20, 1997: the Blue Ox, Freeze, Northern Lights, Voyageurs, White Bears and Wild. The Wild was unveiled as the choice of the franchise on January 22, 1998.

In the 2000 NHL Expansion Draft, the Wild used their first selection on goaltender Jamie McLennan, who played for the St. Louis Blues and added goalie Mike Vernon from Florida. The team added veterans like Sean O'Donnell, Filip Kuba and Curtis Leschyshyn on the blue line along with Joe Juneau, Sergei Krivokrasov and Darby Hendrickson up front. With the 3rd pick in the 2000 NHL Draft, the Wild made Marian Gaborik their first selection. Highly respected Jacques Lemaire was installed as the first coach in franchise history.

Minnesota played the first game in franchise history on October 6, 2000 on the road against the Mighty Ducks of Anaheim. Gaborik scored the first goal in franchise history but the team fell 3-1. They played their first home game on October 11, 2000 against the Philadelphia Flyers, with Hendrickson scoring the first home goal in history as the Wild battled to a 3-3 tie. Minnesota recorded the first victory in franchise history with a 6-5 win over Tampa Bay on October 18, 2000. Scott Pellerin led the team with 39 points in 58 games before being dealt to Carolina. Gaborik, Hendrickson and Wes Walz each scored 18 goals to tie for the team lead. Manny Fernandez went 19-17-4 with a 2.24 GAA and a .920 save percentage along with four shutouts.

The Wild made their first playoff appearance in franchise history in their third year of existence. The 2002-03 season saw Minnesota finish the season with a 42-29-10-1 for 95 points. Gaborik scored 30 goals to lead the team and had 65 points. Dwayne Roloson went 23-16-8 with a 2.00 GAA, a .927 save percentage with four shutouts. The Wild played the first playoff game in franchise history on April 10, 2003 on the road against the Colorado Avalanche. Minnesota was victorious, 4-2, and recorded the first playoff win in team history. Minnesota would drop the next three games in the series to go down 3-1 but rallied to win Games 5, 6 and 7, all by 3-2 scores, to eliminate Colorado and pick up the first playoff series win in franchise history. That advanced Minnesota to the Western Conference semifinals against the Vancouver Canucks. Again, Minnesota found themselves in a 3-1 series hole but rallied to win the final three games by a combined score of 16-5 to take the series 4-3 and advance to the Western Conference Finals for the first time in history. The Wild ran out of gas by the time they faced the Mighty Ducks of Anaheim and they scored just one goal in the series as they were swept. Lemaire won the Jack Adams Trophy for Coach of the Year. Roloson won the Roger Crozier Saving Grace Award for the best save percentage in the NHL in 2003-04 as he went 19-18-11 with a 1.88 GAA with a .933 save percentage and five shutouts, but Minnesota missed the playoffs. Minnesota came back in the 2005-06 season after the lockout and missed the postseason again by finishing with a 38-36-8 mark for 84 points.

In the 2006-07 season, Minnesota went 48-26-8 on the season for a franchise record 104 points. Gaborik was second on the team with 30 goals while Brian Rolston was tied for the team lead with 64 points, including 31 goals, while Pavol Demitra added 64 points. Five Wild players scored at least 20 goals on the season. Niklas Backstrom took over in net and went 23-8-6 with a 1.97 GAA and won the Roger Crozier Saving Grace Award with a .929 save percentage. The Wild was knocked out in the first round of the playoffs 4-1 by Anaheim.

The Wild followed that up in 2007-08 with their first, and to date, only, division crown as they posted a 44-28-10 mark for 98 points. Gaborik set franchise records in goals (42) and points (83), Pierre-Marc Bouchard had a franchise record 50 assists while Backstrom was 33-13-8 with a 2.31 GAA, .920 save percentage and four shutouts. On April 3, 2008, Lemaire won his 500th game, making him the 11th coach in NHL history to reach that mark. Despite the terrific performance, the Wild was unsuccessful in the playoffs and they were eliminated in the first round by the Avalanche 4-2.

Lemaire stepped down as coach after the 2008-09 season, leaving with a mark of 29 256-107 in Minnesota. He was replaced by Todd Richards, who coached the team for tw seasons but he was fired after the 2010-11 season after coaching the team to a 77-71-16 ma Mike Yeo was hired on June 17, 2011. The Wild went 35-36-11 in their first season under Ye missing the playoffs for the fourth straight season. Dany Heatley led the team with 24 goa and 53 points on the season.

Minnesota made bold moves in the offseason, bringing in Ryan Suter and Zach Parise o matching 13 year, $98 million deals. The deals paid off as the Wild returned to the playoff and finished 26-19-3 in the lockout shortened season. Parise led the team with 18 goals and 38 points while Suter stabilized the blue line with four goals and 32 points. Backstrom went 24-15-3 with a 2.48 GAA, .909 save percentage and two shutouts. Minnesota was wiped out 4-1 by the Chicago Blackhawks in the first round of the playoffs.

In the 2013-14 season, Minnesota relocated to the Central Division due to the league's realignment. The team clinched the top wild card spot in the playoffs, finishing with 43-27-12 for 98 points. Jason Pominville led the Wild in scoring with 30 goals and 60 points in his first full season with the team. Parise added 29 goals in 67 games for the team while five goaltenders saw action Josh Harding's 29 games were the most of any goalie for the Wild on the season. Minnesota beat Colorado 4-3 in the opening round of the playoffs. The Wild ran out of momentum in the conference semifinals as they were beaten 4-2 by Chicago.

Mikael Granlund #64 of the Minnesota Wild looks on in Game Six of the First Round of the 2014 NHL Stanley Cup Playoffs against the Colorado Avalanche on April 28, 2014 at Xcel Energy Center in St Paul, Minnesota. The Wild defeated the Avalanche 5-2.

CCM
Minnesota
WILD

MONTREAL CANADIENS

First Year of Existence: 1909-10
Owner: Molson Family
Coach: Michel Therrien (June 5, 2012-present)

The Montreal Canadiens are arguably the most storied franchise in the history of the National Hockey League as they date back to the 1909-10 season. The franchise was originally founded on December 4, 1909, by J. Ambrose O'Brien as one of the charter members of the National Hockey Association.

The Canadiens have won a league-high 24 Stanley Cups, with 22 of them coming after the 1927 season, when the Stanley Cup was only competed for by NHL franchises. Their first Stanley Cup victory came in the 1915-16 season as they defeated the Portland Rosebuds of the PCHA, 3-2.

Montreal was one of the charter members of the NHL in the 1917-18 season. The Canadiens finished the first NHL season 13-9, winning the first half of the season to advance to the NHL Finals. They lost the two game series on goals 10-7 to the Toronto Arenas. Montreal won the NHL Finals in 1918-19 by beating Ottawa 4-1 but with the Stanley Cup Finals even at two wins apiece plus a tie, the rest of the series was canceled thanks to the Spanish flu epidemic; Joe Hall died from it. This was the only time in NHL history that the Stanley Cup was not awarded once the playoffs had gotten underway.

The Canadiens were defeated 3-1 by the Victoria Cougars of the PCHL in the 1924-25 Stanley Cup Finals. It was the last time a non-NHL franchise won the Stanley Cup. Montreal wouldn't win another Stanley Cup until 1929-30. Montreal knocked off Chicago on total goals 3-2 in the quarterfinals before bouncing the New York Rangers in the semifinals. In the Stanley Cup Final, the Canadiens beat the Boston Bruins to win the Cup. They would repeat as champions in 1930-31, defeating the Bruins 3-2 in the semifinals and beating the Chicago Black Hawks 3-2 in the Stanley Cup Finals.

In 1943-44, the second year of the Original Six era, the Canadiens put up a stellar 38-5-7 mark. Montreal whipped Toronto 4-1 in the semifinals before sweeping Chicago to win the Stanley Cup. The Canadiens won the Cup again in 1945-46 as they swept Chicago before defeating the Bruins 4-1 to win the Stanley Cup.

The Canadiens appeared in the Stanley Cup Finals in ten straight seasons from 1950-51 through 1959-60. Montreal lost four of the first five Stanley Cup Finals in the decade, dropping the 1951 Stanley Cup Finals 4-1 to Toronto in a series that saw all five games go to overtime. Montreal was swept by Detroit in 1952, beat the Bruins 4-1 in 1953 and lost to Detroit 4-3 in both 1954 and 1955.

Montreal won five straight Stanley Cups, a feat that has never been surpassed or even matched in NHL history. The Canadiens defeated the Red Wings 4-1 in the 1956 Stanley Cup Finals, beat the Bruins 4-1 in 1957 and 4-2 in 1958, knocked off Toronto 4-1 in 1959 and swept the Leafs in 1960. Their impressive run ended in the 1960-61 season as the Canadiens were defeated 4-2 by Chicago in the semifinals.

Montreal closed out the Original Six era with three straight Stanley Cup Final appearances. The Canadiens defeated Chicago 4-3 in the 1965 Stanley Cup Finals, knocked off Detroit 4-2 in 1966 and lost to Toronto 4-2 in 1967. In the first year after expansion, the Canadiens won their third Stanley Cup in four years with a sweep of the St. Louis Blues.

The Canadiens won the Stanley Cup in 1968-69 as they swept the Blues. Al MacNeil led the Canadiens to a Stanley Cup championship with a 4-3 win over Chicago. Rookie goalie Ken Dryden was the team's starter in the postseason and won the Conn Smythe Trophy as the postseason's MVP.

Montreal posted a NHL record 132 point season in 1976-77 when they went 60-8-12. The Canadiens won five Stanley Cups under Bowman; they defeated Chicago 4-2 in the 1973 Stanley Cup Finals, swept the Flyers in 1976, swept the Bruins in 1977, beat Boston 4-2 in 1978 and dusted the Rangers 4-1 in 1979, giving them four straight Stanley Cup victories.

Montreal put things together again in 1985-86. In the postseason, Montreal brushed aside Boston 3-0 in the Adams Division semifinals and followed that up with a 4-3 series win over the Hartford Whalers in the Adams Finals. In the conference finals, Montreal defeated the Rangers in 4-1 before upending the Calgary Flames 4-2 to win their 23rd Stanley Cup. Roy was named the Conn Smythe winner as playoff MVP.

The 1992-93 season was special for Montreal as the team was 48-30-6 on the season. Montreal won a NHL record 10 overtime games in the postseason; after dispatching Quebec 4-2 and the Sabres in four to reach the conference finals, Montreal handled the New York Islanders 4-1 to advance to the Stanley Cup Finals.

Montreal trailed 1-0 and was down 2-1 late in Game 2 when Jacques Demers called for measurement on the curve of the blade of Kings defenseman Marty McSorely's stick and it wa found to be illegal. The Canadiens tied the game on the ensuing power play before winning overtime. The measurement proved to be the turning point in the series and Montreal wo the next three games to win the Stanley Cup. Roy won his second Conn Smythe Trophy. It's th most recent Stanley Cup win for the franchise and the last one by a Canadian team.

Montreal missed the playoffs in 1994-95. It was just the third time in 55 years that the playoffs went on without Montreal. Montreal was forced to deal Roy on December 6, 1995 to the Colorado Avalanche after he was left for nine goals on 26 shots in an 11-1 loss to Detroit. Roy told team president Ronald Corey that it was his last game in Montreal.

The Canadiens had a solid season in 2013-14, finishing 46-28-8. Max Pacioretty led the team with 39 goals and 60 points while defenseman P.K. Subban had a team high 43 assists. Carey Price was the team's top goalie in the regular season, posting a 34-20-5 record in 59 games with a 2.32 GAA, .927 save percentage and six shutouts. Montreal swept the Tampa Bay Lightning in the quarterfinals and then eliminated the Boston Bruins 4-3 to reach the conference finals. Price was injured in Game 1 of the series against the New York Rangers and didn't return. Dustin Tokarski took over the goaltending duties but Montreal was eliminated 4-2.

Thomas Vanek #20 of the Montreal Canadiens plays the puck against the New York Rangers during Game Six of the Eastern Conference Final in the 2014 NHL Stanley Cup Playoffs at Madison Square Garden on May 29, 2014 in New York City.

WARRIOR
CCM

NASHVILLE PREDATORS

First Year of Existence: 1998-99
Owner: Predators Holdings LLC
Coach: Peter Laviolette (May 6, 2014-present)

The Nashville Predators entered the National Hockey League as the 27th franchise in time for the 1998-99 season. Nashville had originally tried to lure the New Jersey Devils to town but the attempt failed, creating a second attempt to bring hockey to Tennessee. On June 25, 1997, Nashville, Atlanta, Columbus and Minnesota were awarded franchises contingent on selling 12,000 season tickets before March 31, 1998.

David Poile was named the team's first general manager and Barry Trotz was selected as the first coach of the franchise. On September 25, 1997, Craig Leipold and team president Jack Diller revealed the logo and mascot for the franchise, a saber-toothed tiger. After the logo was revealed, the choices for team name was narrowed to three: the Fury, Ice Tigers and Attack with Leipold throwing his own idea, the Predators, into the mix. As it turned out, his submission won.

The Predators took part in the expansion draft for the initial population of their roster, taking one player from each of the other 26 franchises. Nashville ended up with goaltenders Tomas Vokoun and Mike Dunham along with wingers Scott Walker and Andrew Brunette.

Nashville was officially awarded their franchise on May 4, 1998. With the 2nd pick in the 1998 NHL Draft, they selected David Legwand. In Nashville's first game in franchise history on October 10, 1998 at the Bridgestone Arena in Nashville, the Predators were blanked 1-0 by the Florida Panthers. On October 13, 1998, Nashville received their first win with a 3-2 win over the Carolina Hurricanes. Andrew Brunette scored the first goal.

Nashville finished the year 28-47-7 for 63 points, leaving them with the fourth worst record overall. Cliff Ronning, who was acquired early in the season from the Phoenix Coyotes, led the team with 53 points while Sergei Krivokrasov led with 25 goals. Dunham was 16-23-3 with a .908 save percentage, 3.08 GAA plus one shutout in 44 games while Vokoun played 37 games, going 12-18-4 with a 2.95 GAA, .908 save percentage and one shutout.

On March 1, 2003, Trotz coached his 392nd game with the franchise, setting a new NHL record for games coached by an expansion team's first coach, breaking Terry Crisp's mark of 391 he set with the Tampa Bay Lightning. The 2003-04 season saw the Predators post their first season with a winning mark as they went 38-29-11-4. It was good enough for the Predators to earn their first playoff berth. Walker led the team with 25 goals and 67 points while the defense corps got a boost from Marek Zidlicky. Vokoun was 34-29-10 with a 2.53 GAA, a .909 save percentage and three shutouts as he played 73 games.

The Predators played their first playoff game on April 7, 2004 in Detroit and they were defeated 3-1 with Adam Hall scoring for Nashville. The Predators played the first home playoff game on April 11, winning 3-1 to cut their deficit to 2-1. Vokoun recorded the first playoff shutout in team history in Game 4 but Nashville dropped the next two games to lose the series 4-2.

After a year off for the lockout, Nashville was solid in 2005-06, going 49-25-8 for 106 points. Five players scored at least 20 goals on the year for Nashville, with Paul Kariya and Steve Sullivan each bagging 31 to lead the team. Vokoun went 36-18-7 with a 2.67 GAA, .919 save percentage and four shutouts. Despite having home ice advantage for the first time, the Predators were knocked out in the first round as the San Jose Sharks beat them 4-1.

In 2006-07, Nashville set a franchise record for victories (51) and points (110); Kariya led the team in assists (52) and points (76) while Legwand posted 27 goals en route to a career high 63 point season. Vokoun (27-12-4, 2.40 GAA, .920 save percentage, 5 shutouts) had a near even split in playing time with Chris Mason (24-11-4, 2.38 GAA, .925 save percentage, 5 shutouts) on the year. Nashville was ousted again in the first round, falling 4-1 to the Sharks for the second straight year.

Nashville slipped to a 41-32-9 mark in 2007-08 but qualified for the postseason for the fourth consecutive season. They were ousted in the opening round 4-2 by Detroit. The Predators returned to the playoffs in 2009-10 thanks to the third 100 point season in franchise history. The end result once the playoffs began was the same as they fell in the opening round 4-2 to the Chicago Blackhawks.

The Predators posted 99 points in the 2010-11 season behind strong play from goalie Pekka Rinne, who was 33-22-9 with a 2.12 GAA, a .930 save percentage and six shutouts. Sergei Kostitsyn led the team with 23 goals and tied Martin Erat for the team lead in point with 50. Nashville picked up the first playoff series win in franchise history by dispatching th Anaheim Ducks 4-2 in the opening round before being eliminated by the Vancouver Canuck 4-2 in the conference semifinals.

Nashville returned to the playoffs in 2011-12 after picking up 104 points. Nashville bea Detroit 4-1 in the first round before losing to the Phoenix Coyotes 4-1 in the conferenc semifinals. During the offseason, Ryan Suter signed a 13 year, $98 million deal with th Minnesota Wild. Once the lockout ended, Nashville struggled: Weber led the team with 28 points and only three Nashville players scored double digit goals. The Predators missed the postseason, finishing 16-23-3-6 for 41 points.

The 2013-14 season didn't go well either. Rinne was able to play just 24 games, leaving young goalies Carter Hutton and Marek Mazanec to carry the load. Craig Smith led the team with 24 goals while Weber had 23 goals and 56 points, both are franchise records for a defenseman. Nashville couldn't get things going as they finished the year with a winning record at 38-32-12 but missed the playoffs by three points.

After the season, Nashville made the decision to fire Trotz, who was the longest-tenured coach in the NHL. Trotz finished his Nashville coaching career with a record of 577-479-60-100. On May 6, 2014, the Predators announced that Peter Laviolette would replace Trotz as the head coach of the franchise.

Shea Weber #6 of the Nashville Predators skates against the Phoenix Coyotes at Bridgestone Arena on April 10, 2014 in Nashville, Tennessee.

CCM
Reebok
WEBER
BAUER
TOTALONE
Reebok
CCM

NEW JERSEY DEVILS

First Year of Existence: 1974-75
Owner: New Jersey Devils, LLC
Coach: Peter DeBoer (July 19, 2011-present)

The New Jersey Devils have had a long, circuitous route to becoming the franchise that they are today. The franchise was originally awarded on June 8, 1972 to Kansas City, Missouri. After a contest to name the team took place, the new name, the Scouts, was revealed.

Kansas City took part in the 1974 NHL Expansion Draft along with the Washington Capitals to populate their initial rosters. The Scouts selected players like goaltender Michel Plasse, defensemen Brent Hughes, Paul Terbenche and Brian Lefley along with forwards Simon Nolet, Gary Croteau, Randy Rota and Real Lemieux. With the second pick in the 1974 NHL Draft, the Scouts made Wilf Paiement their first draft choice. Bep Guidolin was the team's first head coach while Nolet was the first captain in team history.

The Scouts played their first game on October 9, 1974 against the Toronto Maple Leafs and lost 6-2, with Nolet scoring the team's first goal. On November 3, 1974, the Scouts picked up their first win with a 5-4 road win over Washington. Kansas City finished their first season 15-54-11 record and was last in the Smythe Division.

The Scouts were even worse in 1975-76. On December 28, 1975, the Scouts were one point out of a playoff spot in the Smythe. They went through a 0-14-2 stretch before beating the Capitals on February 7. That was followed by a 0-21-6 mark the rest of the year, meaning that the Scouts went just 1-35-8 in their last 44 games. With ownership in debt, the decision was made to sell the franchise. The team was sold to a group led by Jack Vickers, who moved the team to Denver and renamed the team the Colorado Rockies.

In 1977-78, the Rockies were 19-40-21 but made the playoffs as Chicago was the only team in the division with a .500 record. The Rockies' time in the playoffs was short-lived as they were eliminated in two games in the preliminary round. With the Brendan Byrne Arena completed in 1982, the franchise was sold to John McMullen. He moved the team to New Jersey in time for the 1982-83 season. On June 30, 1982, the franchise was renamed the New Jersey Devils and was moved from the Smythe Division to the Patrick Division with the realignment.

In 1987-88, the Devils posted a 38-36-6 mark. The Devils won the first playoff series in franchise history by eliminating the New York Islanders 4-2 in the Patrick Division semifinals and followed that up with a 4-3 series win in the Patrick Finals over the Capitals. That sent the Devils to the conference finals for the first time but they lost 4-3 to the Boston Bruins.

The Devils returned to the conference finals in 1993-94. New Jersey edged the Buffalo Sabres 4-3 in the quarterfinals and followed that up with a 4-2 defeat of the Bruins in the semifinals. In the conference finals, the Devils led the Rangers 3-2 and were ahead 2-0 in Game 6 only to see Mark Messier score a natural hat trick in the third period en route to a 4-2 Rangers win. They dropped Game 7 in double overtime.

The Devils won their first Stanley Cup in 1994-95. The team dispatched the Bruins 4-1 in the quarterfinals and followed that up with a 4-1 elimination of the Pittsburgh Penguins in the conference semifinals. New Jersey knocked off the Philadelphia Flyers 4-2 in the conference finals for their first trip to the Stanley Cup Finals. They swept the Detroit Red Wings to win the Cup; Claude Lemieux won the Conn Smythe as the postseason MVP.

New Jersey found their playoff groove again in 1999-00. New Jersey swept the Florida Panthers in the Eastern Conference quarterfinals. They followed that up with 4-2 victory over the Toronto Maple Leafs and then eliminated the Flyers 4-3 in the Eastern Conference Finals. New Jersey rallied from a 3-1 deficit in the series; it was the first time it happened in the conference finals in league history. In the Stanley Cup Finals, the Devils knocked off the Dallas Stars 4-2.

It was a solid year for New Jersey; Scott Stevens won the Conn Smythe for playoff MVP, Ken Daneyko was awarded the Masterton Trophy and Scott Gomez won the Calder as the rookie of the year. New Jersey returned to the Stanley Cup Finals in 2000-01 after setting a franchise record with 111 points but couldn't close out the Colorado Avalanche. After leading 3-2 and having Game 6 on home ice, the Devils scored just one goal in the final two games to lose the series 4-3.

New Jersey returned to the Stanley Cup Finals for the third time in four years in 2002-03 under Pat Burns. The Devils went 46-20-10-6 for 108 points and won the Atlantic Division fo[r] the fifth time in seven seasons. New Jersey dispatched Boston 4-1 in the quarterfinals an[d] wiped out the Tampa Bay Lightning 4-1 to advance to the conference finals. New Jersey near[ly] squandered a 3-1 series lead before beating the Ottawa Senators 4-3. In the Stanley Cup Final[s] New Jersey was again forced to a Game 7 but Brodeur led the team to the Stanley Cup with [a] shutout in Game 7 to win the series 4-3.

In 2011-12, New Jersey got back on track as they posted a 48-28-6 mark. New Jerse[y] knocked the Florida Panthers off 4-3 in the Eastern Conference quarterfinals and followe[d] that up with a 4-1 triumph over the Flyers. The Devils beat the Rangers 4-2 in the conference finals but lost in the Stanley Cup Finals as they were defeated by the Los Angeles Kings 4-2.

At the 2013 NHL Draft, the Devils dealt the 9th overall pick to the Vancouver Canucks for goaltender Cory Schneider. Kovalchuk announced his retirement from the NHL on July 11, 2013 and stated his intentions of playing in the KHL. On August 13, 2013, the team announced that Josh Harris and David Blitzer bought the team for upward of $320 million.

New Jersey finished 2013-14 with 88 points, five points out of the final playoff spot in the East. Adam Henrique led the team with 25 goals while Jaromir Jagr posted a team high 67 points on the season. Schneider played 45 games, posting a 16-15-12 record with a 1.97 GAA, .921 save percentage and three shutouts while Brodeur logged 39 games, going 19-14-6 with a 2.51 GAA, .901 save percentage and three shutouts.

Steve Bernier #18 of the New Jersey Devils skates against the Calgary Flames at the Prudential Center on April 7, 2014 in Newark, New Jersey. The Flames shutout the Devils 1-0.

18
DEVILS
NHL.COM
18
Morristown
Medical Center
ATLANTIC HEALTH SYSTEM

NEW YORK ISLANDERS

First Year of Existence: 1972-73
Owner: Charles Wang
Coach: Jack Capuano (November 15, 2010-present)

The New York Islanders came into the National Hockey League as part of a two team expansion along with the Atlanta Flames. The NHL awarded a franchise to Roy Boe in an effort to prevent the WHA from putting a franchise in the new Nassau Veterans Memorial Coliseum.

New York took part in the 1972 expansion draft to piece together their initial roster. The Islanders picked up goalies Gerry Desjardins and Billy Smith, defensemen Bryan Lefley, John Schella and Bill Mikkelson along with forwards Terry Crisp, Ed Westfall and Brian Spencer. The team selected Billy Harris with the first overall pick in the 1972 NHL Draft while also adding Lorne Henning and Bob Nystrom in the second and third rounds.

Phil Goyette was the first coach in franchise history and he wouldn't last the season. Bill Torrey was the team's first general manager and opted to make very few trades, choosing to build the team through the draft. The team played their first game on October 7, 1972 at home against the Flames. Westfall scored the first goal but the Islanders fell to the Flames 3-2. The team recorded their first win on October 12, 1972 as they posted a 3-2 win over the Los Angeles Kings.

Goyette was fired on January 29, 1973 after 48 games. The team didn't do much better under Earl Ingarfield's guidance and they finished last in the league with a record of 12-60-6. Since the Islanders finished last, they had the top pick in the 1973 NHL Draft, which they used to select defenseman Denis Potvin.

In the offseason, New York made a bold move by bringing Al Arbour in to coach. Potvin won the Calder Trophy as the league's rookie of the year. In the 1974 NHL Draft, the Islanders continued to add talent, bringing in Clark Gillies in the first round and Bryan Trottier in the second. The Islanders wouldn't have another losing season until 1988-89.

In 1974-75, the Islanders made the playoffs for the first time as they posted a record of 33-25-22. The goaltending combination of Smith (21-18-17, 2.78 GAA, three shutouts) and Chico Resch (12-7-5, 2.47 GAA, three shutouts) was solid in net. The Islanders won their first playoff series with a 2-1 series win over the Rangers in the preliminary round and followed that up by becoming just the second team in NHL history to rally from a 3-0 series deficit to win as they beat the Pittsburgh Penguins 4-3. New York fell to the defending champion Philadelphia Flyers in the semifinals, 4-3.

Trottier won the Calder Trophy in 1975-76 as the Islanders went 42-21-17 but the team was knocked off in the semifinals 4-1 by the Montreal Canadiens. They posted 106 points in 1976-77 but again fell to Montreal in the semifinals 4-2. With the 15th overall pick in the 1977 NHL Entry Draft, the Islanders added another piece to their puzzle in sniper Mike Bossy.

Bossy scored 53 goals in his rookie campaign and won the Calder Trophy as the Islanders posted a 48-17-15 record and won their first division title. The Isles won the President's Trophy in 1978-79 with the league's best record as they went 51-15-14. Trottier won the Hart Trophy as the league's MVP in addition to the Art Ross Trophy with a league high 134 points, including 47 goals. Resch went 26-7-10 with a 2.50 GAA and two shutouts while Smith was 25-8-4 with a 2.87 GAA and one shutout. The Islanders were knocked off by the Rangers in the semifinals, 4-2.

In 1979-80, the Isles finished with 91 points and made a big trade before the deadline as Harris and Dave Lewis were traded to the Los Angeles Kings for Butch Goring. They knocked off the Kings 3-1 in the preliminary round and followed that up with a 4-1 win over the Boston Bruins in the quarterfinals. New York edged the Buffalo Sabres 4-2 to reach the Stanley Cup Finals for the first time. The Islanders upended the Philadelphia Flyers, 4-2, with Nystrom recording the Cup-winning goal at 7:11 of overtime in Game 6.

The Islanders would go on to win the next three Stanley Cups, giving them four straight titles. The Islanders beat the Minnesota North Stars 4-1 in 1980-81 as Bossy bagged 68 goals. In 1981-82, they would set franchise records for wins with 54 and points with 118, after edging the Penguins 3-2 in the first round, the Islanders cruised. They knocked off the Rangers 4-2, then swept the Quebec Nordiques in the conference finals and swept the Canucks in the Stanley Cup Finals. Bossy scored 64 goals and had 147 points while Trottier potted 50 goals of his own.

In 1982-83, the Islanders were 42-26-12 as Bossy scored another 60 goals. It was busines as usual in the playoffs as New York steamrolled the Washington Capitals 3-1 in the openin round, the Rangers 4-2 in the Patrick Division Finals and the Boston Bruins 4-2 in the conferen finals. In a matchup with Wayne Gretzky and the Edmonton Oilers, it was no contest; th Islanders won their fourth straight championship in a sweep. The Islanders would make the way to the a fifth straight Stanley Cup Finals appearance in 1983-84 but ran out of steam a Gretzky and the Oilers took the series 4-1.

The Islanders' last run at glory came in the 1992-93 season when the team went 40-37-7. Ray Ferraro scored a pair of overtime winners in the first round as the Islanders dispatched the Capitals 4-2. Pierre Turgeon, the Isles star center who was obtained in a deal that sent LaFontaine to Buffalo two years earlier, was drilled after the play by Dale Hunter, separating his shoulder. Hunter was suspended a then-league record 21 games for the incident. The Islanders were heavy underdogs to the Penguins in the conference semifinals, especially without Turgeon but stunned the Penguins 4-3 to go to the conference finals. They were eliminated 4-1 by the Canadiens and haven't won a playoff series since.

The Islanders have made the playoffs just six times since that run. In the 2013-14 season, the Islanders finished 34-37-11 for 79 points. Kyle Okposo led the Islanders with 27 goals, 42 assists and 69 points while Evgeni Nabokov was the top goaltender, posting a 15-14-8 mark with a 2.74 GAA, .905 save percentage and four shutouts.

Thomas Hickey #14 of the New York Islanders skates against the Ottawa Senators at the Nassau Veterans Memorial Coliseum on April 8, 2014 in Uniondale, New York.

14
EASTON
EASTON
14
BAUER

NEW YORK RANGERS

First Year of Existence: 1926-27
Owner: The Madison Square Garden Company
Coach: Alain Vigneault (June 21, 2013-present)

The New York Rangers are one of the Original Six franchises of the National Hockey League. Tex Rickard was awarded the team for the 1926-27 season to compete with the then-active New York Americans, who had begun play in Madison Square Garden the year before. The Rangers tabbed Lester Patrick, who helped found the PCHA, to be the team's first head coach.

The Rangers played their first game in front of a crowd of nearly 13,000 against the Montreal Maroons on November 16, 1926. Captain Bill Cook scored the lone goal of the game to give the Rangers a 1-0 victory with Hal Winkler recording the shutout win. New York won the American Division in their first season, posting a 25-13-6 mark for 56 points. The Rangers were knocked off by the Boston Bruins in the playoffs, losing by goal differential, 3-1.

The Rangers were a playoff team in 1927-28. New York advanced past the quarterfinals by outscoring the Pittsburgh Pirates 6-4 and upended the Bruins in the semifinals by a 5-2 goal differential to advance to the Stanley Cup Finals for the first time. Chabot suffered an eye injury in Game 2 of the series. In that era, teams didn't have to dress a backup goalie. Patrick put himself between the pipes and he played 46 minutes in the game, allowing one goal, the Rangers won the game in overtime. The Rangers won the Stanley Cup by taking the series 3-2. They became the first American team in NHL history to win the Stanley Cup.

In 1932-33, the Rangers returned to the Stanley Cup Finals and beat the Leafs 3-1 to win their second Stanley Cup. In 1939-40, the Rangers went 27-11-10 in the regular season. New York knocked off Boston, 4-2, in the semifinals and then defeated Toronto, 4-2, to win their third Stanley Cup. They wouldn't win another Stanley Cup for 54 years.

In the 25 year span of the Original Six era from 1942-43 through 1966-67, the Rangers were doormats for the majority of that time. New York made the playoffs only seven times, finishing last in the NHL eight times. The one time the Rangers made the Stanley Cup Finals in the Original Six era came in 1949-50. New York finished 28-31-11. In the playoffs, the Rangers upset the Montreal Canadiens, 4-1, in the semifinals and lost to Detroit 4-3 in the Stanley Cup Finals.

New York made the playoffs in nine straight seasons from the 1966-67 season through the 1974-75 campaigns, including three straight seasons with at least 100 points but struggled in the playoffs. In 1971-72, the Rangers made the Stanley Cup Finals. New York posted a 48-17-13 mark in the regular season but lost 4-2 to the Bruins. The following season, the Rangers became the first Original Six team to lose a playoff series to an expansion team as they fell 4-3 to the Philadelphia Flyers.

New York made the Stanley Cup Finals in the 1978-79 season. New York beat the Los Angeles Kings 2-0 in the preliminary round, followed with a 4-1 series win over the Flyers to advance to the conference finals. The Rangers knocked off the Islanders 4-1 to advance to the Stanley Cup Finals but fell short as they lost 4-1 to the Canadiens.

New York's next good run came in 1985-86 when they finished that season 36-38-6. New York stunned the Flyers 3-2 in the Patrick semifinals and followed that up with a 4-2 win over the Washington Capitals in the Patrick Finals. In the conference finals the Rangers were knocked off 4-1 by the Canadiens.

In 1993-94 with Mike Keenan at the helm, the Rangers set franchise records with 52 victories and 112 points. The Rangers swept the New York Islanders in the quarterfinals. New York whipped the Capitals in five games to advance to the conference finals.

With the Rangers trailing 3-2 against the New Jersey Devils in the conference finals, Mark Messier guaranteed a New York win in Game 6. The Rangers trailed 2-0 after one period and cut the lead in half after 40 minutes thanks to an Alexei Kovalev marker. Messier scored a natural hat trick in the third period, including an empty net goal that sealed a 4-2 win to extend the series. In Game 7 Stephane Matteau scored the series clinching goal in double overtime to give the Rangers a 2-1 win and a 4-3 series win to advance to the Stanley Cup Finals.

The Rangers led the Vancouver Canucks 3-1 in the Finals, only to see Vancouver tie the series. In Game 7 the Rangers led 2-0 after one period, with Messier scoring to make it 3-1 and that proved to be the decisive goal as the Rangers won 3-2 for their first Stanley Cup since 1940. Brian Leetch was the first American player to be awarded the Conn Smythe Trophy a the MVP in the playoffs. Kovalev, Sergei Nemchinov, Zubov and Alexander Karpovtsev becam the first Russians to have their names engraved on the Stanley Cup.

New York reached the conference finals in 1996-97 but was bounced 4-1 by the Flyer. New York advanced to the conference finals in the 2011-12 season after 4-3 series wins ov the Ottawa Senators and the Washington Capitals before they were beaten 4-2 by the Devi in the conference finals.

In 2013-14, the Rangers finished with a 45-31-6 mark. Rick Nash scored a team-high 26 goals while Mats Zuccarello had team highs in assists (40) and points (59) on the season. Henrik Lundqvist played 63 games in net, going 33-24-5 with a 2.36 GAA, .920 save percentage and 5 shutouts. The Rangers knocked off the Flyers 4-3 in the quarterfinals and followed that up by rallying from a 3-1 deficit to knock off the Pittsburgh Penguins 4-3. In the conference finals, the Rangers beat the Montreal Canadiens 4-2 to advance to the Stanley Cup Finals for the first time since 1993-94.

In the Stanley Cup Finals, the Rangers were defeated 4-1 by the Los Angeles Kings. The Rangers were unable to close out games; they lost Game 1 3-2 in overtime and Game 2 5-4 in double overtime. New York was blanked in Game 3 to fall behind 3-0. They rallied to win Game 4 2-1 to send the series back to Los Angeles. In Game 5, the Rangers blew another third period lead. Alec Martinez's goal at 14:43 of the second overtime gave the Kings a 3-2 win and ended the series.

Chris Kreider #20 of the New York Rangers scores a second period goal past goaltender Jonathan Quick #32 of the Los Angeles Kings during Game Five of the 2014 Stanley Cup Final at Staples Center on June 13, 2014 in Los Angeles, California.

VAUGHN
32
VAUGHN
VAUGHN
2
KREIDER
20

OTTAWA SENATORS

First Year of Existence: 1992-93
Owner: Eugene Melnyk
Coach: Paul MacLean (June 4, 2011-present)

The Ottawa Senators came into existence in the 1992-93 NHL season as one of two expansion teams that year with the other being the Tampa Bay Lightning. The franchise was awarded to the Terrace Investments Ltd. Group on December 6, 1990 at a cost of $50 million. Mel Bridgman was named the team's first general manager after being rebuffed by Scotty Bowman and John Muckler. Rick Bowness was the first head coach in team history.

Ottawa took part in the 1992 NHL Expansion Draft with the Lightning and had their laptop fail, leaving them with no alternative plan. The Senators tried to select a series of ineligible players due to the issue and ended up with a series of journeymen. Ottawa took goalies Peter Sidorkiewicz and Mark LaForest, defenseman Brad Shaw and forwards Sylvain Turgeon, Mike Peluso, Laurie Boschman and Rob Murphy. With their first pick in franchise history, the Senators took Alexei Yashin with the 2nd overall pick in the 1992 NHL Draft.

The Senators played their first game on October 8, 1992 at home against the Montreal Canadiens. Ottawa shocked Montreal 5-3 with Neil Brady scoring the first goal. It was the lone highlight for the Senators that season as they finished the season 10-70-4 and tied with the San Jose Sharks for last place in the league with 24 points. The Senators set NHL records for most consecutive home losses with 11, the longest road losing streak with a 38 game skid and tied the league record for the fewest road wins with 1. Turgeon led the team with 25 goals while Norm MacIver had 46 assists and 63 points. Sidorkiewicz played in 64 games, going 8-46-3 with a 4.43 GAA and a .856 save percentage on the season. The poor performance was to be expected as owner Bruce Firestone expected the team to struggle to pick up high draft picks.

Ottawa struggled over the next three seasons, failing to record more than 41 points. The team selected Alexander Daigle with the top overall pick in the 1993 NHL Draft, Radek Bonk in the 1994 NHL Draft and Bryan Berard in the 1995 draft. Berard informed the Senators he wouldn't play for the franchise and was dealt with Martin Straka to the New York Islanders for goaltender Damian Rhodes and defenseman Wade Redden. The Senators added Chris Phillips in the 1996 draft and would pick up Marian Hossa in the 1997 draft.

The Senators made the postseason for the first time in franchise history in the 1996-97 season with a 31-36-15 record. Yashin led the team with 35 goals and 75 points. Rhodes was in net for 50 games, going 14-20-14 with a 2.72 GAA, .890 save percentage and one shutout while Ron Tugnutt was 17-15-1 with an .895 save percentage, a 2.80 GAA and three shutouts in 37 games. The Senators were the 7th seed in the Eastern Conference playoffs but were beaten 4-3 by the Buffalo Sabres. Yashin made a crucial gaffe in Game 7, putting the puck in his own net to tie the game. Derek Plante's overtime goal clinched the series for Buffalo. It was the first of 11 straight playoff appearances for the Senators.

The Senators won the first playoff series in franchise history in 1997-98 as they ousted the New Jersey Devils 4-2 in the Eastern Conference quarterfinals but were knocked out 4-1 by the Washington Capitals in the conference semifinals. The following season saw the Senators post the first division title in franchise history with a 44-23-15 record in 1998-99 but Ottawa was swept by the Sabres. It was the first of three straight first round exits for the Senators. The team lost in the conference semifinals in 2001-02.

Ottawa reached the conference finals for the first time in 2002-03 as they set a franchise record with 52 victories and 113 points. Hossa led the team with 45 goals and 80 points as five players scored at least 22 goals. Patrick Lalime was the anchor in net, playing 67 games, going 39-20-7 with a .911 save percentage, a 2.16 GAA and eight shutouts while Martin Prusek was 12-2-1 with a .911 save percentage and a 2.37 GAA in 18 outings. Ottawa rolled over the New York Islanders 4-1 in the Eastern Conference quarterfinals and knocked off the Philadelphia Flyers 4-2 in the semifinals. In the conference finals Ottawa rallied from a 3-1 series deficit against New Jersey to force a Game 7 but fell 3-2 to lose the series 4-3.

The Senators reached the Stanley Cup Finals for the only time in franchise history in 2006-07. Ottawa went 48-25-9 for 105 points and finished second in the Northeast Division Dany Heatley led the team with 50 goals and 105 points, Jason Spezza had 34 goals whil Daniel Alfredsson potted 29 with both players scoring 87 points. Ray Emery was the stalwa in goal, playing in 58 games, going 33-16-6 with a .918 save percentage, a 2.47 GAA and fi shutouts while Martin Gerber was 15-9-3 with a 2.78 GAA, a .906 save percentage and o shutout as the backup. Ottawa took out the Pittsburgh Penguins 4-1 in the Eastern Conferen quarterfinals and followed that up with a 4-1 win over the Devils. The Senators then took o the Sabres 4-1 to advance to the Stanley Cup Finals but were beaten in five games by th Anaheim Ducks.

Ottawa made the playoffs in four of the seven seasons since but they've had little succes in the postseason. The Senators were dropped in the Eastern Conference quarterfinals i three of their four appearances. They were bounced in the Eastern Conference semifinals in their other season. Paul MacLean took over the coaching duties on June 14, 2011 and signed a three year extension on July 4, 2013.

In the 2013-14 season, the Senators struggled to a 37-31-14 record and finished fifth in the Atlantic Division. Kyle Turris led the team with 26 goals while defenseman Erik Karlsson posted a team high 54 assists and 74 points. Craig Anderson got the lion's share of the work in the net, playing in 53 games and posting a 25-16-8 record with a 3.00 GAA, a .911 save percentage and four shutouts. Robin Lehner was the backup, playing in 36 games, going 12-15-6 with a 3.06 GAA, a .913 save percentage and one shutout. The Senators missed the postseason by five points.

Ales Hemsky #83 of the Ottawa Senators skates against the New York Islanders at the Nassau Veterans Memorial Coliseum on April 8, 2014 in Uniondale, New York.

83
BAUER
83

PHILADELPHIA FLYERS

First Year of Existence: 1967-68
Owner: Comcast Spectacor
Head Coach: Craig Berube (October 8, 2013-present)

The Philadelphia Flyers were part of the NHL's initial expansion when the league doubled from six to 12 teams for the 1967-68 season. Ed Snider was interested in purchasing a hockey team after seeing fans flocking to see a last place club in the Boston Bruins. On April 6, 1966, there was a name the team contest announced and on August 3, 1966, the team was unveiled as the Flyers.

The team took part in the first expansion draft in NHL history to populate their roster. Philadelphia selected goaltender Bernie Parent with their first pick. They added goalie Doug Favell, defensemen Ed Van Impe and Joe Watson along with forwards Brit Selby, Leon Rochefort and Gary Dornhoefer.

Philadelphia played their first regular season game on October 11, 1967 on the road against the California Golden Seals. Bill Sutherland scored the first goal but the Flyers lost 5-1 in the contest. The team won their first game on October 18, 1967 with a 2-1 road win over the St. Louis Blues. The Flyers finished the regular season 31-32-11 and won the West Division. They were upended 4-3 in the first round by the Blues.

The Flyers made it out of the first round of the playoffs for the first time in the 1972-73 season, which was the first time they had a winning record. Philadelphia went 37-30-11 and finished second in the West. Rick MacLeish bagged a team-high 50 goals, while Bobby Clarke had 37 goals and a team high 104 points. Favell played in 44 games, going 20-15-4 with a 2.83 GAA and three shutouts; Parent had been dealt to Toronto on February 1, 1971. Philadelphia knocked out the Minnesota North Stars 4-2 in the quarterfinals but was knocked off 4-1 by the Montreal Canadiens. Clarke was awarded the Hart Trophy as the league's MVP after the season.

The 1972-73 season marked the first of 17 straight years in the playoffs and the start of the Broad Street Bullies. The Flyers were 50-16-12 and won the division in 1973-74 as they were led by Clarke's 35 goals and 87 points. Parent returned and played in 73 games, going 47-13-12 with a 1.89 GAA and 12 shutouts. In the playoffs, the Flyers swept the Atlanta Flames and followed that up with a 4-3 win over the New York Rangers to reach the Stanley Cup Finals for the first time. Philadelphia beat the Boston Bruins 4-2 to win their first title.

Philadelphia followed up their Stanley Cup win with a run to the Finals in 1974-75. The Flyers were 51-18-11 and won the Patrick Division after realignment. Reggie Leach led the team with 45 goals while Clarke had 27 goals and 89 assists for 116 points. Parent played in 68 games, going 44-14-10 with a 2.03 GAA and 12 shutouts. Dave "The Hammer" Schultz was the quintessential enforcer with 472 penalty minutes on the season. The Flyers swept the Toronto Maple Leafs in the quarterfinals and recorded a 4-3 series win over the New York Islanders to return to the Stanley Cup Finals. Philadelphia knocked off Buffalo 4-2 for the second Stanley Cup in team history.

The Flyers advanced to the Stanley Cup Finals in 1979-80; Philadelphia went 48-12-20, going undefeated in 35 games in a row (25-0-10) between October 14, 1979 and January 7, 1980. Leach bagged 50 goals to lead the team while Rick MacLeish led the team with 79 points and the goaltending duties were split between Pete Peeters (29-5-5, 2.73 GAA, one shutout in 40 games) and Phil Myre (18-7-15, 3.57 GAA in 41 games) on the year. Philadelphia swept the Edmonton Oilers in the preliminary round, dusted the Rangers 4-1 and followed that up with a 4-1 win over the North Stars to advance to the Finals. Once there, the Flyers lost 4-2 to the Islanders.

Clarke retired following the 1983-84 season. The Flyers won a franchise record 53 games in 1984-85, with Tim Kerr leading the team with 54 goals and 98 points while Brian Propp had 43 goals and 97 points. Pelle Lindbergh was in net, going 40-17-7 with a 3.02 ERA, .899 save percentage and two shutouts. The Flyers swept the Rangers in the Patrick semifinals, followed that up with a 4-1 series win over the Islanders and then beat the Quebec Nordiques 4-2 to advance to the Stanley Cup Finals. The Flyers won the opener over the Oilers but lost the next four.

Lindbergh was killed when he lost control of his car on November 10, 1985 and hit a wall in front of an elementary school. He was taken off life support the following day and died at the age of 26. He was selected as the starter for the Prince of Wales Conference in the All Star Game. It was the first time that a player was chosen to the All Star Game after his death.

Ron Hextall took over in net in 1986-87 and led the team back to the Stanley Cup Finals. Philadelphia knocked off the Rangers 4-2 and the Islanders 4-3 before dispatching the Montre Canadiens 4-2 in a feisty, fight-filled series that included a bench clearing brawl. Philadelph trailed 3-1 in the Stanley Cup Finals against the Oilers, battled back to tie the series but lo in Game 7 to drop the series 4-3. Hextall won the Conn Smythe Trophy as the MVP in th playoffs.

The team missed the playoffs five straight seasons from 1989-90 through 1993-94. Th biggest move that took place was the 1992 acquisition of Eric Lindros from the Quebe Nordiques in exchange for Steve Duchesne, Peter Forsberg, Hextall, Mike Ricci, Chris Simon, Kerry Huffman, two first round picks and $15 million.

The Flyers have made the postseason in 17 of the last 19 seasons but haven't had much success in the playoffs. The team reached the Stanley Cup Finals twice, getting knocked off in four games by the Detroit Red Wings in 1996-97 and the Chicago Blackhawks in six games following in 2009-10.

In 2013-14, the Flyers finished the season with a 42-30-10 mark. Peter Laviolette was fired after three games and replaced by Craig Berube. Wayne Simmonds led the team with 29 goals while Claude Giroux had a team high 86 points. Steve Mason played 61 games in net, going a 33-18-7 record with a 2.50 GAA, .917 save percentage and four shutouts. The Flyers battled the Rangers in the opening round of the Eastern Conference playoffs but fell 4-3.

Head coach Craig Berube of the Philadelphia Flyers directs the players after the Florida Panthers scored their second goal of the third period at the BB&T Center on April 8, 2014 in Sunrise, Florida. The Flyers defeated the Panthers 5-2.

zimmerman
zimmerman
93
24
ACEK
28
Hotel
Planner
Reebok
GIROUX
28
22
BAUER

PITTSBURGH PENGUINS

First Year of Existence: 1967-68
Owner: Mario Lemieux, Ronald Burkle
Coach: Mike Johnston (June 25, 2014-present)

The Pittsburgh Penguins were part of the NHL's first expansion from the Original Six era as they joined the league with five other teams in time for the 1967-68 season. Pittsburgh was awarded a franchise on February 8, 1966 at the price of $2.5 million, along with $750,000 in additional costs for the start-up costs of the franchise.

When it came to naming the franchise, 700 entries of the nearly 26,000 received came up with Penguins. The team took part in the NHL's first expansion draft in 1967. The team drafted Andy Bathgate, who was once a prolific scorer but was in the twilight of his career along with defenseman Leo Boivin.

Red Sullivan was the team's first coach as the Penguins took the ice for the first time on October 11, 1967 against the Montreal Canadiens. The Penguins suffered a 2-1 loss with Bathgate scoring the team's first goal. On October 13, the Penguins picked up their first win, beating the St. Louis Blues 3-1. On October 21, 1967, the Penguins were the first expansion team to beat an Original Six franchise as they beat the Chicago Black Hawks 4-2. Pittsburgh finished the season 27-34-13 for 67 points and finished two points behind the Minnesota North Stars for the last playoff spot.

The Penguins made their first playoff appearance in 1969-70 in their first season under new coach, Hall of Famer Red Kelly. Pittsburgh finished the regular season 26-38-12 and picked up their first playoff win 2-1 on April 8, 1970, over the Oakland Seals. The Penguins swept the Seals before being ousted 4-2 in the West Division Finals by the Blues.

Rookie Michel Briere contributed 44 points and was second in rookie scoring behind Philadelphia's Bobby Clarke, who finished second in the Calder Trophy voting to Chicago goaltender Tony Esposito. Sadly, Briere's career came to an end after that season as he was involved in a car crash on May 15, 1970 and suffered brain trauma. He went into a coma and died on April 13, 1971 at the age of 21. Briere's #21 was never issued again and was formally retired by the team in 2001.

Pittsburgh was put in bankruptcy in January 1975 as creditors wanted to be paid. The team was in danger of folding before being bailed out by a group that included Wren Blair, the former coach of the Minnesota North Stars. Pittsburgh became the second NHL team to lose a playoff series after leading 3-0 as they dropped four straight to the New York Islanders in 1974-75.

Pittsburgh finished with the league's worst mark in 1982-83 and 1983-84. The Penguins were in dire financial straits and seemed poised to fold again. Late in the 1983-84 season, the Penguins made some terrible moves in an effort to tank the season to get the first pick in the 1984 NHL Draft. Pittsburgh succeeded and drafted Mario Lemieux. It's been speculated that Pittsburgh would have folded had they not selected Lemieux. Lemieux made an immediate impact, scoring on his first shot on his first shift in his first NHL game. He finished with 43 goals and 100 points in his rookie campaign.

The team won their first division crown in 1990-91 even with Lemieux playing just 26 games due to a herniated disc in his back. Lemieux was healthy at playoff time and had 44 points in 23 games as the Penguins won their first Stanley Cup by beating the Minnesota North Stars 4-2. Pittsburgh followed that up with a second straight Stanley Cup in 1991-92 as they swept Chicago.

The Penguins posted a franchise record with 119 points in 1992-93 and won the only President's Trophy in team history. The Penguins were ousted in the Patrick Division Finals by the Islanders 4-3. A dark cloud was coming to hover over the Penguins once again.

At the end of the 1996-97 season, Lemieux announced his retirement due to health issues. The Penguins' ownership was being harassed by creditors as they owed over $90 million due to their free-wheeling spending habits. The team filed for bankruptcy for the third time and Pittsburgh was facing folding up or relocating. In 1999, Lemieux was the biggest creditor of the franchise, as the team owed him $32.5 million in deferred money. The team offered to convert what he was owed into equity to become majority owner and he took control of the franchise on September 3, 1999. He came out of retirement on December 27, 2000 and was the first player-owner in the history of the NHL. Pittsburgh advanced to the Eastern Conference Finals in 2000-01 but lost 4-1 to the Devils.

Pittsburgh ended up with high picks in 2003 when they took Marc-Andre Fleury, in 200 when they selected Evgeni Malkin 2nd overall and in 2006 when the team took Sidney Crosb with the top overall selection. Lemieux retired on January 27, 2006 after developing an irregula heartbeat. Crosby broke Lemieux's rookie record for points with 102 and the Penguins ende up with another top two pick and they selected Jordan Staal.

Pittsburgh returned to the playoffs in 2006-07 only to lose in the first round. Pittsburg made a charge in 2007-08, advancing to the Stanley Cup Finals but was upended 4-2 by th Detroit Red Wings. Pittsburgh exacted revenge by hoisting the Stanley Cup a year later with a 4-3 series win over Detroit.

Pittsburgh finished 2013-14 with a 51-24-7 mark for 109 points, which was good enough to win the Metropolitan Division. Crosby led the team in the major offensive categories with 36 goals, 68 assists and 104 points while Fleury was the stalwart in net. He played 64 games, going 39-18-5 with a .915 save percentage, a 2.37 GAA and five shutouts. Pittsburgh knocked off the Columbus Blue Jackets 4-2 in the Eastern Conference quarterfinals. After taking a 3-1 series lead over the New York Rangers in the conference semifinals, the Penguins fell apart, dropping the final three games to lose the series 4-3. General manager Ray Shero was fired on May 16, 2014.

On June 6, 2014, the Penguins announced that they had fired head coach Dan Bylsma. The same day, they announced the hiring of Jim Rutherford as the team's general manager. Pittsburgh announced the hiring of Mike Johnston as their new head coach on June 25, 2014.

Sidney Crosby #87 of the Pittsburgh Penguins waits to take a face off against the New York Rangers in Game Five of the Second Round of the 2014 NHL Stanley Cup Playoffs on May 9, 2014 at CONSOL Energy Center in Pittsburgh, Pennsylvania.

87
Reebok
C

SAN JOSE SHARKS

First Year of Existence: 1991-92
Owner: San Jose Sports and Entertainment Enterprises
Coach: Todd McLellan (June 11, 2008-present)

The San Jose Sharks joined the National Hockey League in time for the 1991-92 season and came around as a form of compromise. Gordon and George Gund were brothers and minority owners of the old California Golden Seals and were part of the team's move to Cleveland in 1976 and eventual merger with the Minnesota North Stars in 1978.

The Gunds became majority owners of the North Stars with that transaction and attempted to move the team to California in 1990 but were turned down by the league. Former Hartford Whalers owner Howard Baldwin was trying to get the league to put a team in San Jose. As a compromise, the Gunds sold their stake in the North Stars to Baldwin and the league awarded them the expansion team in San Jose.

In a name the franchise contest, the most popular choice for the team's name was the Blades but the Gunds didn't like the potential negative light that could associated with the term. The second place finisher in the contest was the Sharks. San Jose was allowed to select 14 skaters and two goaltenders from unprotected players on the North Stars roster and both teams would select ten players from the pool of unprotected players around the league. Key personnel that the Sharks took included goaltenders Arturs Irbe and Jeff Hackett along with winger Shane Churla, who was important for who he was traded for. The Sharks received Kelly Kisio in return for sending Churla back to Minnesota. With the second overall pick in the 1991 NHL Draft, the Sharks selected right wing Pat Falloon.

George Kingston was the team's first head coach and when the team swung a deal with the Chicago Blackhawks on September 6, 1991 for defenseman Doug Wilson, he was named the first captain in franchise history. San Jose played their first game on October 4, 1991 on the road against the Vancouver Canucks. The Sharks fell 4-3 with Craig Coxe scoring the first goal. One night later, they played the first home game in franchise history and lost 5-2 to Vancouver. On October 8, the Sharks recorded the first win in franchise history 4-3 over the Calgary Flames. The Flames were the Sharks' first road victory; they were 0-13-1 away from home before a 2-1 win on November 30 in Calgary.

San Jose finished the season with 17-58-5 and was last in the Smythe Division. They were 42 points behind fourth place Winnipeg, who secured the final playoff spot in the division. Falloon led the team in scoring with 25 goals and 59 points. Hackett was the primary goaltender; he went 11-27-1 with a 3.82 GAA and a .892 save percentage while playing in 42 games.

As bad as things were in their inaugural season, they were worse for the Sharks in 1992-93. They endured a 17 game losing skid at one point during the season and finished the year with an 11-71-2 record for 24 points. The 71 losses set a NHL record. Kisio led the team with 26 goals and 78 points. After the season, Kingston was fired and replaced by Kevin Constantine.

San Jose turned things around in a big way in Constantine's first season as they went 33-35-16 for 82 points, a NHL record 58 point improvement. The Sharks made the playoffs for the first time in franchise history as the eighth seed in the Western Conference. They stunned the Detroit Red Wings 4-3 in the opening round. San Jose then had the Toronto Maple Leafs on the ropes but lost Game 6 in overtime before falling in Game 7 to lose the series 4-3. Sergei Makarov led the team with 30 goals and 68 points while Irbe played in 74 games, going 30-28-16 with a 2.84 GAA, a .899 save percentage and three shutouts.

The Sharks made the playoffs again in 1994-95 and posted a 4-3 series victory over the Calgary Flames in the opening round before getting swept by the Red Wings in the conference semifinals. Constantine's magic wore off; he was fired 25 games into the 1995-96 season with the team 3-18-4. They would turn to Jim Wiley for the rest of the season. He went 17-37-3, leaving the team with 47 points.

San Jose made the playoffs five straight seasons under Darryl Sutter, reaching in each of his full seasons at the helm. Evgeni Nabokov won the Calder Trophy as Rookie of the Year in the 2000-01 season as the Sharks goaltender. San Jose won their first division title in 2001-02 in the Pacific Division as they went 44-27-8-3. The problem was San Jose fizzled in the postseason. They were knocked out in the opening round of the playoffs three times and were ousted in the conference semifinals the other two times.

The Sharks have qualified for the playoffs in each of the last ten seasons. San Jose reache the conference finals for the first time in 2003-04 after winning their second division crow The Sharks knocked off the St. Louis Blues 4-1 in the opening round and followed that up wi a 4-2 elimination of the Colorado Avalanche. San Jose ran out of gas in the conference fina as they were eliminated 4-2 by the Calgary Flames. Early in the 2005-06 season, the Shark dealt Brad Stuart, Wayne Primeau and Marco Sturm to the Boston Bruins for Joe Thornton. Thornton would win the Hart Trophy has the league's MVP while winning the Art Ross Trophy with 126 points. Jonathan Cheechoo led the league in goals with 56, winning the Maurice "Rocket" Richard Trophy.

In the 2013-14 season, the Sharks posted a 51-22-9 mark for 111 points and they finished second in the Pacific Division. Joe Pavelski led the team with 41 goals and 79 points while Thornton had a team high 65 assists with 11 goals for 76 points. Antti Niemi was solid in net for the Sharks, going 39-17-7 with a 2.39 GAA, a .913 save percentage and four shutouts in 64 games. Despite another solid campaign for the Sharks in the regular season, they struggled in the playoffs. The Sharks became just the fourth team to lead 3-0 in a playoff series only to lose. After scoring 17 goals in the first three games, San Jose was held to five in the next four as they to the Kings, 4-3.

Alex Stalock #32 of the San Jose Sharks takes a break from play during the second period in Game Six of the First Round of the 2014 NHL Stanley Cup Playoffs at Staples Center on April 28, 2014 in Los Angeles, California.

32
NHL

ST. LOUIS BLUES

First Year of Existence: 1967-68
Owner: St. Louis Blues Hockey Club Inc.
Coach: Ken Hitchcock (November 6, 2011-present)

Part of the NHL's first wave of expansion from the Original Six era, the St. Louis Blues joined the National Hockey League in time for the 1967-68 season along with five other teams as the league doubled in size. The Blues ended up with a franchise mainly at the behest of the Wirtz family, who owned the Chicago Blackhawks. The family also owned the St. Louis Arena and wanted to get rid of it. The city had not formally put in a bid but ended up with a team.

In the expansion draft, which saw the Original Six teams protect the majority of their top tier talent, the Blues selected goaltender Glenn Hall from the Chicago Blackhawks with their initial selection. They had Al Arbour, Rod Seiling and Jim Roberts on defense while picking up Ron Schock, Red Berenson and Gerry Melnyk up front. The Blues played their first game on October 11, 1967 at home against the Minnesota North Stars. Larry Keenan scored the first goal as the Blues battled the North Stars to a 2-2 tie. They recorded their first win on October 14 on the road in Pittsburgh as they defeated the Penguins 4-1. Their first home victory came November 1 with a 5-2 win over the Boston Bruins.

Patrick resigned on November 19 after a loss to the Philadelphia Flyers with the team 4-10-2 and he was replaced by assistant Scotty Bowman. The team went 23-21-14 under Bowman to finish their first season in third place in the West with a 27-31-16 mark. Berenson led the team with 22 goals and 51 points while playing in 55 games. Hall went 19-21-8 with a 2.48 GAA and five shutouts in 49 games at age 36 as the anchor in the nets. St. Louis made the playoffs, edging the division champion Flyers 4-3 and followed that up with a 4-3 series victory against the North Stars. With the way that the playoffs were set up, an expansion team had to play in the Stanley Cup Finals and that was the Blues. They were swept by the Montreal Canadiens. Hall was awarded the Conn Smythe Award as the most valuable player in the playoffs.

The Blues won their first division title in 1968-69 as they went 37-25-14. Berenson led the team with 35 goals and 82 points. Hall went 19-12-8 with a 2.17 GAA and eight shutouts while splitting time with Jacques Plante, who was 18-12-6 with a 1.96 GAA and five shutouts. Hall and Plante shared the Vezina Trophy while Berenson was the first player in NHL history to score six goals in a road game on November 7, 1968 against the Flyers. St. Louis swept the Flyers and then took out the Los Angeles Kings in four straight to return to the Stanley Cup Finals. Once again, the Blues were swept by the Canadiens.

St. Louis picked up their second straight division title by posting a 37-27-12 mark. Phil Goyette led the Blues with 78 points while Berenson was high man in goals as he potted 33. Plante went 18-9-5 with a 2.19 GAA and five shutouts while Ernie Wakely was 12-9-4 with a 2.11 GAA and four shutouts. The Blues knocked off the North Stars 4-2 and recorded a 4-2 win over the Penguins to advance to the Stanley Cup Finals for the third straight year. The Blues were swept in the Finals, this time by the Boston Bruins.

In 1971-72, St. Louis beat Minnesota 4-3 in the opening round before being dusted by the Bruins in the second round of the postseason. The Blues posted a 107 point season in 1980-81 and edged the Penguins 3-2 in the preliminary round before being ousted in the quarterfinals 4-2 by the New York Rangers. That season was the first of 25 consecutive years that the Blues made the playoffs.

While St. Louis consistently made the playoffs, they struggled. The team advanced to the conference finals just twice in that quarter century while they were eliminated in the opening round on ten occasions. When the Blues did reach the conference finals, they were knocked out 4-3 by the Calgary Flames in the 1985-86 season and then 4-1 by the Colorado Avalanche in the 2000-01 campaign. Brett Hull set a NHL record for goals by a right wing when he tallied 86 markers in the 1990-91 season. He won the Hart Trophy as the league's most valuable player. More often than not, the Blues saw their talented players flourish elsewhere as the team didn't have the resources to retain them.

St. Louis posted a franchise record 114 points and won the President Trophy for the league's best record in the 1999-00 season but ended up getting knocked off 4-3 by the San Jose Sharks, who finished the season 27 points behind the Blues. In 2005-06, the Blues had the worst record in the league and snapped their postseason streak.

Early in 2011-12, the Blues fired head coach Davis Payne and brought in Ken Hitchcoc as head coach. Hitchcock's style and leadership worked for the Blues as they went 43-15-1 under his guidance, winning the Central Division title. The Blues beat the Sharks 4-1 in th opening round for their first playoff series win in a decade before being swept by the Lo Angeles Kings.

The Blues were 29-17-2 in the lockout shortened 2012-13 season and made the playoff but were upended in the opening round 4-2 by the Kings. The 2013-14 season was one ful of promise for the Blues as they finished the season 52-23-7, setting a franchise mark fo victories in the process. Alex Steen led the team with 33 goals and 62 points while star defenseman Alex Pietrangelo contributed a team high 43 assists. Jaroslav Halak was 24-9-4 with a 2.23 GAA, a .917 save percentage and four shutouts in net. He was dealt to the Buffalo Sabres along with Chris Stewart, William Carrier and a pair of draft choices for Ryan Miller and Steve Ott.

Brian Elliott was in net for 31 games, going 18-6-2 with a .922 save percentage, a 1.96 GAA and four shutouts. Miller was 10-8-1 in 19 games with the team, posting a 2.47 GAA, a .903 save percentage and one shutout. In the playoffs, the Blues jumped to a 2-0 lead against the Chicago Blackhawks and promptly dropped the next four to lose the series. After the season, the Blues signed Elliott to a three year contract extension and announced that he would be part of the goaltending tandem with young goalie Jake Allen.

T.J. Oshie #74 of the St. Louis Bluesshoots against the Chicago Blackhawks in Game Four of the First Round of the 2014 NHL Stanley Cup Playoffs at the United Center on April 23, 2014 in Chicago, Illinois.

74
BAUER
CCM
COVERT

TAMPA BAY LIGHTNING

First Year of Existence: 1992-93
Owner: Tampa Bay Sports and Entertainment
Coach: Jon Cooper (March 25, 2013-present)

The Tampa Bay Lightning came into existence as one of two teams that joined the NHL in the expansion of 1992-93 along with the Ottawa Senators. The original ownership group was fronted by Hockey Hall of Famers Tony and Phil Esposito cost $50 million.

The team tapped former Calgary Flames coach Terry Crisp as the first head coach in franchise history while Phil Esposito put himself in the general manager's role. Tampa Bay took part in the 1992 NHL Expansion Draft with the Senators to put their initial roster together. The team selected Roman Hamrlik with their first pick in the 1992 NHL Draft.

Tampa Bay put themselves on the map during the preseason when Manon Rheaume became the first woman to play in a NHL game, playing one period and allowing two goals against the St. Louis Blues. She played in a preseason game in 1993 against the Boston Bruins but never played in the regular season.

The Lightning played the first game in franchise history on October 7, 1992 at home against the Chicago Blackhawks. Tampa Bay surprised with a 7-3 victory as Chris Kontos tallied four goals in the victory. The Lightning finished the season with a mark of 23-54-7. Bradley finished the season with 42 goals and 44 points for a team leading 86 points. Jean-Claude Bergeron and Pat Jablonski tied for the team lead in victories with eight.

The 1995-96 season saw Tampa Bay put up the first winning season in franchise history by going 38-32-12 and earned their first playoff berth. Bradley led the team with 79 points, Alexander Selivanov potted a team best 31 goals and Daren Puppa was solid in net, going 29-16-9 with a 2.46 ERA, a .918 save percentage and five shutouts.

The Lightning played their first playoff game in team history on April 16, 1996 on the road against the Philadelphia Flyers and were hammered 7-3. They picked up their first playoff win with a 2-1 overtime win two days later and won their first home playoff game 5-4 in overtime on April 21. The Lightning scored a total of three goals over the next three games and lost the series 4-2.

Tampa Bay wouldn't make the playoffs the next six seasons as the team became a circus off-ice. Forbes Magazine wrote an article in 1997 about how the Lightning was a financial nightmare with a debt equal to 236 percent of its franchise value. The team did select Vincent Lecavalier with the first overall pick in the 1998 NHL Draft. The Lightning became the first team in NHL history with four consecutive seasons with at least 50 losses between 1997-98 and 2000-01.

The Lightning won the first division title in franchise history in 2002-03 with a 36-25-16-5 mark to make their first playoff appearance in seven seasons. Vinny Prospal led the team with 79 points while Lecavalier and Martin St. Louis each had 33 goals to lead the team. Nikolai Khabibulin led the team with a 30-22-11 record, a 2.47 GAA, a .911 save percentage and four shutouts. The Lightning picked up the first playoff series win by dispatching the Washington Capitals 4-2. They were knocked out in the conference semifinals 4-1 by the New Jersey Devils.

In 2003-04, the Lightning was 46-22-8-6 en route to their second straight division title. St. Louis led the team with 38 goals and 94 points, Cory Stillman added 25 goals and 80 points while Brad Richards had 26 goals and 79 points. Khabibulin went 28-19-7 with a 2.33 GAA, a .910 save percentage and three shutouts. Tampa Bay knocked off the New York Islanders 4-1 in the first round. The Lightning swept the Montreal Canadiens in the conference semifinals and followed that up with a 4-3 series win over the Philadelphia Flyers. Tampa Bay advanced to the Stanley Cup Finals and battled the Calgary Flames, winning their only Stanley Cup with a 4-3 series win.

In the 2005-06 season, Tampa Bay finished with 93 points in a season where six Eastern Conference teams posted at least 100 points. They were upended by the Ottawa Senators in five games. In 2006-07, the Lightning posted 92 points and was eliminated in six games by the New Jersey Devils. Lecavalier set franchise records with 52 goals, which led the league and 108 points.

Tampa Bay fell to the league's worst record in the 2007-08 season with a record of 31-42-9 and Tortorella was fired after the season. The Lightning ended up with the first pick in the 2008 NHL Draft and they chose Steven Stamkos. Barry Melrose was hired as the team's coac to replace Tortorella; he lasted just 16 games in 2008-09 before getting fired. Rick Tocchet too over as head coach. The Lightning finished 24-40-18 and ended up second last in the leagu Tampa Bay used that pick to select Victor Hedman.

Tocchet coached the team in 2009-10; Tampa Bay missed the playoffs as they finished 3 36-12. He was replaced by Guy Boucher as the head coach. Boucher led the team to a 46-2 11 mark in 2010-11. St. Louis led the team with 99 points, including 31 goals; Stamkos potte a team high 45 goals and 91 points. Dwayne Roloson led the way in net; he went 18-12-4 wit a 2.56 GAA, .912 save percentage and four shutouts. Tampa Bay edged Pittsburgh 4-3 in the opening round of the playoffs and followed that up with a sweep of the Washington Capitals to return to the Eastern Conference Finals for the first time since 2003-04. The Lightning battled the Boston Bruins but dropped Game 7, 1-0, to lose the series 4-3.

The Lightning had to deal with injuries, as Stamkos broke his tibia in November 2013 and missed 45 games. On March 5, 2014, St. Louis was dealt to the New York Rangers in exchange for Ryan Callahan, a first round selection in 2015 and a conditional second round pick in the 2014. Tampa Bay was 46-27-9, good for second in the Atlantic Division. St. Louis led the team with 29 goals and 61 points before being dealt.

Ben Bishop, who was acquired from Ottawa a year before, was the stalwart between the pipes for Tampa Bay. He played in 63 games, going 37-14-7 with a 2.23 GAA, a .924 save percentage and five shutouts. Tampa Bay didn't have any luck in the playoffs as they were swept by the Montreal Canadiens.

Nikita Kucherov #86 of the Tampa Bay Lightning celebrates his goal with teammates J.T. Brown #23 and Matt Carle #25 as P.K. Subban #76 of the Montreal Canadiens reacts in Game One of the First Round of the 2014 Stanley Cup Playoffs at the Tampa Bay Times Forum on April 16, 2014 in Tampa, Florida.

CCM
BAUER
BAUER
CCM
25
BAUER

TORONTO MAPLE LEAFS

First Year of Existence: 1917-18
Owner: Maple Leaf Sports and Entertainment, Ltd.
Coach: Randy Carlyle (March 2, 2012-present)

The Toronto Maple Leafs are one of the Original Six franchises in the National Hockey League, having been awarded a franchise on November 22, 1917. The franchise was awarded when the Ottawa Senators, Montreal Wanderers, Quebec Bulldogs and the Montreal Canadiens had a fall out with Eddie Livingstone. The other four teams formed the National Hockey League and chose not to incorporate Livingstone in the mix. When the Bulldogs suspended operations, the NHL needed a fourth team to balance the schedule and Toronto was awarded what at the time was supposed to be a temporary franchise.

Dick Carroll was the franchise's first coach and the team finished 13-9-0 and second in the league standings. The team lost their first game 10-9 to the Wanderers. Reg Noble tallied the first goal in franchise history; Noble led the team with 30 goals and a team-high 40 points on the season; Hap Holmes was 9-7 with a 4.73 GAA in 16 games in net. The team won the Stanley Cup in their first season, beating the Montreal Canadiens on goal differential, 10-7.

The Arena Company went in bankruptcy due to the lawsuit and the team was sold. The franchise took on the name of the Toronto St. Patricks, with the colors of the team going from blue and white to green and white. Toronto won their second Stanley Cup by edging the Senators in goal differential 5-4 in the 1921-22 season.

In 1927, the franchise was up for sale and despite a $200,000 offer on the table from a group in Philadelphia, the St. Patricks' ownership sold the team to Conn Smythe for $160,000. Smythe took control of the team in February 1927 and renamed the team the Maple Leafs. The team finished 1926-27 wearing green and white before opening the 1927-28 season wearing the blue and white uniforms that have been the trademark of the franchise.

From 1931-32 through 1941-42, which was the final season before the advent of the Original Six era, Toronto was in the Stanley Cup Finals eight times in 11 seasons but won just two championships. Toronto had some terrific talent during that period, including Busher Jackson, Charlie Conacher and Joe Primeau. Ace Bailey was one of Toronto's top forwards but he had his career come to an end in 1933 when he was checked into the boards by Bruins' defenseman Eddie Shore at full speed. Toronto held the first All Star Game in NHL history to help benefit Bailey.

In the 1941-42 season the Leafs trailed the Detroit Red Wings 3-0 in the Stanley Cup Finals. The Leafs rallied to win the next four games and the Stanley Cup 4-3. It was the first time in history that a team rallied from a 3-0 deficit to win a best of seven playoff series.

Toronto was a dynasty in the NHL between 1944-45 and 1950-51. The Maple Leafs won five Stanley Cup championships. Toronto knocked off Detroit 4-3 in 1944-45, handled Montreal 4-2 in 1946-47, swept Detroit in 1947-48 and 1948-49 to complete a three-peat and defeated Montreal 4-1 in the 1950-51 season in a series that saw all five games go to overtime. Bill Barilko scored the Cup winning goal in overtime of Game 5 in the final game of his career. He would be killed in a plane crash four months later.

The Maple Leafs won four Stanley Cups in the final six seasons of the Original Six era, including another three-peat in the 1961-62, 1962-63 and 1963-64 seasons. Toronto dispatched the Chicago Black Hawks 4-2 in 1961-62 and knocked off Detroit in 1962-63 and 1963-64.

The Maple Leafs won the last Stanley Cup of the Original Six era in 1966-67 as they knocked off the Canadiens, 4-2. Keon won the Conn Smythe Trophy as the playoff MVP. It marked the last time the team has won the Stanley Cup or made the Stanley Cup Finals. Their 47 year drought is currently the longest in NHL history. Toronto didn't reach the conference finals again until 1992-93.

The Maple Leafs made the conference finals in 1992-93 after gritty 4-3 series wins over Detroit and the St. Louis Blues. Toronto led the conference finals 3-2 and in overtime of Game 6, Wayne Gretzky clipped Doug Gilmour in the face with his stick but no penalty was called. He scored the winning goal shortly after. Gretzky scored a hat trick in Game 7 as the Kings won the series.

Toronto returned to the conference finals in 1993-94 after a 4-2 series win over Chicago and a 4-3 series win over the scrappy San Jose Sharks. The series win over San Jose may have drained Toronto and they were beaten 4-1 by the Vancouver Canucks. Since then, the Mapl Leafs have advanced as far as the conference finals just twice.

Behind Pat Quinn's leadership, the Maple Leafs made the conference finals in 1998-9 After knocking off the Philadelphia Flyers 4-2, Toronto dispatched the Pittsburgh Penguins 4 to face the Buffalo Sabres in the conference finals. Things didn't go Toronto's way as Buffa won the series 4-1. The Leafs made the conference finals again in 2001-02 but were upende by the Carolina Hurricanes 4-2.

Toronto set a franchise record with 103 points in 2003-04. After knocking off the Ottaw Senators in 4-3 in the opening round behind Ed Belfour, who set a record with three shutout in the series, Toronto was knocked out 4-2 by the Flyers in the conference semifinals. The playoff series win over Ottawa is the most recent in team history. Toronto trailed 3-1 in the opening round to the Bruins, rallied to tie the series and led Game 7 4-1 in the third period before fading. Boston would tally twice in the final two minutes to tie the game and won in overtime to end the Leafs' season.

In 2013-14, Toronto finished the season 38-36-8 and missed the postseason. Toronto faded late as they dropped 12 of their final 14 games. Phil Kessel had a solid season, leading the team with 37 goals, 43 assists and 80 points. Jonathan Bernier, who was acquired from the Los Angeles Kings prior to the season, was solid in net, playing 55 games and posting a 26-19-7 record with a .922 save percentage and one shutout. On April 11, 2014, the Maple Leafs announced that Brendan Shanahan would be the team's president and alternate governor.

Dave Bolland #63 of the Toronto Maple Leafs skates up the ice during NHL action against the Boston Bruins at the Air Canada Centre April 3, 2014 in Toronto, Ontario.

63
Reebok
A
63
WARRIOR
TORONTO
MAPLE
LEAFS
Reebok

VANCOUVER CANUCKS

First Year of Existence: 1970-71
Owner: Canucks Sports and Entertainment
Coach: Willie Desjardins (June 23, 2014-present)

The Vancouver Canucks were one of two expansion teams in 1970-71 along with the Buffalo Sabres. It was the second time that Vancouver had applied for a NHL franchise; they had submitted a bid when the league expanded in 1967 but it was sloppily put together and rejected.

Vancouver got their team as part of a deal where they wouldn't file a lawsuit for being blocked from trying to relocate the Oakland Seals and the cost was $6 million. Tom Scallen, who led the ownership group, bought the Western Hockey League Canucks for an initial talent pool. He kept some of the roster and the rest were added through the expansion draft.

Vancouver took part in the 1970 NHL Expansion Draft along with the Sabres. Buffalo won the right to have the first pick in both the expansion draft and the 1970 NHL Entry Draft. Vancouver's first selection in the expansion draft was Gary Doak. The team also added Orland Kurtenbach, who was the team's first captain and defenseman Pat Quinn among others. With the 2nd overall selection in the 1970 NHL Entry Draft, the Canucks selected Dale Tallon. Hal Laycoe was hired as the team's first coach.

The Canucks played their first game on October 9, 1970 at home against the Los Angeles Kings. Vancouver lost 3-1 with Barry Wilkins scoring the team's first goal. Two days later, the Canucks picked up their first win 5-3 over the Toronto Maple Leafs. Vancouver completed the season 24-46-8 and finished 6th in the East, one point ahead of Detroit.

Prior to the 1974-75 season, Scallen and his group sold the team to Frank Griffiths for $9 million. Thanks to realignment, the Canucks moved out of the East and into the Smythe Division. Vancouver put together their first winning season as they went 38-32-10 for 86 points. They won their first division title by two points over the St. Louis Blues. Vancouver played their first playoff game on April 13, 1975, and lost 6-2 to the Montreal Canadiens. Vancouver got the first playoff win 2-1 on April 15 and lost the next three games and the series, 4-1.

Vancouver made the playoffs again in 1975-76 but was beaten in the preliminary round, losing two straight games to the New York Islanders. The Canucks would not post a winning record again until 1991-92, a span of 16 seasons. They made the playoffs nine times despite their ineptitude.

The 1981-82 season was a breakthrough despite the team posting a 30-33-17 mark during the regular season. The Canucks won their first playoff series 3-0 over the Calgary Flames in the Smythe semifinals and took a 4-1 win over the Kings in the Smythe Finals. Vancouver beat Chicago 4-1 in the Campbell Conference Finals for their first trip to the Stanley Cup Finals; the Canucks were swept by the Islanders.

In 1991-92, Quinn's first full season as head coach, Vancouver went 42-26-12 and won their first division title since 1974-75. The Canucks edged the Winnipeg Jets 4-3 in the Smythe semifinals before getting ousted 4-2 by the Oilers. Vancouver would repeat as division champs in 1992-93, going 46-29-9. They knocked off the Jets 4-2 but were eliminated in the Smythe Finals 4-2 by the Kings.

Vancouver had better luck in the postseason, despite dropping to 85 points in 1993-94. The Canucks edged the Flames 4-3 in the conference quarterfinals and followed that up with a 4-1 trouncing of the Dallas Stars in the semifinals. Vancouver then handled Toronto 4-1 in the conference finals to go to the Stanley Cup Finals. Vancouver rallied from a 3-1 series deficit to force a Game 7. A 3-2 loss gave the New York Rangers their first Stanley Cup since 1940. Quinn stepped down to focus on his general manager duties; he was replaced by Rick Ley.

The Canucks made the playoffs in 1994-95, and after edging the Blues 4-3, Vancouver was swept by Chicago. Their next playoff series win came in 2002-03; after edging the Blues 4-3, Vancouver lost to the Minnesota Wild 4-3 in the conference semifinals. Vancouver won the Pacific Division crown in 2003-04 but lost in the first round. They won another division crown in 2006-07, beating the Stars 4-3 in the opening round before getting rolled by the Anaheim Ducks 4-1.

Vancouver won five straight division titles and a pair of President's Trophies in 2010-11 and 2011-12 under Alain Vigneault. Playoff success was hard to come by and Vancouver was ousted in the conference semifinals twice while losing in the opening round twice in that span

The 2010-11 season was the lone one where Vancouver had much success in the playoffs Despite a franchise record 117 points and a 3-0 series lead in the opening round against th Blackhawks, Vancouver wilted and ended up in a Game 7 before Alexandre Burrows tallied overtime to eliminate Chicago 4-3. Vancouver then bounced the Nashville Predators 4-2 ar followed that with a 4-1 win over the San Jose Sharks to advance to the Stanley Cup Final Vancouver took a 2-0 series lead over the Boston Bruins and led 3-2 but dropped Game 6 5 and Game 7 at home by a score of 4-0 to lose the series and the Stanley Cup, 4-3.

Vigneault was let go after the 2012-13 season and was replaced by John Tortorella. The Canucks dealt goaltender Cory Schneider to New Jersey for the 9th pick in the 2013 NHL Draft. Right before the 2013-14 trade deadline, Vancouver dealt Roberto Luongo to the Florida Panthers with Steven Anthony for Jacob Markstrom and Shawn Matthias. The Canucks finished the season 36-35-11 for 83 points and missed the playoffs. Ryan Kesler paced the team with 25 markers. Henrik Sedin was the team leader with 39 assists and 50 points. Luongo went 19-16-6 with a 2.38 GAA, a .917 save percentage and three shutouts while Eddie Lack was 16-17-5 with a 2.41 GAA, .912 save percentage and four shutouts.

General Manager Dave Gillis was fired one day after the team was eliminated from playoff contention and on May 1, 2014, Tortorella was let go after one season. On May 21, 2014, the Canucks announced that Jim Benning would be the new general manager. On June 23, 2014, the Canucks announced the hiring of Willie Desjardins as their new head coach.

Dan Hamhuis #2 of the Vancouver Canucks skates with the puck while being pressured by Paul Stastny #26 of the Colorado Avalanche during NHL action on April 10, 2014 at Rogers Arena in Vancouver, British Columbia.

BAUER
HAMHUIS 2
BAUER

WASHINGTON CAPITALS

First Year of Existence: 1974-75
Owner: Monumental Sports and Entertainment
Coach: Barry Trotz (May 26, 2014-present)

The Washington Capitals joined the NHL as part of an expansion in the 1974-75 season along with the Kansas City Scouts. Washington was awarded the franchise on June 9, 1972. The team was originally owned by Abe Pollin, who owned the NBA's Baltimore Bullets (now the Washington Wizards) at that time. The team played in the Capital Center, built in Landover, Maryland as the home venue for both franchises.

On June 12, 1974, the league held an expansion draft for the Scouts and Capitals to put together their rosters. Washington's first pick in the expansion draft was goaltender Ron Low from Toronto. The Capitals added defensemen Yvon Labre and Gord Smith along with forwards Steve Atkinson, Denis Dupere and Jack Egers. Washington made Greg Joly their first pick in the 1974 NHL Entry Draft; he played just two seasons with the team.

The Capitals played their first game on October 9, 1974 at Madison Square Garden against the New York Rangers. Washington was defeated, 6-3, with Jim Hrycuik netting the first goal. On October 15 the Capitals played their first home game in a 1-1 tie with the Los Angeles Kings and Labre scored the team's first goal at home. On October 17, the Capitals recorded their first win with a 4-3 win over the Chicago Blackhawks and it was a rare highlight. They finished the season with a record of 8-67-5 and their .131 winning percentage is the worst in NHL history. Washington was 1-39 on the road. They set league records for the most losses on the road in a season, the most consecutive road losses with 37 and the most losses in a row in any fashion with 17.

Washington failed to post a winning record in their first eight seasons. This allowed Washington to stockpile high draft choices that the Capitals used to select players like Mike Gartner, Bengt Gustafsson, Bobby Carpenter, Rick Green, Ryan Walter and Gaetan Duchesne. The team brought in David Poile from the Flames to be the team's general manager.

On September 9, 1982, Poile engineered a major deal that helped put the Capitals on the right track as he dealt Green and Walter to the Montreal Canadiens in exchange for solid two-way defenseman Rod Langway, Brian Engblom, Doug Jarvis and Craig Laughlin. Langway, coupled with the drafting of Scott Stevens in the 1982 NHL Draft, helped the Capitals defensively. The Capitals improved from 65 points in 1981-82 to 94 points in 1982-83 and earned their first playoff berth. Washington was defeated 3-1 by the three-time defending Stanley Cup champion New York islanders.

The 1982-83 season was the first of 14 straight playoff appearances for the Capitals. They were second in the Patrick Division in the next five seasons before breaking through for their first division title in franchise history in 1988-89 with a 41-29-10 mark. The problem was that the Capitals could never get to the conference finals in that run. They were beaten in the Patrick Division semifinals four times and three times in the Patrick Finals under coach Bryan Murray.

Murray was fired midway through the 1989-90 season and replaced by his brother Terry Murray. Under Terry Murray's guidance the team went 18-14-2 down the stretch to finish 36-38-6 for 80 points and third in the Patrick Division. Washington knocked off the New Jersey Devils 4-2 in the Patrick semifinals and then blasted the Rangers 4-1, in the Patrick Finals to advance to their first conference finals. Things didn't pan out as Washington had hoped as they were swept by the Boston Bruins.

Murray lasted three full seasons with the team before being fired and replaced by Jim Schoenfeld during the 1993-94 season. Schoenfeld coached the team for three full years after that half season stint but was let go after the Capitals missed the playoffs for the first time since 1981-82 when they stumbled to a 33-40-9 mark in 1996-97, leaving them two points out of a playoff spot. The team appointed Ron Wilson as the new head coach for 1997-98.

Washington went 40-30-12 in 1997-98, finishing third in the Atlantic Division. The Capitals upended the Bruins 4-2 in the Eastern Conference quarterfinals and followed that up with a 4-1 series win over the Ottawa Senators in the conference semifinals. In the conference finals, the Capitals managed a 4-2 series win over the Buffalo Sabres for their first conference championship and trip to the Stanley Cup Finals. Things didn't go Washington's way in the Stanley Cup Finals and they were defeated by the Detroit Red Wings.

In the 15 seasons since that run to the Stanley Cup Finals, the Caps have had limite success in the playoffs. Despite winning seven division titles, Washington hasn't advance past the Eastern Conference Semifinals. They've fizzled despite Alexander Ovechkin winnin three Hart Trophies as the league MVP since 2008; in 2009-10, when they won the President Trophy with 121 points thanks to a 54-15-13 mark; they lost in the quarterfinals, 4-3, afte holding a 3-1 series advantage.

The 2013-14 season was a disappointing one for Capitals fans as they missed the playoffs with a 38-30-14 record. Ovechkin led the team with 51 goals and tied with Nicklas Backstrom for the team lead with 79 points. Braden Holtby was the team's top goaltender as he played in 48 games, going 23-15-4 with a .915 save percentage, a 2.85 GAA and four shutouts.

The team was active at the trade deadline, dealing Martin Erat and John Mitchell to Phoenix in exchange for Rostislav Klesla, Chris Brown and a fourth round pick in 2015. A day later, they shifted Klesla and Michal Neuvirth to the Buffalo Sabres for Jaroslav Halak and a third round pick. After the season came to an end, the decision was made to fire general manager George McPhee and head coach Adam Oates.

On May 1, 2014, the Capitals dealt Halak to the New York Islanders in exchange for Chicago's 4th round draft pick in the 2014 NHL Entry Draft. On May 26, 2014, the Capitals announced that Barry Trotz would be the team's new head coach. The team announced that Brian MacLellan would be promoted from assistant general manager to general manager.

Braden Holtby #70 of the Washington Capitals tends net against the New York Islanders at the Nassau Veterans Memorial Coliseum on April 5, 2014 in Uniondale, New York.

CCM

WINNIPEG JETS

First Year of Existence: 1999-2000
Owner: True North Sports and Entertainment
Coach: Paul Maurice (January 12, 2014-present)

The Winnipeg Jets are in their second incarnation, having originally been a franchise from 1972 through 1996 before moving to Phoenix. This version of the Jets came into existence originally as the Atlanta Thrashers as part of four cities granted expansion teams on June 25, 1997 provided they could sell 12,000 season tickets by March 31, 1998. The Thrashers began play in the 1999-2000 season.

The franchise originally picked up the nickname Thrashers in respect to the state bird of Georgia, the brown thrasher but it actually was the second choice in a poll among the fans. The choice that fans wanted was the Flames in tribute to the Atlanta Flames, who left town in 1980 and became the Calgary Flames.

Atlanta populated their roster for the first time in the 1999 NHL Expansion Draft, taking one player from each of the other franchises except for the Nashville Predators, who entered the league the season before. The Thrashers picked up veterans like goalie Trevor Kidd and winger Kelly Buchberger, who was the first captain in team history.

The Thrashers had the top pick in the 1999 NHL Entry Draft and picked Patrik Stefan. Curt Fraser was named the first head coach in franchise history. Atlanta played their first game in franchise history on October 2, 1999 against the New Jersey Devils at home and lost 4-1 with Buchberger tallying the first goal. They picked up the first victory on October 14, 1999 along with the first shutout with a 2-0 win over the New York Islanders behind 20 saves by Damian Rhodes.

Atlanta struggled all season long and finished the year 14-57-7-4 to finish last in the league. Andrew Brunette led the team in scoring with 23 goals and 27 assists for 50 points. Four goaltenders played at least 15 games for the Thrashers but Rhodes led the team in wins. He was 5-19-3 with a 3.88 GAA, an .874 save percentage and one of the team's two shutouts.

The Thrashers didn't have much luck on the ice though they did have success in the draft; they selected Dany Heatley with the second overall pick in the 2000 NHL Draft and Ilya Kovalchuk with the top overall pick in the 2001 NHL Draft. Heatley won the Calder Trophy for the Rookie of the Year in the 2001-02 season after posting a line of 26 goals and 41 assists for 67 points. The assist and point totals led the Thrashers while he was second in goals.

Atlanta failed to make the playoffs in the 2002-03 season either though they improved to 31-39-7-5; Fraser was fired 33 games into the season with the team sitting with a record of 8-20-1-4. Don Waddell went behind the bench for 10 games before bringing in Bob Hartley. Heatley scored 41 goals while posting 89 points and Kovalchuk potted 38 goals of his own. Pasi Nurminen was the main goaltender for the Thrashers, going 21-19-5 with a .906 save percentage, 2.88 GAA and two shutouts.

In 2003-04, the Thrashers finished 33-37-8-4. Kovalchuk tied Heatley's franchise mark with 41 goals and finished with 87 points. Heatley was involved in a car accident on September 29, 2003 when he crashed his Ferrari and teammate Dan Snyder was killed. Heatley suffered a broken jaw, a torn ACL and MCL, a broken arm and a sprained wrist. He played in 31 games, scoring 13 goals with 12 assists for 25 points.

After the lockout, the Thrashers posted went 41-33-8 in 2005-06. Kovalchuk scored 52 goals with 46 assists for 98 points while Marc Savard added 97 points. Heatley was dealt to Ottawa and the trade brought Marian Hossa and Greg de Vries to Atlanta. Hossa potted 39 goals and added 53 assists for 92 points in his first season with the team. The Thrashers missed the playoffs again.

Atlanta won their only division title in 2006-07 as they posted a 43-28-11 record. Hossa scored 43 goals and a franchise record 100 points and Kovalchuk had 42 goals. Kari Lehtonen, who had taken over the goaltending duties, was 34-24-9 with a 2.79 GAA, a .912 save percentage and four shutouts. The Thrashers made their first postseason appearance but were swept in four games by the New York Rangers.

The Thrashers slumped in the 2007-08 season and fired Hartley six games in. Waddell took over for the rest of the season and went 34-34-8 but the Thrashers missed the postseason. J.C. Anderson coached the team in the 2008-09 and 2009-10 seasons and failed to impress before he was fired. Kovalchuk was dealt to the New Jersey Devils on February 4, 2011.

Craig Ramsay coached the team and went 34-36-12 but Atlanta again missed the playoffs in the 2010-11 season. The team was sold to True North Sports and Entertainment with th intent of moving the franchise from Atlanta to Winnipeg. On May 31, 2011, the league an True North Sports and Entertainment had a press conference in Winnipeg to announce th sale of the franchise. On June 21, 2011, the NHL and its Board of Governors approved the sa and the relocation of the team and approved the use of the nickname Jets for the team.

The Jets made their re-debut on October 9, 2011 at home against the Montreal Canadien The Jets were defeated 5-1. Claude Noel was the first coach in the history of the Jets' secon coming with the team picking up their first victory on October 17, 2011 with a 2-1 win over the Pittsburgh Penguins. Winnipeg finished the season 37-35-10. Evander Kane led the team with 30 goals while Blake Wheeler had a team high 64 points. The Jets inherited the Thrashers' spot in the Southeast Division and stayed there until the realignment of the league in the 2013-14 season.

Winnipeg has not made the playoffs in their first three seasons back in Manitoba despite being above .500 in each of those campaigns. In 2013-14, the Jets finished with a 37-35-10 mark. Noel was fired with the team sporting a record of 19-23-5 and he was replaced by Paul Maurice on January 12, 2014. Winnipeg rallied to go 18-12-5 under Maurice but fell short in the playoff race. Wheeler led the team with 28 goals and 69 points while Ondrej Pavelec was the stalwart in net, going 22-26-7 with a 3.01 GAA, a .901 save percentage and a shutout. Maurice was given a four year extension on April 16, 2014.

Dustin Byfuglien #33 of the Winnipeg Jets skates down the ice during second period action of an NHL game against the Pittsburgh Penguins at the MTS Centre on April 3, 2014 in Winnipeg, Manitoba.

33
CCM
33
Jets

IMMORTALS

MIKE BOSSY

There may not have been a more prolific goal scorer in the NHL than the New York Islanders' Mike Bossy. An explosive player with a deadly accurate shot, Bossy lit the lamp with amazing regularity and only issues with his back slowed him. Had he been completely healthy and not had his career end at age 30 in his prime, he very well could have surpassed Wayne Gretzky's mark of 894 goals when it was all said and done.

Bossy played his junior hockey in the Quebec Major Junior Hockey League (QMJHL) with the Laval National. After playing in just four games as a 16 year old, when he scored one goal and added two assists along with three assists in three playoff games in the 1972-73 campaign, Bossy became a key member of the team for the next four seasons. In the 1973-74 campaign, Bossy posted 70 goals along with 48 assists for 118 points with 45 penalty minutes in 68 games. He continued his offensive assault with six goals and 16 assists for 22 points in 11 postseason games but Laval was knocked off in the QMJHL semifinals in six games by the Quebec Remparts, who would go on to win the President's Cup. Bossy would win the Michel Bergeron Trophy as the league's rookie of the year.

In the 1974-75 campaign, Bossy continued his tear through the QMJHL as he scored 84 goals and added 65 assists for 149 points along with 42 penalty minutes to finish fourth in the league in scoring. In the postseason, Bossy played in 16 playoff games, scoring 18 goals while adding 20 assists for 38 points plus two penalty minutes. The National defeated the Trois-Rivières Draveurs in six games in the quarterfinals and followed that up with a five game elimination of the Montreal Bleu Blanc Rouge in the semifinals. In the QMJHL Finals, the National were defeated, four games to one, by the Sherbrooke Castors; Bossy was the leading scorer in the postseason and was a First Team All-QMJHL selection.

In 1975-76, Bossy again was fourth in the league in scoring as he lit the lamp 79 times while collecting 57 assists for 136 points with 28 penalty minutes. The National finished last in the West Division and missed the playoffs; Bossy was named a First Team West Division selection. In his final season in the QMJHL, Bossy played in 61 games, scoring 75 goals and adding 51 assists for 126 points along with just 12 penalty minutes. He added five goals and five assists for 10 points in seven postseason games but the National was eliminated by Sherbrooke in the quarterfinals. Bossy was a Second Team All-QMJHL selection and finished his junior career with 309 goals and 223 assists for 532 points in 263 games.

Bossy was selected with the 15th overall pick in the 1977 NHL Entry Draft after being passed over by 12 teams; the Toronto Maple Leafs and New York Rangers passed him over twice in favor of other players. Coach Al Arbour convinced Bill Torrey to take Bossy, saying that it would be easier to teach a player that could score how to check. Bossy came out and said that he would score 50 goals as a rookie. As it turned out, Bossy was correct, as he tallied 53 goals along with 38 assists for 91 points with just six penalty minutes while recording a +31 plus/minus rating. He scored two goals and added two assists for four points with two penalty minutes in seven games as the Islanders fell in the quarterfinals in seven games to the Toronto Maple Leafs. Bossy won the Calder Trophy as the league's best rookie and was named a Second Team All-NHL selection for his efforts.

In 1978-79, Bossy led the league with 69 goals, including league highs in even strength goals (42) and power play markers (27) while tacking on 57 assists for 126 points; he was a +63 and had 25 penalty minutes in 80 games. In the playoffs, Bossy added six goals and two assists for eight points in ten playoff games as the Islanders were eliminated in the semifinals in six games by the New York Rangers. Bossy was once again a Second Team All-NHL selection for his performance on the ice. He followed that up with a 51 goal, 41 assist performance for 92 points in 75 games in 1979-80, recording a +28 rating and 12 penalty minutes. The Islanders won the first Stanley Cup in franchise history; Bossy contributed 10 goals and 13 assists for 23 points in 16 postseason games, leading all playoff scorers with six power play goals.

Bossy led the league in goals again in 1980-81 as he scored 68 times along with 51 assists for 119 points in 79 games. He recorded a +37 rating while logging just 32 penalty minutes. He became just the second player in NHL history and the first in 36 years to score 50 goals in 50 games. In the playoffs, Bossy led all playoff scorers with 17 goals, 18 assists and 35 points in 18 games with nine power play goals and three game winning markers. The Islanders won their second straight Stanley Cup and Bossy was named a First Team All-NHL selection for the season.

In 1981-82, Bossy set a NHL record for points by a right winger when he scored 64 goals and added 83 assists for 147 points while recording a +69 rating and 22 penalty minutes; he played all 80 games. The record would stand until Pittsburgh's Jaromir Jagr posted 149 points in the 1995-96 season. In the playoffs, Bossy again led all postseason scorers with 17 goals plus 10 assists for 27 points in 19 games as the Islanders recorded their third straight Stanley Cup victory. He was named a First Team All-NHL selection for the second straight year; he also won the Conn Smythe Trophy as the league's most valuable player in the playoffs.

Bossy kept racking up the goals in the 1982-83

50

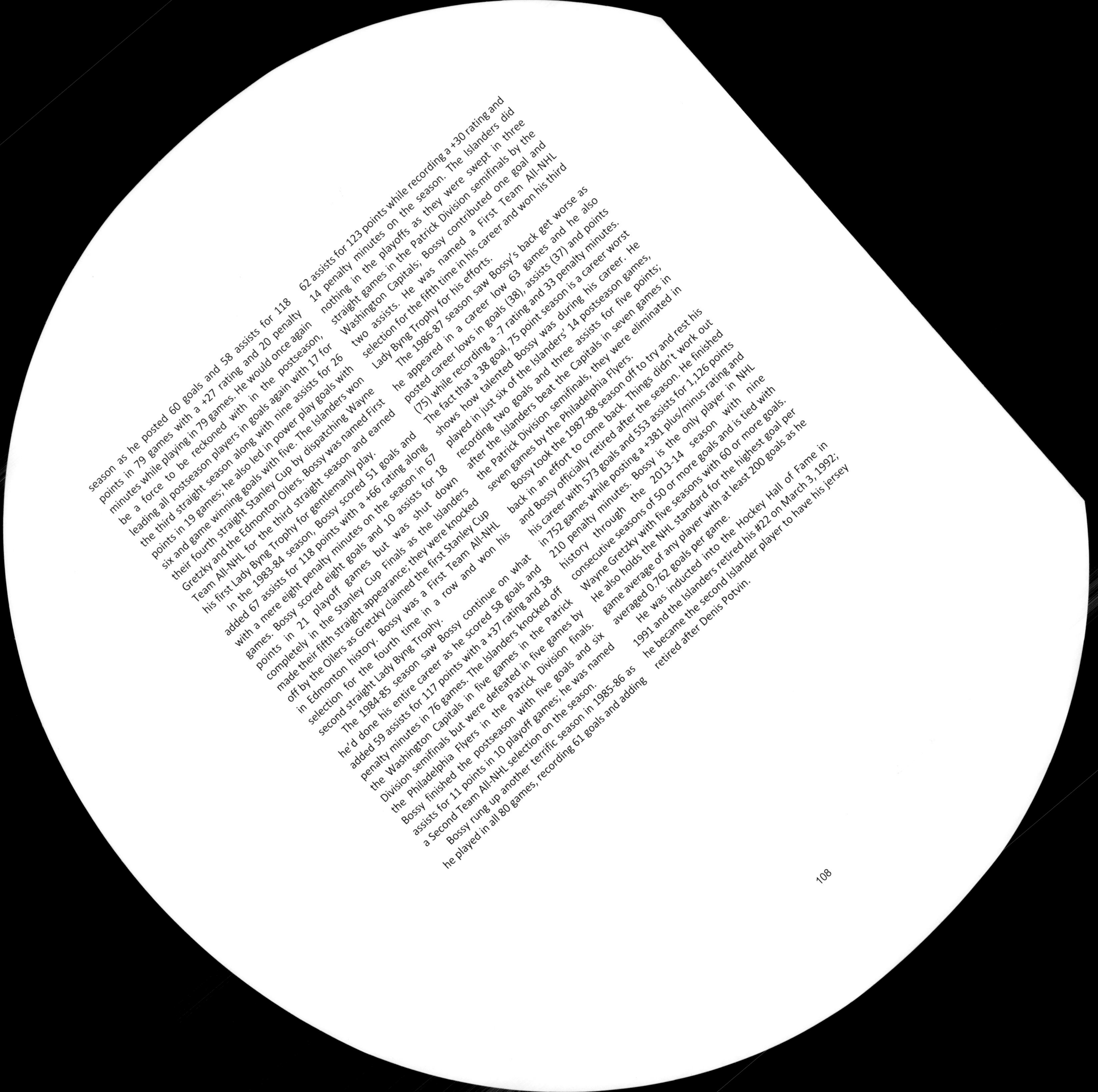

season as he posted 60 goals and 58 assists for 118 points in 79 games with a +27 rating and 20 penalty minutes while playing in 79 games. He would once again be a force to be reckoned with in the postseason, leading all postseason players in goals again with 17 for the third straight season along with nine assists for 26 points in 19 games; he also led in power play goals with six and game winning goals with five. The Islanders won their fourth straight Stanley Cup by dispatching Wayne Gretzky and the Edmonton Oilers. Bossy was named First Team All-NHL for the third straight season and earned his first Lady Byng Trophy for gentlemanly play.

In the 1983-84 season, Bossy scored 51 goals and added 67 assists for 118 points with a +66 rating along with a mere eight penalty minutes on the season in 67 games. Bossy scored eight goals and 10 assists for 18 points in 21 playoff games but was shut down completely in the Stanley Cup Finals as the Islanders made their fifth straight appearance; they were knocked off by the Oilers as Gretzky claimed the first Stanley Cup in Edmonton history. Bossy was a First Team All-NHL selection for the fourth time in a row and won his second straight Lady Byng Trophy.

The 1984-85 season saw Bossy continue on what he'd done his entire career as he scored 58 goals and added 59 assists for 117 points with a +37 rating and 38 penalty minutes in 76 games. The Islanders knocked off the Washington Capitals in five games in the Patrick Division semifinals but were defeated in five games by the Philadelphia Flyers in the Patrick Division finals. Bossy finished the postseason with five goals and six assists for 11 points in 10 playoff games; he was named a Second Team All-NHL selection on the season.

Bossy rung up another terrific season in 1985-86 as he played in all 80 games, recording 61 goals and adding 62 assists for 123 points while recording a +30 rating and 14 penalty minutes on the season. The Islanders did nothing in the playoffs as they were swept in three straight games in the Patrick Division semifinals by the Washington Capitals; Bossy contributed one goal and two assists. He was named a First Team All-NHL selection for the fifth time in his career and won his third Lady Byng Trophy for his efforts.

The 1986-87 season saw Bossy's back get worse as he appeared in a career low 63 games and he also posted career lows in goals (38), assists (37) and points (75) while recording a -7 rating and 33 penalty minutes. The fact that a 38 goal, 75 point season is a career worst shows how talented Bossy was during his career. He played in just six of the Islanders' 14 postseason games, recording two goals and three assists for five points; after the Islanders beat the Capitals in seven games in the Patrick Division semifinals, they were eliminated in seven games by the Philadelphia Flyers.

Bossy took the 1987-88 season off to try and rest his back in an effort to come back. Things didn't work out and Bossy officially retired after the season. He finished his career with 573 goals and 553 assists for 1,126 points in 752 games while posting a +381 plus/minus rating and 210 penalty minutes. Bossy is the only player in NHL history through the 2013-14 season with nine consecutive seasons of 50 or more goals and is tied with Wayne Gretzky with five seasons with 60 or more goals. He also holds the NHL standard for the highest goal per game average of any player with at least 200 goals as he averaged 0.762 goals per game.

He was inducted into the Hockey Hall of Fame in 1991 and the Islanders retired his #22 on March 3, 1992; he became the second Islander player to have his jersey retired after Denis Potvin.

22
URBO
TIT

RAY BOURQUE

When the discussion of the best defensemen in NHL history comes around, several names inevitably come into the discussion. There's Doug Harvey of the Montreal Canadiens, Paul Coffey, Larry Murphy and Bobby Orr. Of course, the name that gets bandied about more often than anyone else is that of Ray Bourque. The fact that Boston went from having the talented Orr to the equally talented Bourque on the blue line is an embarrassment of riches.

Bourque played three seasons in the QMJHL for two different teams in his junior career. He started his junior career in 1976-77 with the Trois-Rivières Draveurs; he played 39 games for the team, scoring three goals with 20 assists for 23 points and 27 penalty minutes. Bourque was dealt to the Sorel Eperviers in exchange for high scoring forward Benoit Gosselin; he scored 9 goals with 16 assists for 25 points and 29 penalty minutes in 30 games. Sorel missed the postseason, leaving Bourque on the outside looking in.

In the 1977-78 season, Sorel moved to Verdun to become the Verdun Eperviers. Bourque played in 72 regular season games, scoring 22 goals with 57 assists for 79 points and 90 penalty minutes on the season. Bourque was named a First Team All-QMJHL selection; Verdun made the playoffs but was swept by the Montreal Juniors in four straight games. He scored two goals with an assist in the series with both goals coming on the power play.

The 1978-79 season saw Bourque play in 63 games, scoring 22 goals with 71 assists for 93 points and 54 penalty minutes on the season. He was named a First Team All-QMJHL selection for the second straight season; he won the Emilie Bouchard Trophy as the defenseman of the year and also won the Frank J. Selke Memorial Trophy as the league's most sportsmanlike player. Verdun defeated the Cornwall Royals in seven games in the quarterfinals before being defeated in four straight games by the Sherbrooke Castors. Bourque finished with three goals and 16 assists for 19 points with 18 penalty minutes in 11 playoff games.

Bourque was selected with the 8th overall pick in the 1979 NHL Draft by the Boston Bruins; Boston acquired that pick in a 1977 deal with the Los Angeles Kings that sent Ron Grahame to Los Angeles. He made his NHL debut for the Bruins on October 11, 1979 at home against the Winnipeg Jets; he scored a goal in Boston's 4-0 victory. Bourque played in all 80 regular season games, scoring 17 goals with 48 assists for 65 points while recording a +52 plus/minus rating and 73 penalty minutes on the year. He was named a First Team All-NHL selection; he became the first rookie non-goaltender to be named a First Team All-NHL choice. Bourque also won the Calder Trophy as the league's best rookie. Boston defeated the Pittsburgh Penguins in five games in the preliminary round before being defeated in five games in the quarterfinals by the New York Islanders. Bourque scored two goals with nine assists and 27 penalty minutes in 10 games.

In the 1980-81 season, Bourque played in 67 games in the regular season, scoring 27 goals with 29 assists for 56 points with a +29 rating and 96 penalty minutes. He was named a Second Team All-NHL selection on the season; Boston was swept by the Minnesota North Stars in three games in the preliminary round. Bourque finished with one assist and two penalty minutes in the series.

The 1981-82 season saw Bourque play in 65 regular season games, scoring 17 goals plus 49 assists for 66 points, a +22 rating and 51 penalty minutes. He was named a First Team All-NHL selection for the second time in his career. In the playoffs, Boston defeated the Buffalo Sabres in four games in the Adams Division semifinals and then was defeated by the Quebec Nordiques in seven games in the Adams Division Finals. Bourque played in nine of Boston's playoff games, scoring one goal with five assists and 16 penalty minutes.

The 1982-83 season saw Bourque play 65 games, tallying 22 goals with 51 assists for 73 points with a +49 rating and 20 penalty minutes. He was named a Second Team All-NHL selection for his efforts; Boston beat Quebec in four games in the Adams Division semifinals and eliminated Buffalo in seven games in the Adams Division Finals before getting eliminated by the Islanders in the conference finals in six games. Bourque played in all 17 playoff games, scoring eight goals with 15 assists for 23 points and 10 penalty minutes in the postseason.

In 1983-84, Bourque scored a career-high 31 goals along with 65 assists for a career-high 96 points to go with a +51 rating and 57 penalty minutes. Bourque was named a First Team All-NHL selection for the third time in his career; Boston won the Adams Division but was swept in three games by the Montreal Canadiens in the Adams Division semifinals. Bourque finished with two assists in the series and a -3 rating in the series. Bourque continued his strong play in the 1984-85 season, scoring 20 goals with 66 assists for 86 points, a +30 rating and 53 penalty minutes in 73 games; he was named a First Team All-NHL selection for the fourth time in his career. Boston was knocked off in five games by the Canadiens in the Adams Division semifinals; Bourque finished the series with three assists, a +1 rating and four penalty minutes.

Bourque was rock solid again during the 1985-86 season, playing in 74 games; he scored 19 goals with 58 assists for 77 points, a +17 rating and 68 penalty minutes. He was named a Second Team All-NHL

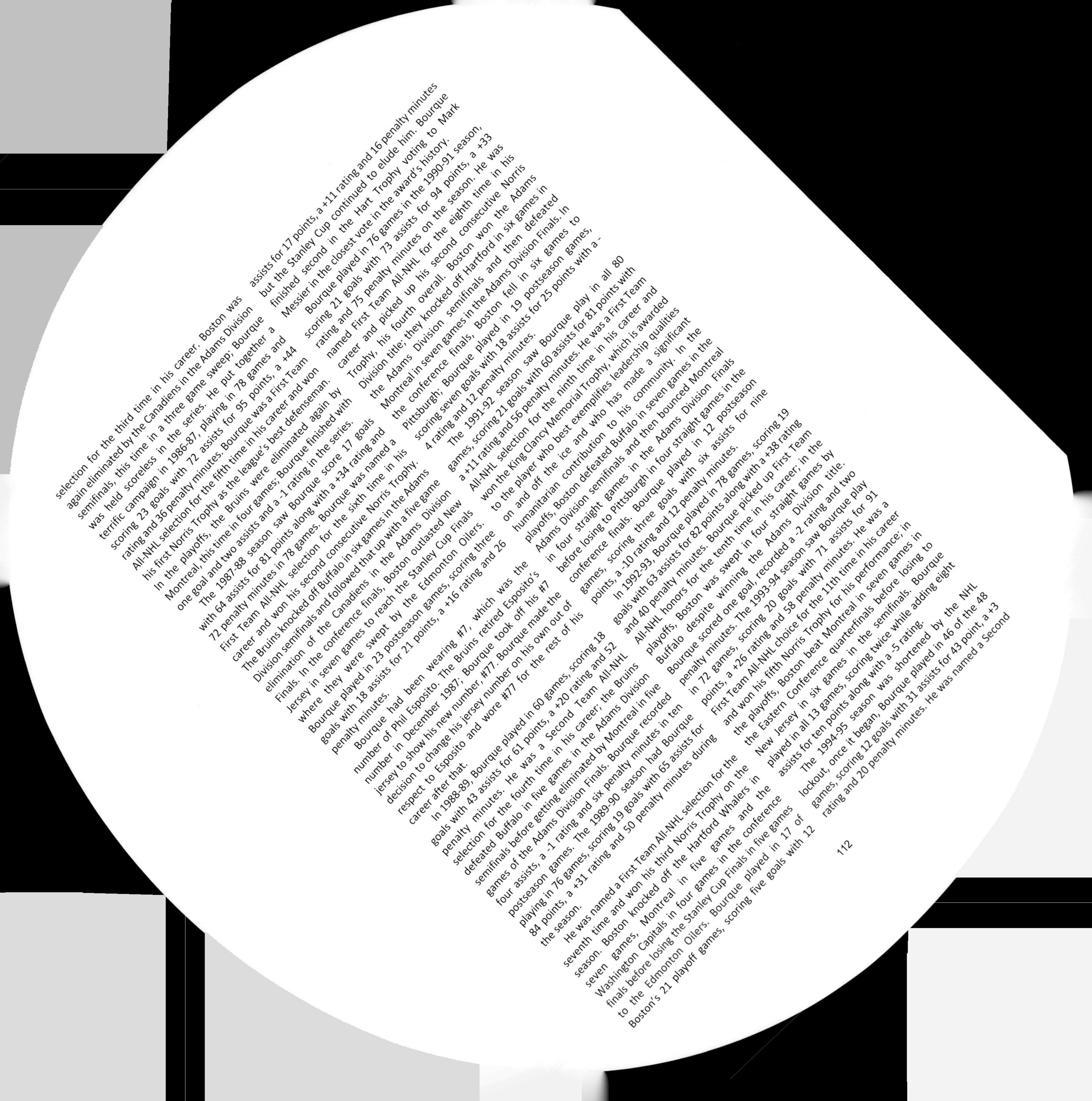

selection for the third time in his career. Boston was again eliminated by the Canadiens in the Adams Division semifinals, this time in a three game sweep; Bourque was held scoreless in the series. He put together a terrific campaign in 1986-87, playing in 78 games and scoring 23 goals with 72 assists for 95 points, a +44 rating and 36 penalty minutes. Bourque was a First Team All-NHL selection for the fifth time in his career and won his first Norris Trophy as the league's best defenseman.

In the playoffs, the Bruins were eliminated again by Montreal, this time in four games; Bourque finished with one goal and two assists and a -1 rating in the series.

The 1987-88 season saw Bourque score 17 goals with 64 assists for 81 points along with a +34 rating and 72 penalty minutes in 78 games. Bourque was named a First Team All-NHL selection for the sixth time in his career and won his second consecutive Norris Trophy. The Bruins knocked off Buffalo in six games in the Adams Division semifinals and followed that up with a five game elimination of the Canadiens in the Adams Division Finals. In the conference finals, Boston outlasted New Jersey in seven games to reach the Stanley Cup Finals where they were swept by the Edmonton Oilers. Bourque played in 23 postseason games, scoring three goals with 18 assists for 21 points, a +16 rating and 26 penalty minutes.

Bourque had been wearing #7, which was the number of Phil Esposito. The Bruins retired Esposito's number in December 1987; Bourque took off his #7 jersey to show his new number, #77. Bourque made the decision to change his jersey number on his own out of respect to Esposito and wore #77 for the rest of his career after that.

In 1988-89, Bourque played in 60 games, scoring 18 goals with 43 assists for 61 points, a +20 rating and 52 penalty minutes. He was a Second Team All-NHL selection for the fourth time in his career; the Bruins defeated Buffalo in five games in the Adams Division semifinals before getting eliminated by Montreal in five games of the Adams Division Finals. Bourque recorded four assists, a -1 rating and six penalty minutes in ten postseason games. The 1989-90 season had Bourque playing in 76 games, scoring 19 goals with 65 assists for 84 points, a +31 rating and 50 penalty minutes during the season.

He was named a First Team All-NHL selection for the seventh time and won his third Norris Trophy on the season. Boston knocked off the Hartford Whalers in seven games, Montreal in five games and the Washington Capitals in four games in the conference finals before losing the Stanley Cup Finals in five games to the Edmonton Oilers. Bourque played in 17 of Boston's 21 playoff games, scoring five goals with 12 assists for 17 points, a +11 rating and 16 penalty minutes but the Stanley Cup continued to elude him. Bourque finished second in the Hart Trophy voting to Mark Messier in the closest vote in the award's history.

Bourque played in 76 games in the 1990-91 season, scoring 21 goals with 73 assists for 94 points, a +33 rating and 75 penalty minutes on the season. He was named First Team All-NHL for the eighth time in his career and picked up his second consecutive Norris Trophy, his fourth overall. Boston won the Adams Division title; they knocked off Hartford in six games in the Adams Division semifinals and then defeated Montreal in seven games in the Adams Division Finals. In the conference finals, Boston fell in six games to Pittsburgh; Bourque played in 19 postseason games, scoring seven goals with 18 assists for 25 points with a -4 rating and 12 penalty minutes.

The 1991-92 season saw Bourque play in all 80 games, scoring 21 goals with 60 assists for 81 points with a +11 rating and 56 penalty minutes. He was a First Team All-NHL selection for the ninth time in his career and won the King Clancy Memorial Trophy, which is awarded to the player who best exemplifies leadership qualities on and off the ice and who has made a significant humanitarian contribution to his community. In the playoffs, Boston defeated Buffalo in seven games in the Adams Division semifinals and then bounced Montreal in four straight games in the Adams Division Finals before losing to Pittsburgh in four straight games in the conference finals. Bourque played in 12 postseason games, scoring three goals with six assists for nine points, a -10 rating and 12 penalty minutes.

In 1992-93, Bourque played in 78 games, scoring 19 goals with 63 assists for 82 points along with a +38 rating and 40 penalty minutes. Bourque picked up First Team All-NHL honors for the tenth time in his career; in the playoffs, Boston was swept in four straight games by Buffalo despite winning the Adams Division title. Bourque scored one goal, recorded a -2 rating and two penalty minutes. The 1993-94 season saw Bourque play in 72 games, scoring 20 goals with 71 assists for 91 points, a +26 rating and 58 penalty minutes. He was a First Team All-NHL choice for the 11th time in his career and won his fifth Norris Trophy for his performance; in the playoffs, Boston beat Montreal in seven games in the Eastern Conference quarterfinals before losing to New Jersey in six games in the semifinals. Bourque played in all 13 games, scoring twice while adding eight assists for ten points along with a -5 rating.

The 1994-95 season was shortened by the NHL lockout, once it began, Bourque played in 46 of the 48 games, scoring 12 goals with 31 assists for 43 point, a +3 rating and 20 penalty minutes. He was named a Second

CCM
CCM
GP·1500
SHER-WOOD
VAUGHN

Team All-NHL selection for the fifth time in his career. Boston was eliminated in five games in the quarterfinals by New Jersey; Bourque had three assists and a -5 rating in the series. That was followed up by a terrific 1995-96 season at age 35; he played in all 82 games, scoring 20 goals with 62 assists for 82 points, a +31 rating and 58 penalty minutes. He earned First Team All-NHL honors for the 12th time in his career; Boston was eliminated in the quarterfinals again, this time in five games by the Florida Panthers. Bourque finished with one goal and six assists for seven points, a -2 rating and two penalty minutes in the series.

In 1996-97, Bourque played in 62 games, scoring 19 goals with 31 points for 50 points, a -11 rating and 18 penalty minutes. Boston missed the playoffs for the first time in 29 seasons as they finished sixth in the Northeast Division. The 1997-98 season saw Bourque play in all 82 games, scoring 13 goals with 35 assists for 48 points, a +2 rating and 80 penalty minutes. Boston returned to the postseason but was eliminated in the quarterfinals in six games by the Washington Capitals; Bourque had one goal and four assists, a -2 rating with two penalty minutes in the series.

Bourque played in 81 games in the 1998-99 season, scoring 10 goals with 47 assists for 57 points, a -7 rating and 34 penalty minutes. Bourque picked up Second Team All-NHL honors for the sixth time in his career. Boston defeated the Carolina Hurricanes in six games in the quarterfinals before losing in the conference semifinals by Buffalo in six games. Bourque played in all 12 playoff games, scoring one goal with nine assists for ten points, a +1 rating and 14 penalty minutes.

The 1999-00 season would lead to the end of Bourque's long tenure with the Bruins. He played in 65 games with Boston, scoring 10 goals with 28 assists for 38 points, a -11 rating and 20 penalty minutes. Bourque requested a trade to try and win a Stanley Cup as the Bruins were fading at the time. He initially asked to be dealt to a team on the East Coast but general manager Harry Sinden swung a deal with the Colorado Avalanche. On March 6, 2000, Boston traded Bourque and Dave Andreychuk to Colorado in exchange for Brian Rolston, Martin Grenier, Samuel Pahlsson and New Jersey's first round draft pick in the 2000 NHL Entry Draft.

In 14 regular season games with the Avalanche to close out the regular season, Bourque scored eight goals while adding six assists for 14 points, a +9 rating and six penalty minutes. Colorado dispatched the Phoenix Coyotes in five games and the Detroit Red Wings in five games in the semifinals before getting knocked off by the Dallas Stars in seven games in the conference finals. Bourque hit the goalpost in the final minute of Game 7 with Colorado down one. He played 13 playoff games, scoring one goal with eight assists for nine points, a +4 rating and eight penalty minutes.

The 2000-01 season saw Bourque play in 80 of Colorado's 82 regular season games, scoring seven goals with 52 assists for 59 points, a +25 rating and 48 penalty minutes. He earned First Team All-NHL honors for the 13th time in his career. In the playoffs, Colorado knocked off the Vancouver Canucks in four straight games in the quarterfinals, the Los Angeles Kings in seven games in the semifinals and the St. Louis Blue in five games in the conference finals to advance to the Stanley Cup Finals. The Avalanche knocked off the New Jersey Devils in seven games to win the Stanley Cup and give Bourque that elusive championship. In 21 postseason games, Bourque had four goals and six assists for 10 points, a +9 rating and 12 penalty minutes.

On June 26, 2001, Bourque, after winning his Stanley Cup, announced his retirement at the age of 40. He played in 1,612 regular season NHL games, scoring 410 goals with 1,169 assists for 1,579 points, a +528 rating and 1,141 penalty minutes. As of the 2013-14 season, Bourque owns NHL records for goals, assists and points for a defenseman; he's 11th in NHL history in points and is 8th all-time in games played. Bourque won a silver medal in the 1981 Canada Cup and gold medals in the 1984 and 1987 Canada Cups.

Bourque was enshrined in the Hockey Hall of Fame in 2004; he was awarded the Lester Patrick Trophy for his contributions to ice hockey in the United States in 2003.

CHAMPIONS

It's often said that lightning doesn't strike twice in the same place but the Pittsburgh Penguins would be the deviation from the norm when it comes to that phenomenon. More than two decades after ending up with the first pick in the NHL Draft that would bring Mario Lemieux to the franchise, the team ended up picking first again and adding a superstar in Sidney Crosby to the mix.

Crosby played for the Rimouski Oceanic in the Quebec Major Junior Hockey League (QMJHL) before playing in the NHL. In his first season with Rimouski, he scored 54 goals and added 81 assists for 135 points in 59 games to win the Jean Beliveau Trophy as the league's leading scorer. He also won the RDS/JVC Trophy awarded to the league's best rookie and the Michel Briere Memorial Trophy awarded to the league's most valuable player; he was the first player in QMJHL history to win all three awards in the same season. The Oceanic knocked off the Shawinigan Cataractes in the playoffs before being eliminated by the Moncton Wildcats in the semifinals; Crosby posted seven goals and nine assists in nine playoff games.

In 2004-05, Crosby again was dominant, scoring 66 goals and adding 102 assists for a league leading 168 points in just 62 games. He again won the Jean Beliveau Trophy and the Michel Briere Memorial Trophy for his efforts. In the postseason, Crosby led Rimouski to the QMJHL title as they defeated the Halifax Mooseheads in the finals, giving the team a berth in the Memorial Cup. Rimouski reached the Memorial Cup Final where they were shut out 4-0 by the London Knights of the Ontario Hockey League. Crosby still picked up the Ed Chynoweth Trophy as the leading scorer of the Memorial Cup with six goals and five assists in five games.

Crosby was the first overall pick in the 2005 NHL Entry Draft by the Penguins, who won the draft lottery that was held due to the lockout erasing the 2004-05 season. The lottery was weighted by the number of playoff appearances and draft lottery wins by teams in the previous four seasons. Crosby made his NHL debut for the Penguins on October 5, 2005 and registered his first career point on an assist of a Mark Recchi goal as Pittsburgh lost 5-1. He scored his first NHL goal three days later in a 7-6 overtime defeat to the Bruins as he beat Hannu Toivonen. Crosby began the year playing alongside Lemieux, who had to retire after 26 games due to an irregular heartbeat. He finished the season with 39 goals and rookie team records with 63 assists and 102 points. Crosby is the youngest player in NHL history to score at least 100 points in a season through the 2013-14 campaign; he finished 24th in the Hart Trophy voting for the league's most valuable player and 2nd in the Calder Trophy voting for Rookie of the Year behind only Alexander Ovechkin of the Washington Capitals.

In 2006-07, Crosby continued to impress as he scored 36 goals and dished out 84 assists to total a league leading 120 points. The Penguins improved 47 points in the standings, going from 58 points and a fifth place finish in the Atlantic Division the year before to 105 points and a second place finish. Pittsburgh would be knocked off in the Eastern Conference quarterfinals in five games by the Ottawa Senators; Crosby scored 3 goals and added two assists to pace the team in scoring. He won the Art Ross Trophy as the league's leading scorer; in addition, he was named a First Team All-NHL selection while claiming the Hart Trophy and the Lester B. Pearson Trophy, which is awarded to the most valuable player in the league as voted on by the players.

Prior to the 2007-08 season, Crosby signed a five year, $43.5 million deal with the Penguins that kept him with the team through the 2012-13 campaign. The Penguins won their first division title since the 1997-98 season with 102 points. Crosby scored 24 goals and added 48 assists for 72 points while playing just 53 games; he missed 28 games due to a high ankle sprain he suffered crashing into the boards against the Tampa Bay Lightning in January 2008. With him healed for the playoffs, along with the development of Evgeni Malkin and the acquisition of Marian Hossa, the Penguins were loaded offensively. They steamrolled the Senators in four straight games in the quarterfinals then bulldozed the Rangers and Flyers in five games to return to the Stanley Cup Finals for the first time since the 1991-92 season. The Penguins would fall short, losing to the Detroit Red Wings in six games; Crosby tied for the league lead in postseason scoring with Henrik Zetterberg of the Red Wings. He scored six goals and added 21 assists in 20 playoff games.

In 2008-09, Crosby came back with a vengeance as he scored 33 goals and added 70 assists for 103 points, finishing third in the scoring race that was won by teammate Evgeni Malkin. The Penguins finished 45-28-9 for 99 points and finished second in the Atlantic Division. Pittsburgh dispatched the Flyers in six games in the quarterfinals and then eliminated the Washington Capitals in seven games in the semifinals before bouncing the Carolina Hurricanes in four straight in the Eastern Conference Finals. That set up a rematch with the Red Wings in the Stanley Cup Finals and the Penguins ultimately prevailed in seven games to win their first Stanley Cup since 1991-92. Crosby scored 15 goals and added 16 assists for 31 points in 24 postseason games; he became the youngest captain in NHL history through the 2013-14 season to win the Stanley Cup.

Crosby had a tremendous 2009-10 season as he tied for the league lead in goals with Tampa Bay's Steven

87
MOMENTUM

Stamkos by scoring 51 times while adding 58 assists for 109 points. He shared the Maurice "Rocket" Richard Trophy with Stamkos and finished third in the Hart Trophy voting. Pittsburgh was unable to defend their championship; after knocking off Ottawa in six games in the quarterfinals, the Penguins were ousted in seven games by the Montreal Canadiens. Crosby scored 6 goals and added 13 assists in 13 postseason games.

Injuries took their toll on Crosby in the next two years as he played a total of 63 games out of 164 regular season contests in the 2010-11 and 2011-12 seasons combined. Crosby had a 25 game point streak in the first half of the 2010-11 season that saw him score 27 goals and add 24 assists; after taking shots to the head in back to back games in early January, Crosby was sidelined with concussion issues and didn't play the final 41 games of the regular season or in the playoffs. He still led the team in scoring with 32 goals and 34 assists but without him and Malkin, who tore knee ligaments late in the year, the Penguins lost in seven games to Tampa Bay in the quarterfinals. He was plagued by concussion-like symptoms through the 2011-12 season, playing just 22 goals; he posted 8 goals and 29 assists for 37 points as the Penguins exited in the quarterfinals again, dropping a six game series to the Philadelphia Flyers.

Crosby signed a 12 year deal worth $104.4 million that would lock him up with the Penguins through the 2024-25 season barring a trade on June 28, 2012. The lockout between the NHL and the NHL Players Association carried over into January 2013, shortening the season to 48 games. Crosby played in 36 contests, scoring 15 goals and adding 41 assists for 56 points. His regular season was cut short after he was hit in the mouth with a Brooks Orpik slap shot that broke his jaw. He returned for the postseason as the Penguins dispatched the New York Islanders in six games and the Ottawa Senators in five to return to the Eastern Conference Finals; Pittsburgh was no match for the Boston Bruins, who swept them in four games. Crosby played in 14 postseason games, scoring seven goals and eight assists; he won the Lester B. Pearson Trophy for a second time while finishing second in the Hart balloting and second in the league in scoring behind Martin St. Louis.

He stayed healthy in the 2013-14 campaign, playing in 80 games and scoring 36 goals while leading the league in assists with 68 and points with 104. That gave Crosby his second Art Ross Trophy of his career as the Penguins won their third division title in four years. Pittsburgh eliminated the Columbus Blue Jackets in six games in the quarterfinals and led the New York Rangers three games to one in the conference semifinals but was outscored 10-3 in the final three games of the series to lose four games to three. Crosby was held to one goal and eight assists in 13 postseason games. On May 1, 2014, Crosby was named one of the three finalists for the Hart Trophy along with Philadelphia's Claude Giroux and Anaheim's Ryan Getzlaf. On June 24, 2014, Crosby won the Hart Trophy for the second time in his career; he also picked up his third Lester B. Pearson Trophy for his performance. In addition, Crosby was named a First Team All-NHL selection for the season.

For his career, through the 2013-14 season, Crosby has scored 274 goals and added 495 assists for 769 points in 550 NHL games along with 463 penalty minutes. He's played in 95 playoff games, scoring 41 goals while dishing out 73 assists for an additional 114 points. Crosby has also been a part of two Canadian Olympic teams, winning gold medals in the 2010 and 2014 Winter Olympics.

RYAN GETZLAF

The Anaheim Ducks have stockpiled a solid pool of talent in recent years but the heart and soul of their franchise right now is Ryan Getzlaf. The talented center has been a staple with the team since 2005-06 and is one of three players on the roster in 2013-14 that was part of the Stanley Cup winning team in 2006-07 along with Corey Perry and Francois Beauchemin.

Getzlaf played his junior hockey with the Calgary Hitmen in the Western Hockey League and made his debut in junior in the 2000-01 season. In 63 games, Getzlaf scored nine goals and added nine assists for 18 points with a -16 plus/minus rating and 34 penalty minutes. He added two goals and one assists for three points with a -4 rating and four penalty minutes in the playoffs; Calgary was knocked off in seven games in the quarterfinals by the Swift Current Broncos. Getzlaf put together a solid season in the 2002-03 campaign, playing in 70 games; he scored 29 goals with 39 assists for 68 points along with a +8 rating and 121 penalty minutes. In the postseason, Calgary was dispatched in the quarterfinals in five games by the Red Deer Rebels; Getzlaf finished with one goal and one assist in the series with a -2 rating and six penalty minutes.

He would be selected with the 19th overall pick in the 2003 NHL Entry Draft by the Mighty Ducks of Anaheim. The Mighty Ducks sent Getzlaf back to Calgary for the 2003-04 season; he put up 28 goals with 47 assists for 75 points in just 49 games with a +32 rating and 97 penalty minutes. The Hitmen made the playoffs again but were knocked off in the quarterfinals again, this time in seven games by Red Deer; Getzlaf had five goals with one assist for six points with a +4 rating and 12 penalty minutes. When the NHL locked out the players and the 2004-05 season was canceled, Getzlaf stayed in Calgary and had 29 goals with 25 assists for 54 points in 51 games while posting a +22 rating and 102 penalty minutes. In the playoffs, Getzlaf finished with four goals and 13 assists for 17 points in 12 games with a +6 rating and 18 penalty minutes. Calgary defeated the Lethbridge Hurricanes in five games in the quarterfinals before being eliminated in seven games by the Brandon Wheat Kings in the conference semifinals.

After the Hitmen were eliminated, Getzlaf joined the Cincinnati Mighty Ducks of the American Hockey League in the playoffs. In his pro debut, he scored one goal and had four assists for five points with a -3 rating and four penalty minutes in 10 postseason games. He started the 2005-06 season with Anaheim and scored his first NHL point on October 5, 2005 against the Chicago Blackhawks. He recorded his first career point on an assist against the Columbus Blue Jackets on October 14, 2005 and his first NHL goal came on October 21 against the Detroit Red Wings.

He was sent down to the AHL in mid-November to give him more playing time but was called back up in mid-January. He finished the season with 14 goals and 25 assists for 39 points in 57 games, posting a +6 rating and 22 penalty minutes. The Mighty Ducks defeated the Calgary Flames in seven games in the quarterfinals and eliminated the Colorado Avalanche in four games in the semifinals before getting knocked off by the Edmonton Oilers in five games in the conference finals. Getzlaf finished with three goals and four assists for seven points with a -3 rating and 13 penalty minutes in 16 postseason games.

The 2006-07 season saw Getzlaf play in all 82 games; he posted 25 goals and 33 assists for 58 points with a +17 rating and 66 penalty minutes. In the playoffs, the Ducks defeated the Minnesota Wild in five games in the quarterfinals and the Vancouver Canucks in five games in the semifinals before eliminating the Red Wings in six games in the conference finals. In the Stanley Cup Finals, the Ducks defeated the Ottawa Senators in five games to win their first and through 2013-14, only, Stanley Cup championship. Getzlaf played in 21 playoff games, scoring seven goals and adding 10 assists for 17 points with a +1 rating and 32 penalty minutes.

The 2007-08 season saw Getzlaf play in 77 games; he posted 24 goals and 58 assists for 82 points with a +32 rating and 94 penalty minutes. He was named to his first All Star Game for his efforts. The Ducks didn't do much in their effort to defend their title as they were eliminated in the quarterfinals in six games by the Dallas Stars. Getzlaf scored two goals and added three assists for five points in the series with a -2 rating and six penalty minutes. In 2008-09, Getzlaf played in 81 games, scoring 25 goals and setting a franchise record with 66 assists for a career high 91 points en route to his second All Star Game. He was third in the league in assists and sixth in points on the season and finished with a +5 rating and 121 penalty minutes. In the postseason, Getzlaf played 13 games, scoring four goals and adding 14 assists for 18 points with a +3 rating and 25 penalty minutes. The Ducks beat the Stars in six games in the quarterfinals before losing to the Red Wings in seven games in the semifinals.

Getzlaf played in just 66 games in the 2009-10 season as he missed time with a high ankle sprain. He finished the year with 19 goals and 50 assists for 69 points, a +4 rating and 79 penalty minutes but the team fell short of the playoffs. When Scott Niedermayer retired after the season, Getzlaf was named the captain of the Ducks before the 2010-11 season. He contributed 19 goals and 57 assists for 76 points with a +14 rating and 35 penalty minutes in 67 games. The Ducks were again eliminated in the quarterfinals, this time in six

BAUER.

games by the Nashville Predators; Getzlaf had two goals and four assists for six points with nine penalty minutes in the series.

The 2011-12 season saw Getzlaf play all 82 games for the second time in his career; he scored a career low 11 goals along with 46 assists for 57 points with a -11 rating and 75 penalty minutes as the Ducks missed the playoffs. He bounced back in the lockout shortened 2011-12 season, scoring 15 goals with 34 assists for 49 points in 44 games with a +14 rating and 41 penalty minutes. The Ducks returned to the playoffs but were eliminated in the quarterfinals with a seven game series defeat at the hands of the Red Wings; Getzlaf put up three goals and three assists for six points with a +2 rating and six penalty minutes.

In 2013-14, Getzlaf put up a career-high 31 goals along with 56 assists for 87 points to go with a +28 rating and 31 penalty minutes. He finished second in the NHL in points and fifth in assists. In the playoffs, the Ducks eliminated the Stars in six games in the quarterfinals before getting eliminated in seven games in the semifinals by the Los Angeles Kings. Getzlaf finished the playoffs with four goals and 11 assists for 15 points in 12 games with a -2 rating and 10 penalty minutes. He was named a finalist for the Hart Trophy on May 1, 2014 along with Pittsburgh's Sidney Crosby and Philadelphia's Claude Giroux. On June 24, 2014, Getzlaf finished second in the balloting for the Hart Trophy, finishing behind Crosby. He was also named a Second Team All-NHL selection for his performance.

In his career through the 2013-14 season, Getzlaf has played in 633 regular season games; he's scored 183 goals with 425 assists for 608 points, a +109 rating and 564 penalty minutes. Getzlaf is the third leading scorer in franchise history, trailing only Teemu Selanne and Paul Kariya. In the postseason, Getzlaf has played in 81 games; he's scored 25 goals and 49 assists for 74 points with a -1 rating and 101 penalty minutes. In addition, Getzlaf has won two gold medals in the Olympics with Canada, with those coming in 2010 and 2014. He's also won a silver medal with Canada in the 2008 World Championships plus a silver medal in the 2004 World Junior Championships and a gold medal in the 2005 World Junior Championships.

BAUER

CLAUDE GIROUX

Claude Giroux may be one of the most underappreciated top line players in the National Hockey League. He goes about his business and quietly puts up numbers that helps his team win hockey games. While he hasn't won any major awards, there are few players whose contributions are more valuable to their franchise than what Giroux brings to the table for the Philadelphia Flyers.

Giroux was actually a free agent in major junior hockey before he was invited to a walk-on tryout with the Gatineau Olympiques of the QMJHL before the 2005-06 season. Giroux impressed the people in charge and earned a roster spot. In 69 games, Giroux scored 39 goals and added 64 assists for 103 points while posting a +30 plus/minus rating plus 64 penalty minutes. In the playoffs, Gatineau defeated the Drummondville Voltigeurs in seven games in the division quarterfinals and followed that up with a five game elimination of the Chicoutimi Saguenéens in the division semifinals before being defeated by the Moncton Wildcats in five games. Giroux posted five goals and 15 assists for 20 points with a -3 rating and 24 penalty minutes. He was named to the QMJHL All-Rookie Team for his performance.

He would be selected with the 22nd overall pick in the first round of the 2006 NHL Entry Draft by the Philadelphia Flyers. Giroux spent the majority of the 2006-07 season with Gatineau, scoring 48 goals with 64 assists for 112 points with a +12 rating and 46 penalty minutes with 20 of his goals coming on the power play. Giroux finished fourth in the QMJHL in scoring. He did play five games with the Philadelphia Phantoms of the American Hockey League, scoring one goal and adding one assist. In the playoffs, Gatineau was knocked off in five games in the quarterfinals by the Rouyn-Noranda Huskies; Giroux had two goals and five assists for seven points in the series.

Giroux started the 2008-09 season with the Philadelphia Phantoms but was called up after Christmas in 2008 and stuck with the team the rest of the season. He picked up his first NHL point on December 31, 2008 with an assist against the Vancouver Canucks and recorded his first NHL goal against Tomas Vokoun and the Florida Panthers on January 27, 2009. Giroux finished the regular season playing in 42 games, scoring nine goals and adding 18 assists for 27 points with a +10 plus/minus rating and 14 penalty minutes. The Flyers made the postseason but were eliminated in six games in the quarterfinals by the Pittsburgh Penguins; Giroux finished the series with two goals and three assists for five points with a +2 rating and six penalty minutes.

In the 2009-10 season, Giroux played in all 82 games, tallying 16 goals and adding 31 assists for 47 points while recording a -9 rating and 23 penalty minutes on the year. In the playoffs, Giroux was a major factor as the Flyers eliminated the New Jersey Devils in five games in the Eastern Conference quarterfinals and followed that up with an improbable rally from a 3-0 series deficit and a 3-0 hole in Game 7 to stun the Boston Bruins in the semifinals. In the conference finals, the Flyers defeated the Montreal Canadiens in five games to advance to the Stanley Cup Finals, where they were defeated in six games by the Chicago Blackhawks. Giroux played in 23 postseason games, scoring 10 goals and adding 11 assists for 21 points with a +7 rating and four penalty minutes.

The 2010-11 season saw Giroux sign a three year extension worth $11.25 million. He played in all 82 games again and scored 25 goals with 51 assists for 76 points while recording a +20 rating and 47 penalty minutes.

In 2011-12, Giroux took over as the top center on the team with the departures of Jeff Carter and Mike Richards and he responded with his best season to date through the 2013-14 campaign. Giroux scored 28 goals and added 65 assists for 93 points, which was good for third in the league. Giroux played in 10 postseason games, finishing tied for the league lead with eight goals along with nine assists for 17 points with a +2 rating and 13 penalty minutes.

The lockout shortened 2012-13 season saw Giroux play in all 48 games on the year; he scored 13 goals and added 35 assists for 48 points with a -7 rating and 22 penalty minutes. The Flyers missed the playoffs, however, as they were unable to come back from a slow start. In the 2013-14 season, Giroux played in all 82 games, scoring 28 goals and adding 58 assists for 86 points, finishing third in the league in that category for the second time in his career; he also posted a +7 rating and 46 penalty minutes on the season. Philadelphia returned to the playoffs but was knocked off in seven games by the New York Rangers in the quarterfinals; Giroux scored two goals with four assists for six points with a +2 rating and two penalty minutes. He was named one of the three finalists for the Hart Trophy; he finished third in the voting behind Pittsburgh's Sidney Crosby and Anaheim's Ryan Getzlaf for the award.

In his career through the end of the 2013-14 season, Giroux has played in 415 regular season games; he's scored 119 goals and added 258 assists for 377 points with a +25 rating and 181 penalty minutes. He's played in 57 career postseason games, scoring 23 goals and tacking on 38 assists for 61 points with a +15 rating and 33 penalty minutes. Giroux also was part of the 2008 Canadian gold medal winning team in the World Junior Championships.

BAUER

WAYNE GRETZKY

There are plenty of platitudes that are thrown around in the world of professional sports but more often than not, the players or teams don't live up to the hype. In one case where the hype was lived up to and perhaps, in one of the rare occasions in professional sports, exceeded expectations comes in the form of "The Great One", Wayne Gretzky.

Gretzky retired from the NHL holding 61 NHL records and still, as of the 2013-14 season, owns 60 NHL records. There are a slew of unofficial records that he holds as well; the fact that Gretzky has more career assists than any other player in league history has points shows his dominance in the sport over the two decades of his career.

Gretzky played one full season of junior hockey; he played three games as an emergency call-up for the Peterborough Petes of the Ontario Hockey League, recording three assists. He was drafted by the Sault Ste. Marie Greyhounds with the third pick in the 1977 OMJHL Midget Draft; he originally wanted to wear number 9 to pay tribute to his childhood idol Gordie Howe but that number was already in use by Brian Gualazzi. Coach Muzz MacPherson came up with the idea for Gretzky to wear number 99; it marked the first time that he wore the number in his hockey career.

He would play 63 games for the Greyhounds in 1977-78, finishing second in the league in scoring behind Bobby Smith of the Ottawa 67's by posting 70 goals with 112 assists for 182 points with 14 penalty minutes. Gretzky won the Emms Family Award as the OHL Rookie of the Year and also won the William Hanley Trophy as the league's most sportsmanlike player. In the playoffs, Gretzky played in 13 games, scoring six goals and adding 20 assists for 26 points. The Greyhounds defeated the Kingston Canadians, three games to two, in the first round before falling to the Ottawa 67's in the quarterfinals, four games to three, with one tie.

The NHL had a rule in play that players under the age of 20 couldn't be signed but the WHA didn't have those restrictions. Several teams in the WHA were battling for Gretzky's services but in the end, it was Nelson Skalbania, who owned the Indianapolis Racers and would later be part of the ownership group that brought the Flames from Atlanta to Calgary, who inked Gretzky. He signed Gretzky to a seven year personal services contract worth $1.75 million on June 12, 1978.

Gretzky would score his first professional goal against the Edmonton Oilers and goaltender Dave Dryden in the fourth game of the 1978-79 season, a 4-3 loss. He would add his second goal just four seconds after the first. All told, Gretzky would play just eight games with the Racers, scoring three goals and three assists for six points and a -2 rating. The Racers were struggling financially and Skalbania ended up selling Gretzky, goaltender Eddie Mio and Peter Driscoll to the Oilers for a reported price tag of $850,000; the actual price that Peter Pocklington, the owner of the Oilers, paid was actually in the neighborhood of $700,000. As for the Racers, they folded 17 games later, going out of business on December 15, 1978.

With the Oilers, Gretzky would finish out the season playing 72 games for Edmonton, scoring 43 goals with 61 assists for 104 points with a +23 plus/minus rating and 19 penalty minutes. He finished his season playing 80 games, scoring 46 goals with 64 assists for 110 points, a +20 rating and 19 penalty minutes. In the postseason, the Oilers defeated the New England Whalers in six games before falling to the Winnipeg Jets in seven games in the Avco Cup Finals. Gretzky scored 10 goals and added 10 assists for 20 points with a +6 rating and two penalty minutes in 13 playoff games. He was awarded the Lou Kaplan Trophy as the WHA's Rookie of the Year; he was also named a Second Team All-WHA selection.

The WHA merged with the NHL following the season; the Oilers were one of the four teams that joined the NHL. Gretzky could have been forced back into the entry draft but Pocklington pushed the issue, showing that he was on a personal services contract and the league caved.

In the 1980-81 season, Gretzky played in all 80 regular season games, scoring 55 goals along with a league high 109 assists for a league leading 164 points with a +41 rating and 28 penalty minutes. He was named a First Team All-NHL selection, won his second straight Hart Trophy and claimed the Art Ross Trophy as well. Edmonton defeated Montreal in three games in the preliminary round but was defeated in the quarterfinals by the New York Islanders in six games. Gretzky finished the playoffs with seven goals and 14 assists for 21 points with four penalty minutes in nine playoff games.

The 1981-82 season saw Gretzky set a NHL record with 92 goals along with 120 assists for 212 points in 80 games, making him the first player in NHL history to score at least 200 points in a season. Gretzky destroyed the old record of 50 goals in 50 games as he reached the mark in just 39 contests. He was a First Team All-NHL selection for the second straight year, claimed his second straight Art Ross Trophy, his third consecutive Hart Trophy and bagged his first Lester B. Pearson Trophy as the league's most valuable player as voted on by the players. Despite winning the Smythe Division title, the Oilers were defeated in the Smythe Division semifinals, three games to two, by the Los Angeles Kings. Gretzky contributed five goals and seven assists for 12 points with eight penalty minutes in the series.

Los Angeles
KINGS
C
EAS
AIR
99
EASTON
Supra
CCM

Gretzky continued to pile up the points in the 1982-83 season; he played in 80 games, scoring 71 goals and adding 125 assists for 196 points, leading the league in all three categories while recording a +60 rating and 59 penalty minutes.

In 1983-84, Gretzky played in 74 games, leading the league in goals (87), assists (118), points (205) and plus/minus (+76) with 39 penalty minutes. Once again, he was named a First Team All-NHL selection, picked up his fifth straight Hart Trophy, fourth straight Art Ross and a third straight Lester B. Pearson Trophy. In the playoffs, Edmonton dispatched Winnipeg in three games, Calgary in seven and the Minnesota North Stars in four straight games in the conference finals to advance to their second consecutive Stanley Cup Finals.

The 1984-85 season saw Gretzky lead the league in goals (73), assists (135), points (208) and plus/minus (+98) with 52 penalty minutes in 80 games. He was named a First Team All-NHL selection for the fifth straight season, won his sixth straight Hart Trophy, his fifth straight Art Ross Trophy and his fourth Lester B. Pearson Trophy. In the playoffs, Edmonton blew through Los Angeles in three games, Winnipeg in four games and Chicago in six games to reach their third straight Stanley Cup Finals. Once there, Edmonton defeated the Flyers in five games to win their second straight championship. Gretzky played in 18 playoff games, scoring 17 goals along with a playoff high 30 assists and 47 points with a +28 rating and four penalty minutes. He earned the Conn Smythe Trophy as the most valuable player in the postseason for his efforts.

In 1985-86, Gretzky played in all 80 games, scoring 52 goals while adding a NHL record 163 assists and a NHL record 215 points along with a +71 rating and 46 penalty minutes. Gretzky again was a First Team All-NHL selection, won his seventh straight Hart Trophy, his sixth straight Art Ross Trophy and his fifth straight Lester B. Pearson Trophy. Edmonton couldn't win a third straight Stanley Cup; after beating the Vancouver Canucks in three games, the Oilers were beaten in the Smythe Division Finals in seven games by the Calgary Flames; Gretzky finished with eight points and 11 assists for 19 points with two penalty minutes in 10 games.

The 1986-87 season saw Gretzky play in 79 games, leading the league in goals (62), assists (121), points (183) and plus/minus (+70) with 28 penalty minutes. Gretzky was again a First Team All-NHL selection, won his eighth straight Hart Trophy, seventh straight Art Ross Trophy and his sixth straight Lester B. Pearson Trophy. In the playoffs, Edmonton knocked off the Kings in five games, the Jets in four and the Detroit Red Wings in five to return to the Stanley Cup Finals. In the Stanley Cup Finals, the Oilers outlasted the Flyers in seven games for Gretzky's third championship; he played 21 playoff games, scoring five goals with 29 assists for 34 points with a +10 rating and six penalty minutes.

Gretzky's last season in Edmonton would come in the 1987-88 season though at the time, no one knew that would be the case. He played in just 64 games, scoring 40 goals with a league high 109 assists for 149 points, a +39 rating and 24 penalty minutes. He was named a Second Team All-NHL selection on the season and finished second in the league in scoring; the first time in his career that he hadn't finished in at least a tie for first. In the playoffs, the Oilers cruised past the Jets in five games, the Flames in four and the Red Wings in five to reach the Stanley Cup Finals again. Edmonton dispatched the Boston Bruins in four games to win Gretzky's fourth and final championship. He won the Conn Smythe Trophy for the second time as he played in 19 playoff games, scoring 12 goals with 31 assists for 43 points with a +6 rating and 16 penalty minutes.

The Oilers had been shopping Gretzky because Pocklington was in financial straits; Gretzky had converted the personal services deal into a five year player contract with the ability to become an unrestricted free agent after the 1988-89 season.

In Gretzky's first season with the Kings in 1988-89, he played 78 games, scoring 54 goals, a league high 114 assists for 168 points with a +15 rating and 26 penalty minutes. He was named a Second Team All-NHL selection and won the Hart Trophy for the ninth time in his career. The Kings rallied from a 3-1 series deficit to stun the Oilers, four games to three before getting swept by the Flames in the Smythe Division Finals. Gretzky played in 11 games in the postseason, scoring five goals with 17 assists for 22 points and a -4 rating.

The 1989-90 season saw Gretzky play 73 games; he scored 40 goals with a league leading 102 assists and a league best 142 points, a +8 rating and 42 penalty minutes. On October 15, 1989, against the Oilers no less, Gretzky recorded his 1,851st career point, passing Gordie Howe to become the league's all-time leading scorer. The Kings beat the Flames in six games in the Smythe Division semifinals before getting swept by the Oilers in the Smythe Division Finals. He won his eighth Art Ross Trophy and was named a First Team All-NHL selection. In the playoffs, Gretzky played in seven of the ten playoff games, scoring three goals with seven assists for ten points with a -4 rating.

In 1990-91, Gretzky played 78 games as he scored 41 goals with a league leading 122 assists and a league best 163 points, a +30 rating with 16 penalty minutes. He was named a First Team All-NHL selection again, won his ninth Art Ross Trophy and his second Lady Byng Trophy. The Kings eliminated the Canucks in six games in the

HESPE
HESPE
RTX
99
HES

Smythe Division semifinals before losing to the Oilers in six games. Gretzky scored four goals with 11 assists for 15 points with two penalty minutes in 12 postseason games.

Gretzky played in 74 games in the 1991-92 season, scoring 31 goals to go with a league leading 90 assists to finish with 121 points, a -12 rating and 34 penalty minutes. He won his third Lady Byng Trophy for gentlemanly play. The Kings had no success in the playoffs, losing in the Smythe Division semifinals in six games to the Oilers; Gretzky finished with two points, five assists, seven points, a -3 rating and two penalty minutes in the series.

The 1992-93 season saw Gretzky miss nearly half the season with an upper back injury; he played in 45 regular season games, recording 16 goals with 49 assists for 65 points with a +6 rating and six penalty minutes. In the playoffs, the Kings defeated the Flames in six games, the Canucks in six games and survived a seven game series in the conference finals against the Toronto Maple Leafs to advance to the Stanley Cup Finals for the first time in team history. The Kings ultimately fell short, losing four games to one to the Montreal Canadiens; Gretzky played in 24 postseason games, scoring 15 goals, adding 25 assists for 40 points to lead playoff skaters in all three categories. He was a +6 with four penalty minutes in the postseason.

Gretzky put together a terrific season in the 1993-94 campaign, playing in 81 games; he scored 38 goals, racked up a league best 92 assists and led the league in scoring with 130 points with a -25 rating and 20 penalty minutes. He was named a Second Team All-NHL selection, won his tenth Art Ross Trophy and his fourth Lady Byng Trophy for his performance. After making the Stanley Cup Finals, the Kings finished in fifth place in the Pacific Division and missed the playoffs. Gretzky played in all 48 games in the lockout shortened 1994-95 season, scoring 11 goals with 37 assists for 48 points, a -20 rating and six penalty minutes. The Kings missed the playoffs once again.

In 1995-96, Gretzky played 62 games for the Kings, racking up 15 goals and 66 assists for 81 points, a -7 rating and 32 penalty minutes. He was traded to the St. Louis Blues on February 27, 1996; in exchange, the Kings received Craig Johnson, Patrice Tardif, Roman Vopat, the Blues 5th round pick in 1996 and their 1st round selection in 1997. Gretzky logged 18 regular season games with the Blues, scoring eight goals with 13 assists for 21 points, a -6 rating and two penalty minutes. In the playoffs, the Blues defeated the Maple Leafs in six games in the quarterfinals but fell to the Red Wings in seven games in the conference semifinals. Gretzky had two goals and 14 assists for 16 points with a +2 rating in 13 playoff games. On July 21, 1996, Gretzky signed a two year deal worth $8 million plus incentives with the New York Rangers.

Gretzky played in all 82 games for the Blueshirts in the 1996-97 season, scoring 25 goals along with a league leading 72 assists for 97 points, a +12 rating and 28 penalty minutes. He was named a Second Team All-NHL selection for his performance; the Rangers beat the Florida Panthers in the quarterfinals and the New Jersey Devils in five games in the semifinals but were stopped in five games in the Eastern Conference Finals by the Philadelphia Flyers. Gretzky played in all 15 playoff games, scoring 10 goals and adding 10 assists for 20 points, a +5 rating and two penalty minutes. It would mark the last time Gretzky would make the playoffs in his career.

In the 1997-98 season, Gretzky played in 82 games, scoring 23 goals and adding a league high 67 assists en route to 90 points. He posted a -11 rating and recorded 28 penalty minutes; he was named a Second Team All-NHL selection for the season even though the Rangers missed the playoffs. The 1998-99 season would prove to be Gretzky's last; he played in 70 games, recording nine goals and 53 assists for 62 points along with a -23 rating and 14 penalty minutes. He won the Lady Byng for the fifth time in his career. On April 16, 1999, Gretzky announced his retirement from the NHL.

The league waived the three year waiting period for enshrinement into the Hockey Hall of Fame; he was inducted on November 22, 1999, just seven months after playing his final game. Gretzky's #99 was retired league wide at the 2000 NHL All Star Game. He finished his career playing in 1,487 regular season games, scoring 894 goals with 1,963 assists for 2,857 points, a +518 plus/minus rating and 577 penalty minutes. In the playoffs, he added 122 goals plus 260 assists for 382 points, a +67 plus/minus rating and 66 penalty minutes in 208 games.

Gretzky went on after retirement to coach the Phoenix Coyotes for four seasons from the 2005-06 season through the 2008-09 campaign. He posted a 143-161-24 record, never finishing higher than 12th in the Western Conference. In international play, he won a bronze medal in the World Junior Championships in 1978, a bronze in the World Championships in 1982, a silver medal in the Canada Cup in 1982, gold medals in the Canada Cup in 1984, 1987 and 1991. He also was a member of the silver medal winning Canadian World Cup team.

HESPELER
FIBREGLAS
RTX
99
BAUER
CANADA

GORDIE HOWE

When it comes to longevity in the world of professional hockey as a player, there is no one in the history of the sport that epitomizes it better than Mr. Hockey himself, Gordie Howe. He is still recognized as one of the greatest players in NHL history and some of the feats that he pulled off will likely never be repeated again in the sport.

Howe originally had a tryout with the New York Rangers when he was 15 but failed to make the team. Howe himself stated that he was homesick as he came from Saskatchewan and at the time wasn't quite ready for the massive change that the move would have entailed. He was signed by the Detroit Red Wings a year later and assigned to their junior team, the Gait Red Wings. Howe would be bumped up to the United States Hockey League in 1945 and posted 22 goals and 26 assists for 48 points with 53 penalty minutes in 51 games for the Omaha Knights.

He would make his NHL debut in the 1946-47 season, playing his first game for Detroit on October 18, 1946 and scored his first career goal in a 3-3 tie against the Toronto Maple Leafs. In his rookie season, Howe wore number 17; he didn't get his well-known number 9 until the 1947-48 season after Roy Conacher went to Chicago. Howe played in 58 games in his rookie season, scoring seven goals and adding 15 assists for 22 points with 52 penalty minutes. In the playoffs, Howe was held without a point in five games; he racked up 18 penalty minutes as the Red Wings were beaten in five games by the Maple Leafs.

The 1947-48 season saw Howe improve on his rookie season as he played in 60 games, scoring 16 times and adding 28 assists for 44 points along with 63 penalty minutes. The Red Wings beat the New York Rangers in six games in the semifinals but were swept by the Maple Leafs in the Stanley Cup Finals; Howe scored one goal and added one assist to go with 11 penalty minutes in 10 playoff games. The 1948-49 season saw Howe play in just 40 games but he averaged nearly a point a game with 12 goals and 25 assists for 37 points with 57 penalty minutes. The Red Wings eliminated the Montreal Canadiens in seven games but were again swept by the Maple Leafs in the Stanley Cup Finals; Howe led all playoff scorers with eight goals and 11 points while playing in 11 games. He was named a Second Team All-NHL selection for his efforts on the ice.

In 1949-50, Howe, placed on a line with Ted Lindsay and Sid Abel, flourished. In 70 games, he scored 35 goals and added 33 assists for 68 points with 69 penalty minutes. He finished third in the league in scoring behind his two linemates; Lindsay led the way with 78 points while Abel added 69. In the playoffs, the Red Wings got revenge against the Maple Leafs with a seven game win in the semifinals before beating the Rangers in seven games in the Stanley Cup Finals for the first championship in Howe's career. However, he played in just one game in the playoffs; he fractured his skull against Toronto trying to check Ted Kennedy into the boards. He underwent emergency surgery to relieve pressure on his brain but was ready to go at the start of the 1950-51 campaign. He was named a Second Team All-NHL selection once again.

The 1950-51 season was a breakthrough year for Howe; he played in all 70 regular season games and led the league with 43 goals, 43 assists and 86 points along with 74 penalty minutes; he cruised to the scoring title by 20 points. Detroit was unable to defend their championship, losing in six games to the Canadiens in the semifinals. Howe finished with four goals and three assists for seven points with four penalty minutes in the series; he was named a First Team All-NHL selection and won the Art Ross Trophy as the league's leading scorer.

The 1951-52 season saw Howe continue to put up offensive numbers in a defensive minded era; he played all 70 games again and led the league with 47 goals along with 39 points for a league high 86 points. The Red Wings swept through the postseason, knocking off the Maple Leafs in four games and sweeping the Canadiens in the Stanley Cup Finals for the second title of Howe's career. He played in all eight games and scored two goals along with five assists for seven points and two penalty minutes; after the season, he was named First Team All-NHL in addition to winning the Art Ross for the second time and the Hart Trophy as the league's most valuable player.

The 1952-53 campaign saw Howe play 70 games again; he scored a career-high 49 goals along with 46 assists for a league leading 95 points plus 57 penalty minutes. The Red Wings failed to defend their title again, losing in six games to the Boston Bruins in the semifinals; Howe had two goals and five assists for seven points with two penalty minutes. He was named a First Team All-NHL selection again, won his third straight Art Ross Trophy and his second Hart Trophy. Howe won his fourth straight Art Ross Trophy as he scored 33 goals and added 48 assists for 81 points in 70 games with 109 penalty minutes. Detroit defeated Toronto in five games and then won the third Stanley Cup of Howe's career with a seven game triumph over Montreal; he scored four goals and five assists while leading all playoff skaters with 31 penalty minutes. He was named a First Team All-NHL selection for the fourth straight season.

The 1954-55 campaign saw Howe score 29 goals and add 33 assists for 62 points in 64 games to go with 68 penalty minutes. Detroit swept Toronto in the semifinals and then beat Montreal in seven games for the second

straight Stanley Cup and fourth of Howe's career; he had a playoff high nine goals and 20 points along with 24 penalty minutes in 11 games; he wouldn't win another Stanley Cup in his illustrious career. The 1955-56 season saw Howe play all 70 games, score 38 goals and add 41 assists for 79 points with 100 penalty minutes. Detroit defeated Toronto in five games before losing in the Stanley Cup Finals in five games to Montreal; Howe had three goals and nine assists for 12 points with eight penalty minutes in 10 playoff games. He was named a Second Team All-NHL selection for his performance.

The 1958-59 season saw Howe score 32 goals and add 46 assists for 78 points with 57 penalty minutes in 70 games.

In 1960-61, Howe put up 23 goals and 49 assists for 72 points with 30 penalty minutes in 64 games, earning a Second Team All-NHL selection. He added four goals and 11 assists for a playoff high 15 points with 10 penalty minutes in 11 postseason games; Detroit beat Toronto in five games before losing in the Stanley Cup Finals to the Chicago Black Hawks in six games.

The 1962-63 season saw Howe win his sixth Hart Trophy and his sixth Art Ross Trophy as he scored a league leading 38 goals along with 48 assists for 86 points along with 100 penalty minutes in 70 games. He was also a First Team All-NHL selection; in the playoffs, Howe added seven goals and nine assists for playoff leading 16 points with 22 penalty minutes in 11 games.

The 1964-65 season saw Howe post 29 goals, 47 assists and 76 points with 104 penalty minutes in 70 games as he was a Second Team All-NHL selection. Detroit was eliminated in the semifinals by Chicago in seven games; Howe had four goals and two assists plus 20 penalty minutes in the series. He would follow that up with a nearly identical season in 1965-66, scoring 29 goals with 46 assists for 75 points and 83 penalty minutes in 70 games while earning First Team All-NHL honors. The Red Wings eliminated Chicago in six games before losing the Stanley Cup Finals to Montreal in six games; Howe had four goals and six assists with 12 penalty minutes in 12 playoff games.

In the final season of the Original Six era, 1966-67, Howe scored 25 goals and added 40 assists for 65 points with 53 penalty minutes and was named Second Team All-NHL once again.

The 1968-69 season proved to be Howe's greatest scoring output in the NHL as he played 76 games, scoring 44 goals and posting a career-high 59 assists en route to 103 points with 58 penalty minutes; he earned First Team All-NHL honors for his performance. Detroit still couldn't make the postseason however, finishing 5th in the East. Howe played in 76 games in the 1969-70 season, scoring 31 goals with 40 assists for 71 points and 58 penalty minutes while getting named First Team All-NHL again. Detroit made the playoffs for the first time in four years but was swept by Chicago; Howe had two goals and two penalty minutes in the series.

Howe's last season with Detroit came in 1970-71; he played in 63 games, scoring 23 goals and adding 29 assists for 52 points and 38 penalty minutes. The Red Wings missed the playoffs and Howe, who had been battling a chronic wrist injury, retired and moved to the front office of the Red Wings. In 1972, he was offered the head coaching job of the expansion New York Islanders but turned down the offer. Howe was inducted into the Hockey Hall of Fame in 1972.

A season later, in 1973, Howe was offered a contract with the WHA's Houston Aeros, who had signed both of his sons, Mark and Marty Howe, to contracts. Howe underwent wrist surgery, signed the contract and took to the ice. He would play six seasons in the WHA with the Aeros and the New England Whalers, logging 419 regular season games and putting up 174 goals, 334 assists and 508 points with 399 penalty minutes. In the postseason, Howe appeared in 78 WHA playoff games, scoring 28 goals and adding 43 assists for 71 points with 115 penalty minutes. He was part of two Avco Cup winning teams and won a MVP award, which was renamed the Gordie Howe Trophy.

When the WHA merged with the NHL in the 1979-80 season, Howe signed on to play one final season with the Hartford Whalers. He played in all 80 regular season games, scoring 15 goals and 26 assists for 41 points with 42 penalty minutes; he was 52 by the time the season ended. Hartford made the postseason but was eliminated in three games in the preliminary round by Montreal. Howe had one goal and one assist with two penalty minutes in his final playoff series. He retired with 801 goals, 1049 assists, 1850 points and 1685 penalty minutes in his career.

Howe was named an All Star 23 times in his career, 12 times he was a First Team All-NHL selection and nine times he was a Second Team selection. He finished in the top five in scoring in 20 consecutive seasons and scored 20 or more goals in 22 straight seasons. His 786 goals and 1,809 points with Detroit are the most in both categories by any player with one team in league history. Howe is the only player in NHL history to play in five different decades, the oldest player to play and the only player to play beyond the age of 50.

In one last hurrah, Howe signed a one game contract with the Detroit Vipers in September 1997 and played for them on October 3, 1997 at the age of 69, taking one shift against the Kansas City Blades in a game Kansas City took 5-4 in a shootout. That appearance made him the only player to play professional hockey in six different decades.

PATRICK KANE

Patrick Kane has been a major cog in the revitalization of the Chicago Blackhawks franchise and a big reason why they've won two Stanley Cups in four seasons after not winning one for 49 years prior to the 2009-10 season. With Kane only turning 26 years old in November 2014, there's still plenty of time for him to add more hardware to his mantle.

Kane was drafted in the fifth round of the 2004 Ontario Hockey League Midget draft and would play his junior hockey with the London Knights. He didn't report to the team until the 2006-07 season as he continued to hone his craft playing for the United States under-18 National Team Development Program prior to that. In the 2004-05 season, he scored 33 goals and added 37 assists for 70 points and 16 penalty minutes in 63 games while adding seven goals and eight assists for 15 points and two penalty minutes in nine playoff games. In 2005-06, Kane racked up 52 goals and 50 assists for 102 points with 22 penalty minutes in 58 games.

After the 2005-06 season, Kane made the move to the Knights in the OHL. Playing on a line with fellow future NHL players Sam Gagner and Sergei Kostitsyn, Kane put up 62 goals and 83 assists for 145 points, a +42 plus/minus rating and 52 penalty minutes in 58 games.

Kane finished the playoffs with 10 goals and 21 assists for 31 points while recording a +2 rating and 16 penalty minutes in 16 games. He was named a First Team All-OHL selection; in addition, he claimed the Eddie Powers Memorial Trophy as the OHL's leading scorer, the Jim Mahon Memorial Trophy as the right wing with the most points in the OHL and the Emms Family Award as the OHL Rookie of the Year. He finished second in the voting for the Red Tilson Trophy for the MVP of the OHL to John Tavares.

In 2008-09, Kane helped lead the Blackhawks back to the playoffs for the first time in six years; Chicago had made the postseason just once in the ten seasons between 1997-98 and 2007-08. Kane played in 80 games, scoring 25 goals and adding 45 assists for 70 points while recording a -2 rating and 42 penalty minutes. Chicago knocked off the Calgary Flames in six games in the Western Conference quarterfinals and the Vancouver Canucks in six games in the semifinals but was ousted by the Red Wings in five games in the conference finals.

During the 2009-10 season, Kane signed a new five year, $31.5 million deal that would keep him with the Blackhawks through the 2014-15 season. Kane scored 30 goals and added 58 assists for a career-high, through the 2013-14 season, 88 points while recording a +16 rating with 20 penalty minutes. In the playoffs, Kane contributed 10 goals and 18 assists for 28 points while recording a -2 rating with six penalty minutes. Chicago knocked off the Nashville Predators in six games in the quarterfinals and then eliminated the Vancouver Canucks in six games in the semifinals. In the Western Conference finals, the Blackhawks defeated the San Jose Sharks in four straight games to advance to the Stanley Cup Finals. Once there, Chicago defeated the Philadelphia Flyers in six games for their first Stanley Cup since 1960-61. Kane was named a First Team All-NHL selection for his performance.

In the 2010-11 season, Kane played in 73 games, scoring 27 goals and adding 46 assists for 73 points with a +7 rating and 28 penalty minutes. Chicago didn't have success when it came to defending their championship as they were eliminated in the quarterfinals in seven games by the Canucks. Kane scored one goal and added five assists for six points with two penalty minutes and a -1 rating. He followed that up by playing 82 games in the 2011-12 season, scoring 23 goals and adding 43 assists for 66 points while recording a +7 rating and 40 penalty minutes. Chicago was knocked off in the quarterfinals for the second straight year as they were dispatched in six games by the Phoenix Coyotes.

In the lockout shortened 2012-13 season, Kane played in 47 of a possible 48 regular season games and posted 23 goals along with 32 assists for 55 points while recording a +11 rating and eight penalty minutes. In the playoffs, the Blackhawks dispatched the Minnesota Wild in five games in the quarterfinals and then eliminated the Red Wings in seven games in the conference semifinals. In the conference finals, the Blackhawks defeated the Los Angeles Kings in five games to advance to the Stanley Cup Finals. In the finals, the Blackhawks won their second title in four years by defeating the Boston Bruins in six games. Kane scored nine goals and added 10 assists for 19 points in 23 playoff games with a +7 rating and eight penalty minutes. For his efforts, Kane was awarded the Conn Smythe Trophy as the league's most valuable player in the playoffs.

In the 2013-14 season, Kane played in 69 games, scoring 29 goals and adding 40 assists for 69 points. He was a +7 in the plus/minus department and 22 penalty minutes. In the playoffs, the Blackhawks defeated the St. Louis Blues in six games in the quarterfinals and then knocked off the Wild in six games in the conference semifinals. In the Western Conference Finals, Chicago rallied from a 3-1 series deficit and led in the third period of Game 7 before falling 5-4 in overtime. In 19 playoff games, Kane scored eight goals and added 12 assists for 20 points with a +5 rating and eight penalty minutes. He led all postseason players with four game winning goals.

Through the 2013-14 season, Kane has played in 515 regular season games; he's tallied 178 goals and adding 315 assists for 493 points. He's recorded a +41 plus/minus rating with 212 penalty minutes to his credit. In the playoffs, Kane has taken part in 93 postseason games; he's scored 37 goals and added 54 assists for 91 points with a +1 rating and 46 penalty minutes.

BAUER
STANLEY CUP
FINAL
2010
88

MARIO LEMIEUX

There always are those once in a generation types of talents that come through the world of sports. Some never live up to the hype while others make waves that help change the direction of a franchise or a sport all together. In the case of Mario Lemieux, he literally has been a franchise saver on multiple occasions.

Lemieux began his junior career with the Laval Voisin of the Quebec Major Junior Hockey League. He played three seasons with Laval; in his first season with the team in 1981-82, Lemieux played in 64 games, scoring 30 goals with 66 assists for 96 points and 22 penalty minutes on the year. In the round robin playoffs, Laval finished 10-4 to end at the top of the playoff standings but the team was swept by the Sherbrooke Castors in the semifinals. Lemieux scored five goals with nine assists for 14 points and 31 penalty minutes in 18 playoff games.

In the 1982-83 season, Lemieux played in 66 games for Laval, scoring 84 goals with 100 assists for 184 points and 78 penalty minutes. He finished third in the QMJHL in scoring behind Pat LaFontaine and Claude Verret. In the playoffs, Laval defeated the Hull Olympiques in seven games in the quarterfinals before being defeated in five games in the semifinals by the Longueuil Chevaliers. Lemieux finished with 14 goals and 18 assists for 32 points plus 18 penalty minutes in 12 games.

Lemieux put together a record breaking season in the 1983-84 campaign as he scored 133 goals and 149 assists for a league record 282 points and 92 penalty minutes in 70 games. He set the QMJHL record for goals in a season, breaking Guy Lafleur's record of 130 goals by scoring six goals and six assists in the regular season finale. In the playoffs, Laval defeated the Granby Bisons in four games in the quarterfinals, followed that up with a four game sweep of the Drummondville Voltigeurs in the semifinals and defeated the Longueuil Chevaliers in six games to win the President's Cup as the QMJHL champions.

In the 1984 NHL Entry Draft, the Pittsburgh Penguins managed to get the top pick in the draft after playing poorly enough down the stretch to edge the New Jersey Devils. With that pick, the Penguins drafted Lemieux, who they signed to a two year, $600,000 contract with a $150,000 signing bonus. The Penguins had been on the verge of folding and it's been stated that had they not gotten Lemieux that the franchise wouldn't exist at this point in time. He made his NHL debut for the Penguins on October 11, 1984 against the Boston Bruins; on his first shift, he swiped the puck from Ray Bourque and went in to beat Pete Peeters for his first NHL goal. He played 73 games, scoring 43 goals with 57 assists for 100 points, a -35 rating and 54 penalty minutes; he won the Calder Trophy as the league's top rookie for his efforts.

The 1985-86 season saw Lemieux play in 79 games, scoring 48 goals with 93 assists for 141 points to finish second to Wayne Gretzky of the Edmonton Oilers. He recorded a -6 rating with 43 penalty minutes. He was named a Second Team All-NHL selection for the first time in his career and won the Lester B. Pearson Trophy as the most valuable player in the league as voted on by the players. In 1986-87, Lemieux played in 63 games, scoring 54 goals with 53 assists for 107 points with a +13 rating and 57 penalty minutes. Lemieux was named a Second Team All-NHL selection for the second time in his career. Pittsburgh continued to miss the postseason as they were working on building their talent.

In 1987-88, Lemieux played in 77 games, leading the league with 70 goals to go with 98 assists for a league high 168 points, ending Gretzky's seven year run as the league's top scorer. He recorded a +23 rating along with 92 penalty minutes. For his efforts, Lemieux was a First Team All-NHL selection; in addition, he claimed a second Lester B. Pearson Trophy, his first Hart Trophy as the league's most valuable player and his first Art Ross Trophy. The Penguins missed the playoffs again but fell short by just one point in the standings.

The 1988-89 season saw Lemieux explode as he played in 76 games, leading the league in goals (85), assists (114) and points (199) on the season. He recorded a +41 rating and 100 penalty minutes on the season, winning his second straight Art Ross Trophy and was a First Team All-NHL selection for the second time. The Penguins made the playoffs for the first time in Lemieux's career; they swept the New York Rangers in the Patrick Division semifinals before losing to the Philadelphia Flyers in the division finals in seven games. Lemieux scored 12 goals with seven assists for 19 points with a -1 rating and 16 penalty minutes in 11 playoff games.

Lemieux played in 59 games in the 1989-90 season but still put up huge numbers; he scored 45 goals with 78 assists for 123 points, a -18 rating and 78 penalty minutes. He scored a point in 46 consecutive games before leaving with an injury; he sustained a back injury on February 14, 1990 against the Rangers that developed into a herniated disc and an infection. He missed the rest of the season and Pittsburgh missed the postseason. On July 11, 1990, Lemieux underwent back surgery to deal with the issue.

The 1991-92 season saw Lemieux play in 64 games, scoring 44 goals with 87 assists for a league leading 131 points to go with a +27 rating and 94 penalty minutes. He was named a Second Team All-NHL selection for the third time in his career and won his third Art Ross Trophy. Pittsburgh defeated Washington in seven games in the Patrick Division semifinals, bounced the Rangers in

66
KOHO
Supra

six games in the Patrick Division Finals and then crushed the Bruins in four straight conference finals. In the Stanley Cup Finals, the Penguins defeated the Chicago Blackhawks in four games to win their second straight Stanley Cup. Lemieux played in 15 postseason games; he missed time after Adam Graves of the Rangers broke his left hand with a slash in Game 2 of the series. He won his second straight Conn Smythe Trophy by scoring 16 goals and 18 assists for 34 points with a +6 rating with two penalty minutes.

In 1992-93, Lemieux played in 60 games, scoring 69 goals with 91 assists for a league leading 160 points, a league high +55 plus/minus rating and 38 penalty minutes. He announced on January 12, 1993 that he had been diagnosed with Hodgkins' lymphoma. Lemieux missed two months of action while dealing with radiation treatment.

The 1993-94 season was another injury plagued one for Lemieux as he played just 22 games, scoring 17 goals with 20 assists for 37 points, a -2 rating and 32 penalty minutes. He underwent a second back surgery on July 23, 1993 to repair a herniated muscle that caused him to miss the first ten games of the season. He sustained a back injury on November 11, 1993 against the Rangers which would cost him another 48 games. The Penguins made the playoffs but were defeated in six games in the Eastern Conference quarterfinals by the Capitals; Lemieux finished with four goals and three assists, a -4 rating and two penalty minutes in the series. On August 29, 1994, Lemieux said he would miss the 1994-95 season due to fatigue from the radiation treatments for his Hodgkins' lymphoma.

Lemieux returned to the Penguins in the 1995-96 season, playing in 70 games while leading the league with 69 goals, 92 assists and 161 points to go with a +10 rating and 54 penalty minutes. He was named a First Team All-NHL selection for the fourth time in his career; in addition, he won his fifth Art Ross Trophy, his fourth Lester B. Pearson Trophy and his third Hart Trophy. Pittsburgh defeated the Capitals in six games in the quarterfinals and knocked off the Rangers in five games in the semifinals before being defeated by the Florida Panthers in the conference finals in seven games. Lemieux played in 18 games, scoring 11 goals with 16 assists for 27 points, a +3 rating and 33 penalty minutes.

The 1996-97 season saw Lemieux play 76 games, scoring 50 goals with 72 assists for a league leading 122 points, a +27 rating and 65 penalty minutes. Lemieux picked up his sixth Art Ross Trophy and was named a First Team All-NHL selection for the fifth time. On April 5, 1997, Lemieux announced that he would retire after the 1997 NHL playoffs. The Penguins were eliminated in the Eastern Conference quarterfinals in five games by the Flyers; Lemieux had three goals and three assists in the series with a -4 rating and four penalty minutes. He was enshrined in the Hockey Hall of Fame in 1997.

Lemieux came out of retirement in the 2000-01 season and on December 27, 2000 became the third player in history to appear in a NHL game after being inducted into the Hockey Hall of Fame, joining Gordie Howe and Guy Lafleur. He scored a goal and two assists in his first game back en route to scoring 35 goals and 41 assists for 76 points in 43 games with a +15 rating and 18 penalty minutes. He was named a Second Team All-NHL selection for the fourth time in his career; Pittsburgh eliminated Washington in six games in the quarterfinals and bounced the Buffalo Sabres in seven games in the semifinals before losing to the Devils in five games in the conference finals. Lemieux scored six goals and 11 assists for 17 points with a +4 rating and four penalty minutes.

The 2001-02 season saw Lemieux play just 24 games, scoring six goals with 25 assists for 31 points with 14 penalty minutes. He sustained a hip injury on October 29, 2001 and underwent surgery. The Penguins, who had dealt away most of their expensive players in the offseason to cut expenses, missed the postseason. In 2002-03, Lemieux played in 67 games, scoring 28 goals with 63 assists for 91 points with a -25 rating and 43 penalty minutes on the season. He finished eighth in the league in scoring but Pittsburgh again missed the postseason as they tried to build through the draft.

Lemieux saw the 2003-04 season as a washout; he played in just 10 games, scoring one goal with eight assists for nine points with a -2 rating and six penalty minutes. He sustained a hip injury on November 1, 2003 against the Bruins and underwent surgery on January 6, 2004. With the 2004-05 season wiped out with the lockout, Lemieux was torn by being on both sides as an owner and a player. In the 2005-06 season, Lemieux played in 26 games, scoring seven goals with 15 assists for 22 points with a -16 rating and 16 penalty minutes. He retired on January 24, 2006 at the age of 40 due to an irregular heartbeat.

He finished his NHL career playing in 915 regular season games, scoring 690 goals with 1,033 assists for 1,723 points, a +115 plus/minus rating and 834 penalty minutes. In the postseason, Lemieux played in 107 games, scoring 76 goals with 96 assists for 172 points, a +20 rating and 87 penalty minutes. He won a bronze medal in the World Junior Championships in 1983, a silver medal in the 1985 World Championships, a gold medal in the 1987 Canada Cup, a gold medal in the 2002 Winter Olympics and a gold medal in the 2004 World Cup.

BOBBY ORR

There are superstars in the world of professional sports and then there are those that transcend the game; the once in a generation type talents that turn the game on its collective ear and leave us wanting more, even after they've long left the playing surface for the last time.

Bobby Orr is one of those types of players that had he not been hampered by knee injuries late in his career, could have played on for another six or seven years easily. Instead, hockey fans were treated to a decade of greatness before his body broke down. Some of the accomplishments Orr put together in his brilliant NHL career will likely never be accomplished by a defenseman in the National Hockey League again.

Orr played with the Oshawa Generals in the Ontario Hockey League; Oshawa was the junior affiliate of the Boston Bruins at the time. Orr was an all-star in three of four season with the Generals and made his NHL debut in the 1966-67 season, which was the final year of the Original Six era. At the time, the Bruins had not made the postseason since the 1958-59 campaign or won a Stanley Cup since 1940-41. With Orr a major cog in the new Bruins lineup, things were about to change for Boston in a positive fashion.

He played in 61 games in his rookie campaign, recording 13 goals and 28 assists for 41 points with 102 penalty minutes. For his efforts, Orr was named 2nd team All-NHL in addition to winning the Calder Trophy as the league's best rookie. He finished sixth in the Hart Trophy voting in the race for the league's most valuable player and third in the Norris Trophy voting for the league's best defenseman. Despite Orr's hard work, Boston finished the season 17-43-10 to end up last in the league that season and missed the playoffs again.

The 1967-68 season began a reign of dominance by Orr as the league's best defenseman. Despite playing in just 46 games, Orr scored 11 goals and added 20 assists while picking up 63 penalty minutes. For his efforts, Orr was named a First Team All-NHL selection for the first time in his career and won his first Norris Trophy as the league's best defenseman while finishing third in the Hart Trophy voting. He would go on to be named the Norris Trophy winner and a First Team All-NHL selection in eight straight seasons through the 1974-75 campaign. Just as importantly, Boston improved in the standings, going 37-27-10 to finish third in the East Division but was swept by the Montreal Canadiens in the quarterfinals.

He played in all 76 games in the 1969-70 season, scoring 33 goals and leading the league with 87 assists plus 120 points with a +54 in the plus/minus department. Orr also took a league high 413 shots; he won the Art Ross Trophy as the league's leading scorer, the Hart as the league MVP and the Norris Trophy. More importantly, the Bruins won their first Stanley Cup in nearly three decades as they swept the St. Louis Blues in the Stanley Cup Finals. In the playoffs, Orr added nine goals and 11 assists for 20 points in 14 postseason games; he scored the Stanley Cup winning goal in Game Four in overtime. For his efforts, he was awarded the Conn Smythe Trophy as the most valuable player in the postseason.

The 1974-75 season was Orr's last hurrah as it would turn out and he made it memorable. Orr scored 46 goals, which was the NHL record for defensemen until Paul Coffey netted 48 in the 1985-86 season while he led the league with 89 assists, 135 points, a +80 rating and 384 shots on goal. He won his eighth and final Norris Trophy, was named First Team All-NHL for the eighth time, took his second Art Ross Trophy as the league's leading scorer and won the Lester B. Pearson Award as the league's most valuable player as voted on by the players while finishing third in the Hart voting for the third straight season. Boston was knocked out in the preliminary round by the Chicago Black Hawks, two games to one.

Orr underwent knee surgery on September 20, 1975 and would be out of the lineup for the Bruins until November 8. He played 10 games for the team over the next three weeks but after fighting through the pain, he underwent a second knee surgery on November 29 and would be out for the rest of the season after his knee didn't respond to therapy. This led to an acrimonious set of negotiations with Boston's ownership, who wanted to make sure that he could pass a physical at the start of each season if he wanted to get paid. As a result, Orr signed a five year deal with the Chicago Blackhawks worth $3 million on June 8, 1976.

The knee issues that caused Orr to have surgery limited him to just 26 more games with the Blackhawks over three seasons. He suffered through a dozen knee surgeries and after six games in the 1978-79 season, Orr had seen enough. He chose to retire at that point with his final NHL goal and point coming on the road against the Detroit Red Wings on October 28, 1978. Orr retired with 270 goals and 645 assists for 915 points in 657 career games. He was the first defenseman in NHL history to score 30 and 40 goals in a season and is the only defenseman in league history through 2013-14 to win the Art Ross Trophy. He also is the only player in NHL history to win the Norris, Hart, Conn Smythe and Art Ross trophies in the same season.

Orr was enshrined in the Hockey Hall of Fame in 1979 as the league waived the customary three year waiting period after a player retires. His number 4 was retired by the Bruins in front of a capacity crowd on January 9, 1979.

ALEXANDER OVECHKIN

One of the most prolific goal scorers in the NHL over the last decade, Alexander Ovechkin has proven to be able to light the lamp any time he's on the ice. It doesn't matter if it's shorthanded, on the power play or at even strength, whether his team is up in the game, trailing or tied. It doesn't matter if it's the first period or in overtime, home or away or if the opponent is the defending champs or a doormat; Ovechkin finds a way to put the puck in the net.

Ovechkin was selected with the first overall pick in the 2004 NHL Draft by the Washington Capitals. With the NHL lockout that wiped out that season, it allowed Ovechkin one more season with Moscow Dynamo in the Russian Superleague. In four seasons with Moscow Dynamo, Ovechkin played in 152 games, scoring 36 goals while adding 33 assists for 69 points with 104 penalty minutes in the regular season; he finished with two goals and four assists for six points with 35 penalty minutes in 21 postseason games in his career there.

He made his NHL debut on October 5, 2005 at home against the Columbus Blue Jackets. Oveckin scored twice in the game, including a power play marker, on five shots and was a +1 in 17:36 of ice time as the Capitals picked up a 3-2 victory in the contest; Pascal Leclaire was beaten for both of Ovechkin's goals in the game. Ovechkin played in 81 games, leading the Capitals with 52 goals and 106 points plus 52 penalty minutes on the season. Washington finished the season 29-41-12 for 70 points to finish in the basement of the Southeast Division; Ovechkin won the Calder Trophy as the league's best rookie while earning First Team All-NHL honors.

In the 2007-08 season, Ovechkin played in all 82 games for the second straight season and posted a league leading 65 goals to go with 47 assists for a league leading 112 points. Ovechkin continued to terrorize opposing goaltenders in the 2008-09 season as he bagged a league leading 56 goals to go with 54 assists for 110 points; he led the league with 36 even strength goals and 528 shots on net. Washington went 50-24-8 for 108 points and won the Southeast Division once again. The Capitals rallied from a 3-1 series deficit to stun the Pittsburgh Penguins in seven games in the quarterfinals before losing in seven games to the New York Rangers in the conference semifinals. Ovechkin led the team with 11 goals and 10 assists for 21 points in 14 playoff games; he again won the Hart Trophy, the Rocket Richard Trophy and the Lester B. Pearson Award while being named First Team All-NHL.

The 2009-10 season saw Ovechkin play the fewest games he's logged in an 82 game season as he played in 72 games. He tallied 50 goals to hit that mark for the third straight year and fourth time in his first five seasons; he also added 59 assists for 109 points while leading the league with 37 even strength goals and 368 shots on net. Washington rolled to their third straight division title with a 54-15-13 record for 121 points but folded in the playoffs; the Capitals blew a 3-1 series lead, scoring just three goals in the last three games to lose a seven game series to the Montreal Canadiens in the quarterfinals. Ovechkin had five goals and five assists for 10 points in the series. He won the Lester B. Pearson Award for the third straight season while finishing second in the Hart Trophy voting; he was named First Team All-NHL again.

Ovechkin had a down year in the 2010-11 season; while he rebounded to play in 79 games, he scored just 32 goals while racking up 53 assists for 85 points.

The 2011-12 season saw the Capitals' sniper score 38 goals with 27 points for just 65 points in 78 games. The 65 points is the lowest that Ovechkin has recorded in a full 82 game schedule in his career. The Capitals finished second in the Southeast Division and eliminated the Boston Bruins in seven games in the quarterfinals before getting knocked off in seven games in the semifinals by the Rangers. Ovechkin had five goals and four assists for nine points in 14 postseason games.

He followed that up with a solid performance in the lockout shortened 2012-13 season; he scored a league leading 32 goals while adding 24 assists for 56 points. Oveckin led the league with 16 power play goals and 220 shots on goal. The Capitals won the Southeast Division but were eliminated in seven games in the quarterfinals by the Rangers again as they blew 2-0 and 3-2 series leads.

The 2013-14 season saw Ovechkin bounce back offensive; in 78 games he tallied a league leading 51 goals to go with 28 assists for 79 points. He led the team with 24 power play goals and 386 shots on goal. He won the Rocket Richard Trophy for the fourth time in his career but the Capitals finished the season in fifth place in the Metropolitan Division as they went 38-30-14 for 90 points and missed the postseason. Ovechkin did earn Second Team All-NHL honors for his performance.

In his career, Ovechkin has played in 679 NHL games and scored 422 goals in addition to 392 assists for 814 points with 456 penalty minutes. In 58 postseason games, he's scored 31 goals with 30 assists for 61 points and 30 penalty minutes. He's represented Russia in nine World Championships, scoring 27 goals and adding 19 assists for 46 points in 56 games. Ovechkin has won three gold medals, one silver medal and two bronze medals in World Championship play.

BAUER
BAUER

MAURICE RICHARD

Intensity, tenacity, grit and heart are key components of any successful player in the National Hockey League. Whether you loved him or hated him, it was clear that Maurice "Rocket" Richard had all of those components in spades, not to mention a volatile temper that flared up more than once during his extended career in the NHL, all spent with the Montreal Canadiens.

Richard began his hockey career in the Quebec Amateur Hockey Association in 1938-39 playing for the Montreal Paquette Midgets. In 46 games, he scored a mind-blowing 133 goals with seven assists for 140 points; he scored all but 11 of the team's goals on the season. He moved to the Quebec Junior Hockey League in 1939-40, playing for the Verdun Jr. Maple Leafs. Richard played in 10 games, scoring four goals with one assist and two penalty minutes; he added six goals and three assists for nine points and two penalty minutes in four playoff games as the team won the provincial championship. He would add seven goals and nine assists for 16 points with 16 penalty minutes in seven games in the Memorial Cup.

In the 1940-41 season, Richard was promoted to the Montreal Sr. Canadiens of the Quebec Senior Hockey League; he played just one game, recording an assist. In that contest, Richard crashed into the boards and broke his ankle; he missed the rest of the season with the injury. He recovered in time to play in the 1941-42 season, logging 31 games with the Sr. Canadiens, scoring eight goals with nine assists for 17 points and 27 penalty minutes. He suffered a broken wrist that cost him the rest of the regular season but returned for the playoffs; in the postseason, Richard had two goals plus an assist with six penalty minutes in six games.

Richard was offered a tryout with the Montreal Canadiens, who were struggling on the ice and at the gate with their star players being called up for action in World War II. The team also had a lack of French speaking players to draw fan interest; Montreal inked Richard to a contract worth $3,500 for the 1942-43 season on October 29, 1942. Richard scored his first NHL goal on November 8, 1942 but he played just 16 games before breaking his leg on December 27, 1942 in a game against the Boston Bruins. He finished the season with five goals and six assists for 11 points with four penalty minutes on the year.

He would change his number from 15 to 9 in the 1943-44 season. Coach Dick Irvin moved Richard from the left wing to the right, placing him on a line with Elmer Lach and Toe Blake. The group would collectively be known as "The Punch Line" and was one of the most prolific trios of the era. Richard appeared in 46 games in the 1943-44 season, scoring 32 goals with 22 assists for 54 points and 45 penalty minutes. He was named a Second Team All-NHL selection for his performance. In the postseason, Montreal defeated the Toronto Maple Leafs in five games and the Chicago Black Hawks in four to win their first Stanley Cup in thirteen years; it would be the first of eight that Richard would win in his career. He scored 12 goals with five assists for 17 points and 10 penalty minutes in the nine playoff games.

Richard had a record breaking season in the 1944-45 campaign. He scored five goals and added three assists for eight points in a 9-1 Montreal romp over the Detroit Red Wings on December 28, 1944; that would hold as the single game point record until Darryl Sittler of the Maple Leafs had a ten point performance against the Bruins in 1976. On February 25, 1945, Richard tallied his 45th goal of the season against the Maple Leafs in a 5-2 win to break Joe Malone's record of 44 goals in a season. He would score his 50th goal of the season with 2:15 remaining in the season finale, beating Harvey Bennett of the Bruins. As such, he became the first NHL player to score 50 goals in a season, setting the benchmark of 50 goals in 50 games. He added 23 assists for 73 points, finishing second in the league in scoring behind his line mate Lach; Blake was third. Richard was named a First Team All-NHL selection but Montreal couldn't defend their title; they were ousted in six games by Toronto despite Richard's six goals, two assists and 10 penalty minutes in the series.

In the 1945-46 season, with talent coming back into the league as World War II had come to a close, Richard saw his offensive numbers of the season before decline. He played in all 50 games, scoring 27 goals with 21 assists for 48 points with 50 penalty minutes. He was a First Team All-NHL selection for his performance for the second straight season. Montreal swept Chicago before upending Boston in five games for the second Stanley Cup of Richard's career; he scored seven goals and added four assists for 11 points with 15 penalty minutes in the nine postseason games.

The 1946-47 season saw Richard play in 60 games, posting a league leading 45 goals to go with 26 assists for 71 points with 69 penalty minutes. He was named a First Team All-NHL selection for the third straight season and won the Hart Trophy as the league's most valuable player for the only time in his career. In the postseason, Montreal beat Boston in five games before losing in the Stanley Cup Finals to Toronto in six games. Richard played in 10 of the 11 postseason games, scoring six goals with five assists for 11 points and 44 penalty minutes. He was suspended for Game 3 of the Stanley Cup Finals after being assessed a match penalty in Game 2 for slamming his stick over the head of Toronto's Bill Ezinicki.

Richard held out through training camp in the 1947-48 season angling for a raise along with team captain Emile Bouchard but general manager Frank Selke refused to give in; both players reported when the regular season got underway. Richard played 53 games, scoring 28 goals with 25 assists for 53 points and 89 penalty minutes. He missed the tail end of the season with a knee injury but was named a First Team All-NHL selection for the fourth straight year. The "Punch Line" came to an end as Blake suffered a career-ending leg injury. Without Blake and Richard, the Canadiens missed the playoffs for the first time since the 1939-40 season.

In 1948-49, Richard saw his offensive numbers suffer without Blake in the lineup. He played in 59 games, scoring 20 goals with 18 assists for 38 points and 110 penalty minutes. Richard did manage to earn First Team All-NHL honors again but Montreal lost in the semifinals in seven games to the Red Wings. He managed just two goals and an assist with 14 penalty minutes in the series. The 1949-50 season was a better one for Richard as he led the league in goals for the third time in his career with 43 to go along with 22 assists for 65 points and 114 penalty minutes. He picked up his sixth straight First Team All-NHL selection for his efforts but Montreal was wiped out in five games by the New York Rangers in the postseason. Richard was limited to a goal and an assist plus six penalty minutes in the series.

The 1950-51 campaign saw Richard play in 65 games, scoring 42 times while adding 24 assists for 66 points plus 97 penalty minutes. During the course of the year he scored his 271st career goal with the franchise, making him the team's all-time leader in goals. He was named a Second Team All-NHL selection; Montreal bounced Detroit in six games before falling in five games in the Stanley Cup Finals to Toronto in a series that saw all five games go to overtime. Richard finished the postseason with nine goals and four assists for 13 points plus 13 penalty minutes in 11 games.

In 1951-52, Richard played in 48 games for Montreal, tallying 27 goals with 17 assists for 44 points with 44 penalty minutes, earning Second Team All-NHL honors for the third time in his career. In the playoffs, Richard showed his toughness; he was knocked senseless and was briefly unconscious after being hit by Leo Labine and smacking off Bill Quackenbush's knee in Game 7 of the semifinals against Boston. Despite having a concussion and having a cut over his eye stitched up, Irvin sent Richard out late in the third period with the game tied; Richard netted the winning goal in a 2-1 triumph which spawned an iconic photo of Richard shaking hands with Boston goaltender Jim Henry after the game's conclusion. The Canadiens would be swept by the Red Wings in the Stanley Cup Finals; Richard finished with four goals, two assists and six penalty minutes in 11 playoff games.

Richard played in all 70 games in the regular season in the 1952-53 campaign, scoring 28 times and adding 33 assists for 61 points with a league high 112 penalty minutes. He surpassed Nels Stewart's NHL record of 324 goals when he tallied against Chicago on November 8, 1952. Richard was named a Second Team All-NHL selection for his performance. In the playoffs, Montreal defeated Chicago in four games before whipping Boston in five to win the third Stanley Cup of Richard's career. Richard finished with seven goals and one assist with two penalty minutes in the 12 postseason games.

The 1953-54 season saw Richard lead the league in goals for the fourth time with 37 as he played all 70 games. He added 30 assists for 67 points with 112 penalty minutes and was named a Second Team All-NHL selection for the fourth straight season. In the playoffs, Montreal swept Boston before losing the Stanley Cup Finals in seven games to the Red Wings; Richard was held to three goals and 22 penalty minutes in the playoffs.

In 1954-55, Richard played in 67 games, scoring 38 goals with 36 assists for 74 points and 125 penalty minutes; he tied for the league lead in goals with his teammate, Bernie "Boom Boom" Geoffrion. Richard scored his 400th career goal on December 18, 1954 against the Black Hawks. He was named a First Team All-NHL selection for the seventh time in his career but his season was marred by an ugly incident late in the season. On March 13, 1955, Richard was hit in the head by the Bruins' Hal Laycoe's stick. Richard retaliated by swinging his stick at Laycoe's head and then punched linesman Cliff Thompson when he tried to break up the altercation.

President Clarence Campbell, after two days of mulling over the situation, suspended Richard for the remaining three games of the regular season and the entirety of the playoffs for his actions. When Campbell went to the next Canadiens game at the Montreal Forum, he had eggs, vegetables and trash thrown at him by unruly Montreal fans. One fan threw a tear gas bomb at Campbell that led to the evacuation of the Forum and a forfeit of the night's contest to Detroit. The fleeing fans, coupled with a large group of demonstrators outside the arena, led to the "Richard Riot" which saw more than 50 stores looted, more than 70 arrests and 37 injuries. Damages were estimated at over $100,000 or $872,340 in 2014.

Richard returned to action in the 1955-56 season and welcomed back his "Punch Line" mate in Blake, who took over as head coach. Richard's younger brother, Henri, joined the team that season as well. He played all

70 games, scoring 38 goals while adding 33 assists for 71 points with 89 penalty minutes. He was named a First Team All-NHL selection for the eighth time in his career. In the playoffs, Montreal bounced the Rangers in five games and followed that up with a five game victory over Detroit to win the Stanley Cup. Richard scored five goals and added nine assists for 14 points plus 24 penalty minutes in 10 games.

The 1956-57 season saw Richard play in 63 games, scoring 33 times while adding 29 assists for 62 points plus 74 penalty minutes. He was named a Second Team All-NHL selection for his efforts; in the playoffs, the Canadiens dispatched the Rangers in five games before blitzing the Bruins in five games to win their second straight Stanley Cup and the fifth of Richard's career. He contributed eight goals plus three assists for 11 points with eight penalty minutes in ten postseason games.

Richard would end up playing just 28 games in the 1957-58 season, scoring 15 goals and 19 assists for 34 points with 28 penalty minutes. The season wasn't without milestones however; on October 19, 1957, Richard scored his 500th career goal against Chicago, becoming the first player in NHL history to reach that mark. He suffered a severed Achilles tendon in a game against Toronto on November 13, 1957. Richard returned in time for the postseason, helping Montreal knock off Detroit in four games and Boston in six for their third straight Stanley Cup. Richard potted 11 goals with four assists for 15 points while picking up 10 penalty minutes in the 10 games.

He would be plagued by injuries again in the 1958-59 season as he appeared in just 42 regular season games, scoring 17 goals with 21 assists for 38 points and 27 penalty minutes. He broke his ankle on January 18, 1959 against Chicago and missed extensive time. Montreal rolled past Chicago in six games before beating Toronto in five games for their fourth straight Stanley Cup; Richard was held scoreless in the four postseason games that he played in, picking up two penalty minutes.

The 1959-60 season saw Richard play 51 regular season games, scoring 19 goals with 16 assists for 35 points with 50 penalty minutes. He missed a month during the regular season with a fractured cheekbone but was ready to go in the postseason. In the playoffs, Montreal knocked off Chicago in a sweep and then swept Toronto to win their fifth straight Stanley Cup, a NHL record that has not been equaled through the 2013-14 season. Richard contributed one goal plus three assists along with two penalty minutes in eight postseason games.

Richard would announce his retirement on September 15, 1960. He played in 978 regular season games, scoring 544 goals while adding 421 assists for 965 points with 1,285 penalty minutes. In the playoffs, Richard played in 133 contests, scoring 82 times while adding 44 assists for 126 points and 188 penalty minutes. His career goal mark held until 1963 when Gordie Howe of the Detroit Red Wings passed it; his 50 goals in a season mark was the benchmark until Bobby Hull of the Chicago Black Hawks scored 54 in the 1965-66 season.

Montreal retired Richard's number 9 in 1960 after he retired and the Hockey Hall of Fame waived its five year waiting period, enshrining him in 1961. Richard coached the Quebec Nordiques of the WHA for two games in the 1972-73 season, going 1-1 before resigning after realizing he couldn't handle the stress of coaching. He passed away on May 27, 2000 at the age of 78.

TERRY SAWCHUK

Being a goaltender in the National Hockey League is a challenging feat; becoming a successful one with an extended career is an extremely difficult thing to accomplish. To pull it off in an era where backup goaltenders didn't exist for more than half your career and goalie masks weren't in fashion makes the premise of being a goalie one that ranks up there with skydiving without a parachute: something you wouldn't want to do if you could avoid it.

Terry Sawchuk was the epitome of a hard-nosed goaltender; he played 21 years in the NHL and wasn't afraid to stop the puck with any part of his body that was necessary, including his face. Over the course of his career, Sawchuk dealt with a slew of injuries, including three operations on his right elbow, an appendectomy, cuts and bruises, a broken instep, a collapsed lung, ruptured discs in his back, and severed tendons in his hand. It was estimated that he took over 400 stitches in his face at some point or another in his career, including three in his eyeball after getting gashed. On top of all that, all the years being hunched over in net left Sawchuk with swayback, something that never was fixed.

He finally wore a mask in 1962 after more than a decade in the trenches. A famous 1966 cover of Life Magazine had a makeup artist trying to show all the stitches and scars Sawchuk had on his face during his career; the makeup artist ran out of room trying to depict them all. Still, through all the injuries, all the pucks fired at him and all the problems, Sawchuk laced up the skates when it was game time and gave a stellar performance.

Sawchuk was signed to a professional contract by the Detroit Red Wings in 1947 and played in 30 games for Detroit's junior league team, the Galt Red Wings, posting a 3.13 GAA and four shutouts. He played three games for the Windsor Spitfires in 1947-48, going 3-0-0 with a 1.67 GAA before getting promoted to the Omaha Knights of the United States Hockey League; in 54 games, Sawchuk went 30-18-5 with a 3.24 GAA and four shutouts, earning Rookie of the Year honors. The 1948-49 season saw Sawchuk promoted to the Indianapolis Capitols of the American Hockey League; in 67 games, Sawchuk went 38-17-2 with a 3.06 GAA and two shutouts, earning Rookie of the Year honors in the AHL to go with his USHL honors.

He played the majority of the 1949-50 season with the Capitols, playing 61 games and posting a 31-20-10 record with a 3.08 GAA and three shutouts and going 8-0 with a 1.50 GAA in the AHL playoffs. He was called up in January of 1950 while Harry Lumley was injured and played in seven games for the Red Wings, posting a 4-3-0 mark with a 2.29 GAA and one shutout. Sawchuk showed so much potential in that brief stint in the Motor City that after the season, the Red Wings dealt Lumley to the Chicago Black Hawks, despite the fact that he had backstopped the team to the Stanley Cup.

Sawchuk made the most of his opportunity as he played in all 70 games in his rookie campaign of 1950-51, leading the league in victories as he went 44-13-13 with a 1.99 GAA and a league-high 11 shutouts. He was named a First Team All-NHL selection and won the Calder Trophy as the league's best rookie, making him the first player to win Rookie of the Year honors in three major professional hockey leagues. Sawchuk and the Red Wings lost in six games in the postseason to the Montreal Canadiens; Sawchuk was 2-4 with a 1.68 GAA and one shutout in the series.

The 1951-52 season was much of the same during the regular season for Sawchuk as he again played in 70 games and led the league in wins, going 44-14-12 with a league leading 1.90 GAA and 12 shutouts. During this time, the team that allowed the fewest goals was awarded the Vezina Trophy, so Sawchuk picked up the first one of those in his career. One has to wonder how many he could have won had the current rules been in place. He was named a First Team All-NHL selection again; in the playoffs, Sawchuk was unbeatable, going 8-0 with a 0.62 GAA and four shutouts as the Red Wings swept the Toronto Maple Leafs in the semifinals and then Montreal in the Stanley Cup Finals for the first championship in Sawchuk's career.

In 1952-53, Sawchuk continued to play solid hockey; in 63 games, he led the league in wins for the third straight year, going 32-15-16 with a league leading 1.90 GAA and nine shutouts. He won his second Vezina Trophy and again was a First Team All-NHL selection. Detroit was bounced in six games in the semifinals by the Boston Bruins; Sawchuk was 2-4 with a 3.39 GAA and one shutout in the series. In 1953-54, Sawchuk led the league in wins for the fourth straight year, going 35-19-13 in 67 games with a 1.93 GAA and 12 shutouts. He was named a Second Team All-NHL selection; in the playoffs, Detroit beat Toronto in five games in the semifinals before knocking off Montreal in seven games to win the second championship of Sawchuk's career. He was 8-4 in the playoffs with a 1.60 GAA and two shutouts.

The 1954-55 campaign was much the same as Sawchuk put up his fifth straight season leading the league in victories by posting a 40-17-11 mark in 68 games with a 1.96 GAA and a league best 12 shutouts. He won his third Vezina Trophy and was named a Second Team All-NHL selection for the second time in his career. In the playoffs, Detroit swept Toronto before defeating Montreal in seven games to win their second straight Stanley Cup and the third of Sawchuk's career; he went

8-3 with a 2.36 GAA and one shutout in the postseason. However, Sawchuk's first tenure with the Red Wings would soon come to an end.

In June 1955, the Red Wings dealt Sawchuk along with Vic Stasiuk, Marcel Bonin and Lorne Davis to the Bruins for Ed Sandford, Real Chevrefils, Norm Corcoran, Gilles Boisvert and Warren Godfrey. The rationale for the deal was that Detroit had another young goaltender in Glenn Hall that was ready to transition to the NHL and they felt Sawchuk was expendable. In his first season in Boston, Sawchuk struggled, leading the league in losses as he went 22-33-13 with a 2.60 GAA and nine shutouts over 68 games for a Boston team that was fifth in a six team league.

In 1956-57, Sawchuk was diagnosed with mononucleosis but was back playing for the Bruins in two weeks. He was struggling, in a weakened physical state and in a questionable mental state; on January 16, 1957, he announced his retirement due to nervous exhaustion. He had posted an 18-10-6 mark in 34 games with a 2.38 GAA and two shutouts prior to the announcement; Boston went on to beat Detroit in the playoffs before getting knocked off by Montreal in the Stanley Cup Finals. After being labeled a quitter by several team executives and newspapers, Sawchuk was on his way out of Boston. He was traded back to Detroit on July 10, 1957; in exchange, the Bruins received John Bucyk and cash.

In the 1957-58 season, Sawchuk went 29-29-12 with a 2.95 GAA and three shutouts while playing in all 70 games for Detroit. Hall had been dealt to the Black Hawks after the acquisition of Sawchuk along with Ted Lindsay as both players were proponents of the NHL Players' Association. Detroit made the playoffs but was swept in the semifinals by Montreal; Sawchuk was 0-4 in the postseason with a 4.52 GAA in the series. The Red Wings struggled in the 1958-59 campaign; Sawchuk played in 67 games and led the league in losses, going 23-36-8 with a 3.09 GAA and five shutouts. Detroit missed the playoffs but Sawchuk was named a Second Team All-NHL selection for his performance.

Sawchuk continued to be a workhorse in the 1959-60 season, playing in 58 games and going 24-20-14 with a 2.67 GAA and five shutouts. Detroit was defeated in six games in the semifinals by Toronto as Sawchuk was 2-4 with a 2.96 GAA in the series. In the 1960-61 campaign, Sawchuk played just 37 regular season games, splitting time with Hank Bassen; he went 12-16-8 with a 3.13 GAA and two shutouts. In the playoffs, Detroit beat Toronto in five games but was defeated in six games by Chicago in the Stanley Cup Finals. Sawchuk played in eight of Detroit's 11 playoff games, going 5-3 with a 2.32 GAA and one shutout.

The 1961-62 season again saw Sawchuk split time with Bassen; he went 14-21-8 with a 3.28 GAA and five shutouts in 43 games as the Red Wings missed the playoffs. In 1962-63, Sawchuk saw the majority of the action with Bassen and Dennis Riggin getting some work; he played in 48 games, going 22-16-7 with a 2.55 GAA and three shutouts. He was named a Second Team All-NHL selection; Detroit made the playoffs, beating Chicago in six games in the semifinals before losing to Toronto in five games in the Stanley Cup Finals. Sawchuk played in all 11 games, going 5-6 with a 3.18 GAA during the postseason.

Sawchuk saw his heaviest workload in four years in the 1963-64 season as he played in 53 games, going 25-20-7 with a 2.64 GAA and five shutouts. The Red Wings outlasted Chicago in seven games in the semifinals before losing to Toronto in seven games in the Stanley Cup Finals. Sawchuk appeared in 13 of the Red Wings' 14 postseason games, going 6-5 with a 2.75 GAA and one shutout. After the season, a similar situation to what happened in 1955 took place; Detroit had a promising young goalie in Roger Crozier ready to play in the NHL and Sawchuk was left unprotected in the intra-league waiver draft. He was claimed by the Toronto Maple Leafs on June 10, 1964, ending his second tenure with the Red Wings.

In his first year with Toronto, Sawchuk split time with Johnny Bower; in 36 games, he went 17-13-6 with a 2.56 GAA and one shutout. He picked up his fourth Vezina Trophy for his performance; Toronto was bounced in the semifinals by Montreal in six games with Sawchuk going 0-1 with a 3.00 GAA in his lone appearance in the series. The 1965-66 season saw Sawchuk play in just 27 games, going 10-11-3 with a 3.16 GAA with one shutout; the Leafs made the playoffs again but were wiped out in four straight by Montreal. Sawchuk went 0-2 in the series with a 3.00 GAA.

In the final year of the Original Six era, Sawchuk was part of the "Over the Hill Gang" in Toronto that featured a duo of the 42 year old Bower and the 37 year old Sawchuk between the pipes with 40 year old Allen Stanley and 37 year old Tim Horton on the blue line along with 39 year old Red Kelly and 36 year old George Armstrong up front. Sawchuk went 15-5-4 with a 2.81 GAA and two shutouts in 28 regular season games. In the playoffs, Toronto upended Chicago in six games in the semifinals and then defeated Montreal in six games in the Stanley Cup Finals; it was the fourth championship for Sawchuk and the most recent one, through the 2013-14 season, for the Maple Leafs.

With expansion looming, Sawchuk was left unprotected; he was taken with the first overall pick in the 1967 NHL Expansion Draft by the Los Angeles Kings.

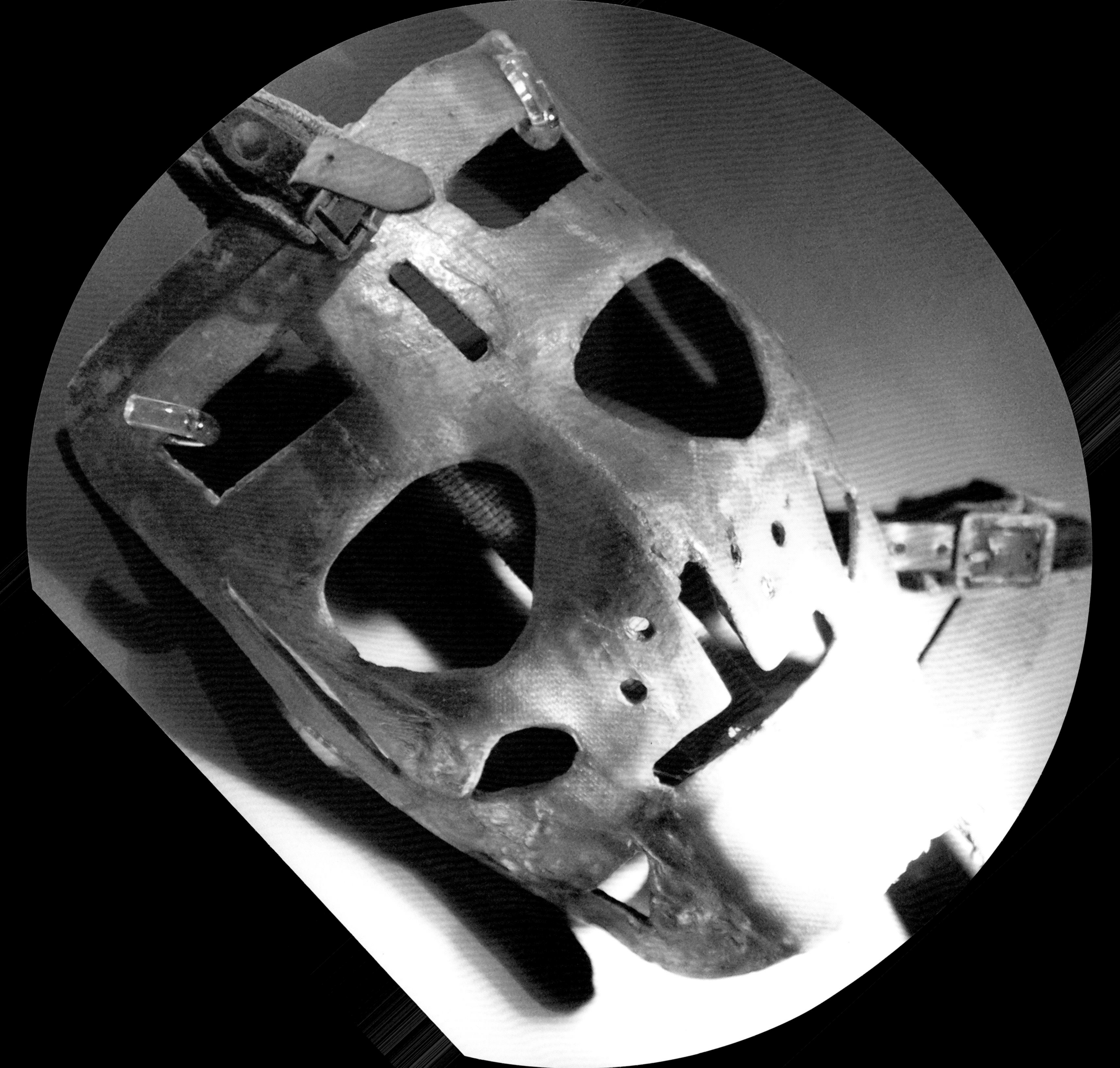

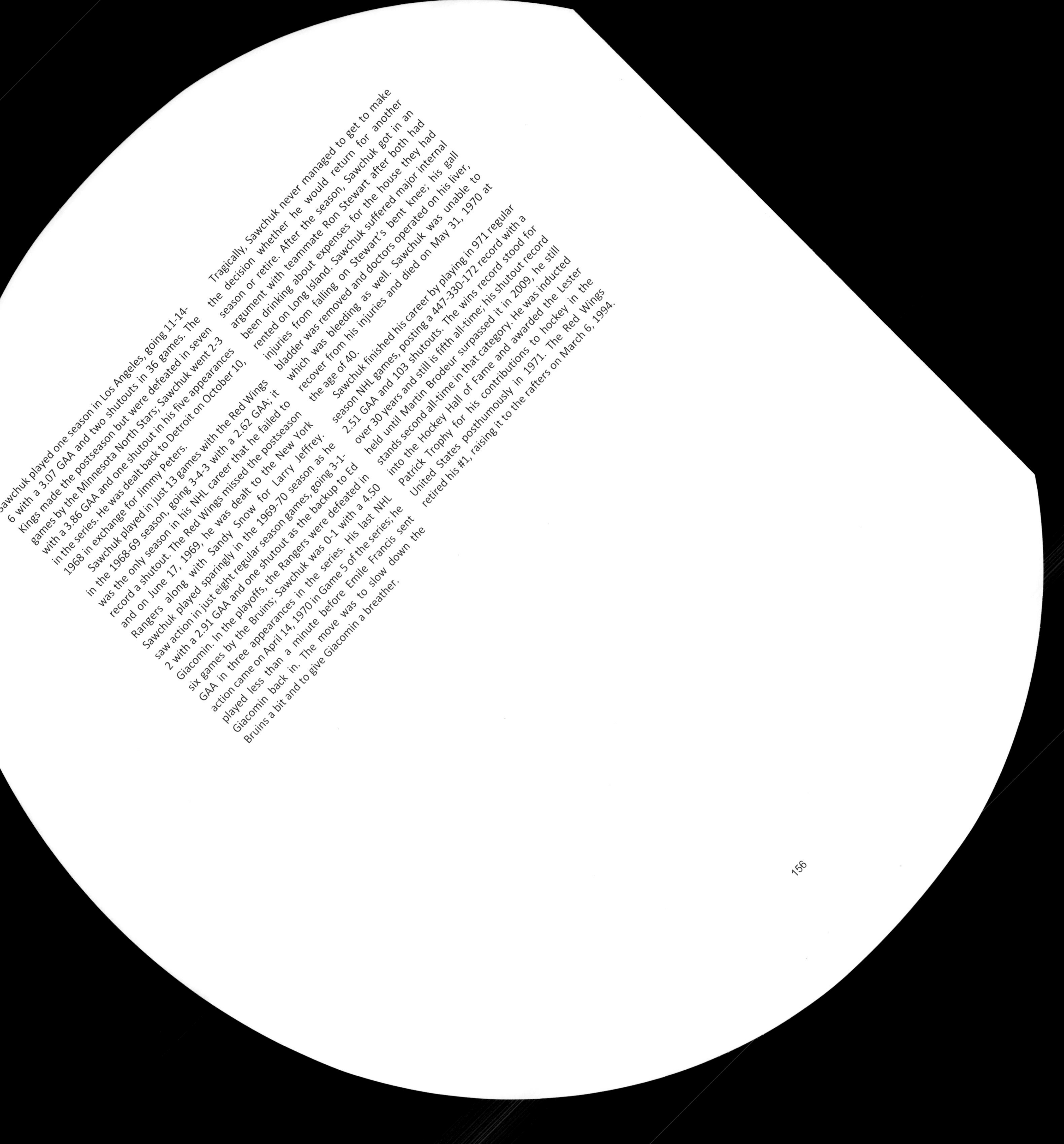

Sawchuk played one season in Los Angeles, going 11-14-6 with a 3.07 GAA and two shutouts in 36 games. The Kings made the postseason but were defeated in seven games by the Minnesota North Stars; Sawchuk went 2-3 with a 3.86 GAA and one shutout in his five appearances in the series. He was dealt back to Detroit on October 10, 1968 in exchange for Jimmy Peters.

Sawchuk played in just 13 games with the Red Wings in the 1968-69 season, going 3-4-3 with a 2.62 GAA; it was the only season in his NHL career that he failed to record a shutout. The Red Wings missed the postseason and on June 17, 1969, he was dealt to the New York Rangers along with Sandy Snow for Larry Jeffrey. Sawchuk played sparingly in the 1969-70 season as he saw action in just eight regular season games, going 3-1-2 with a 2.91 GAA and one shutout as the backup to Ed Giacomin. In the playoffs, the Rangers were defeated in six games by the Bruins; Sawchuk was 0-1 with a 4.50 GAA in three appearances in the series. His last NHL action came on April 14, 1970 in Game 5 of the series; he played less than a minute before Emile Francis sent Giacomin back in. The move was to slow down the Bruins a bit and to give Giacomin a breather.

Tragically, Sawchuk never managed to get to make the decision whether he would return for another season or retire. After the season, Sawchuk got in an argument with teammate Ron Stewart after both had been drinking about expenses for the house they had rented on Long Island. Sawchuk suffered major internal injuries from falling on Stewart's bent knee; his gall bladder was removed and doctors operated on his liver, which was bleeding as well. Sawchuk was unable to recover from his injuries and died on May 31, 1970 at the age of 40.

Sawchuk finished his career by playing in 971 regular season NHL games, posting a 447-330-172 record with a 2.51 GAA and 103 shutouts. The wins record stood for over 30 years and still is fifth all-time; his shutout record held until Martin Brodeur surpassed it in 2009, he still stands second all-time in that category. He was inducted into the Hockey Hall of Fame and awarded the Lester Patrick Trophy for his contributions to hockey in the United States posthumously in 1971. The Red Wings retired his #1, raising it to the rafters on March 6, 1994.

JOHN TAVARES

One of the most talented players in the league right now, John Tavares would be better known if he played for a contending team instead of the struggling New York Islanders. The fact that a terrific talent can fly below the radar even playing (albeit it in the shadows of) New York City is mindboggling at times. If the Islanders ever get some talent to play with him, they could be a dangerous team.

Tavares played his junior hockey with the Oshawa Generals of the Ontario Hockey League. He began his junior career in 2005-06 as a 15 year old; he scored 45 goals and added 32 assists for 77 points with a -13 plus/minus rating and 72 penalty minutes. He was awarded the Emms Family Award as the OHL's Rookie of the Year and was also the CHL Rookie of the Year as the best rookie in all of Canadian junior hockey. Despite his performance, the Generals finished in the basement of the East Division and missed the postseason.

Tavares put together a terrific season in 2006-07 for the Generals, playing in 67 games while scoring 72 goals plus 62 assists for 134 points along with a +25 rating and 60 penalty minutes. He scored a staggering 34 goals on the power play and six shorthanded markers on the season. The Generals made the playoffs, eliminating the Kingston Frontenacs in five games in the quarterfinals before getting swept by the Belleville Bulls. Tavares finished with seven goals and added 12 assists for 19 points with a -4 rating and six penalty minutes in nine games. He finished second in the regular season in the scoring race behind Patrick Kane of London. Tavares did earn the Red Tilson Trophy as the MVP of the OHL and was named the MVP of the CHL as well.

In 2007-08, Tavares put together another strong campaign as he scored 40 goals with 78 assists for 118 points in 59 games while recording a +22 rating and 69 penalty minutes to finish third in the playoff race.

In the 2008-09 season, which was Tavares' final year in the OHL, he was dealt to the London Knights with Michael del Zotto and Darryl Borden in exchange for Scott Valentine, Christian Thomas, Michael Zador and six draft picks on January 8, 2009. Tavares finished the season with 58 goals and 46 assists for 104 points in 56 games to lead the league in scoring while posting a +10 rating and 54 penalty minutes on the season. In the playoffs, London knocked off the Erie Otters in five games in the quarterfinals and then eliminated the Saginaw Spirit in a four game sweep. In the conference finals, the Knights were defeated in five games by the Windsor Spitfires in five games. Tavares scored 10 goals and added 11 assists for 21 points in 14 playoff games while posting a -2 rating and eight penalty minutes. Tavares won the Eddie Powers Memorial Trophy as the OHL's leading scorer. He finished his OHL career with 215 goals in the regular season; through the 2013-14 season, that is the most in OHL history.

The Islanders took Tavares with the first overall pick in the 2009 NHL Entry Draft and he signed his entry level contract on July 15, 2009. He made his regular season debut on October 3, 2009 and scored his first career goal in that game by beating Marc-Andre Fleury of the Pittsburgh Penguins. He would play in all 82 regular season games in the 2009-10 season, scoring 24 goals and adding 30 assists for 54 points while recording a -15 plus/minus rating with 22 penalty minutes.

In the 2010-11 season, Tavares played in 79 games, as he posted 29 goals with 38 assists for 67 points with a -16 rating and 53 penalty minutes. The Islanders continued to struggle as they finished in the basement of the Atlantic Division, missing the playoffs by 20 points.

The 2011-12 season saw Tavares post career highs in goals with 31, assists with 50 and points with 81. He recorded a -6 rating and 26 penalty minutes but the Islanders finished at the bottom of the Atlantic Division again, 23 points behind the fourth place Devils and missed the playoffs.

In the lockout shortened 2012-13 season, Tavares played in all 48 regular season games and scored 28 goals with 19 assists for 47 points while posting a -2 rating and 18 penalty minutes. More importantly, the Islanders made the playoffs for the first time since the 2006-07 season. They didn't last long, however, as they were dispatched in six games in the Eastern Conference quarterfinals to the Pittsburgh Penguins. Tavares scored three goals and added two assists for five points with a -4 rating and four penalty minutes in the series while recording the game winning goal in Game 4 of the series.

The 2013-14 season was a bit of a disappointment for Tavares as he played just 59 games after tearing his MCL and meniscus in his knee on February 19, 2014 in Sochi, Russia while playing for Team Canada in the 2014 Winter Olympics. He missed the rest of the Olympics and the Islanders' season due to the injury. Tavares had posted 24 goals and 42 assists for 66 points on the season with a -6 rating and 40 penalty minutes; he was third in the league in scoring when he went down with the injury. Without their star, the Islanders floundered and missed the playoffs once again.

In his career through the 2013-14 season, Tavares has played in 350 regular season games, scoring 136 goals and adding 179 assists for 315 points. He's recorded a -45 plus/minus rating with 159 penalty minutes. He also earned a gold medal playing in the 2014 Winter Olympics and two gold medals in the World Junior Championships in 2008 and 2009.

CCM
KNIGH
CCM

Bank
EASTON
14
14
67

TD
TD
TD

LA
FINAL
Reebok
QUICK
Reebok
BAUER
LA

LA KINGS
33
2014 STANLEY CUP

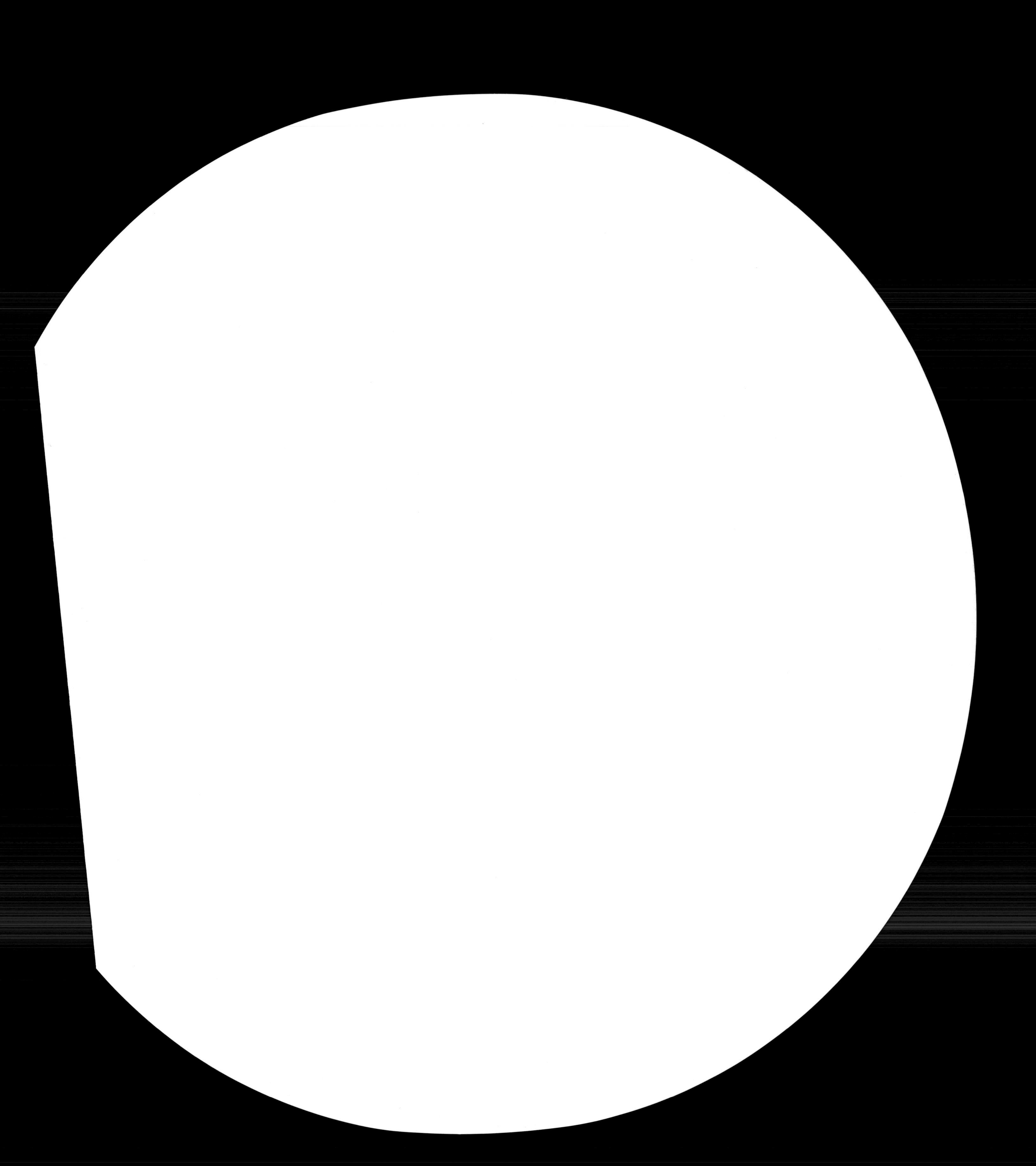

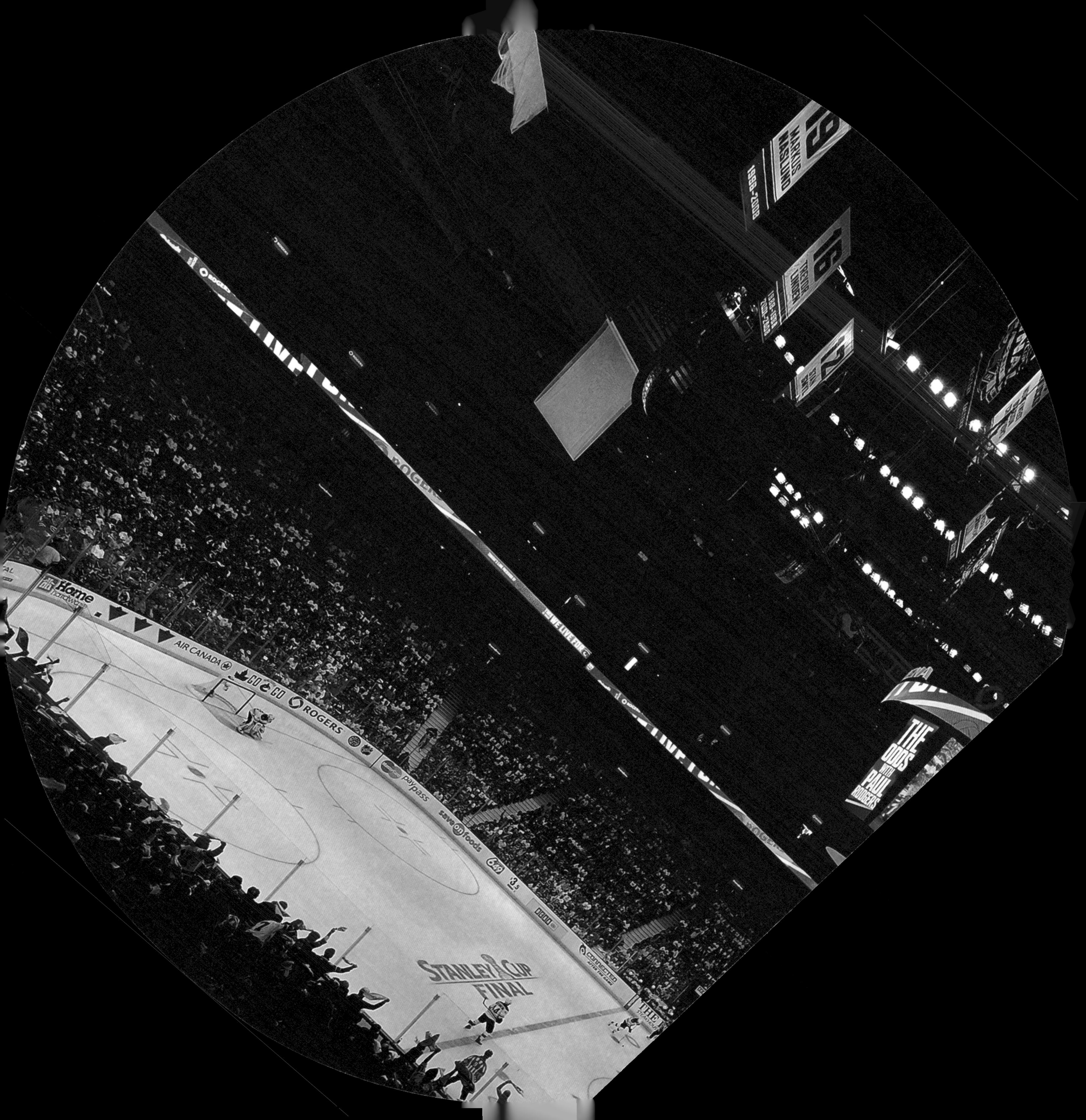
MARKUS NASLUND
1995-2008
AIR CANADA
ROGERS
paypass
save on foods
STANLEY CUP
FINAL
THE ODDS WITH PAUL RODGERS